GOOD GUYS, BAD GUYS

Good Guys, Bad Guys

The Perils of Men's Gender Activism

Emily K. Carian

NEW YORK UNIVERSITY PRESS
New York

NEW YORK UNIVERSITY PRESS
New York
www.nyupress.org

© 2024 by New York University
All rights reserved

Library of Congress Cataloging-in-Publication Data
Names: Carian, Emily K., author.
Title: Good guys, bad guys : the perils of men's gender activism / Emily K. Carian.
Description: New York : New York University Press, [2024] |
Includes bibliographical references and index.
Identifiers: LCCN 2023023421 | ISBN 9781479821006 (hardback ; alk. paper) |
ISBN 9781479821013 (paperback ; alk. paper) | ISBN 9781479820979 (ebook other) |
ISBN 9781479820986 (ebook)
Subjects: LCSH: Male feminists. | Men—Identity. | Men's movement. | Anti-feminism.
Classification: LCC HQ1233 .C35 2024 | DDC 305.31—dc23/eng/20230629
LC record available at https://lccn.loc.gov/2023023421

This book is printed on acid-free paper, and its binding materials are chosen for strength and durability. We strive to use environmentally responsible suppliers and materials to the greatest extent possible in publishing our books.

Manufactured in the United States of America

10 9 8 7 6 5 4 3 2 1

Also available as an ebook

To Mark, the best guy.

CONTENTS

Introduction: Men Gender Activists in the Stalled Revolution   1
1. Playing the Hero   23
2. Straight, White, Cis Men at the Intersection of Privilege   51
3. Making Inequality Unsolvable   89
4. The Limitations of Identity-Driven Activism   127
5. Contexts of Mobilization   158
    Conclusion: Where We Go from Here   191
    Acknowledgments   209
    Appendix: Methods   211
    Notes   231
    Bibliography   241
    Index   255
    About the Author   264

Introduction

Men Gender Activists in the Stalled Revolution

"Men have the power and the rights and the status, and women are still kept down," Charlie told me over the phone. "It is not an equal society. It's not even close. Ask me [whether men and women are equal] when the legislature is made up of 50 percent women or when the CEOs of companies are 50 percent women. This isn't going to be in our lifetime." Charlie is a feminist. He identifies openly with the label among both friends and acquaintances, saying, "I'm completely out. They know I'm a feminist." To Charlie, feminism means understanding that "women's rights must be equal to men's rights." He is especially passionate about protecting women's access to abortion. Toward that end, he is a member of the National Organization for Women and volunteers for his local chapter.

A month before I spoke with Charlie, Brian told me, "About 90 percent of murders are against men, 88 percent of the drug-addicted are men, similarly for suicide. Domestic violence is 70 percent [against] men." Brian explained his belief that patriarchy does not exist but rather is a term made up by feminists to demonize men. He rattled off these statistics to illustrate that men are actually discriminated against in the United States and that feminism has tricked society into giving women special rights and privileges to ameliorate their imagined disadvantage. Brian is a men's rights activist, or a member of a staunchly antifeminist group that organizes around a broad array of "men's issues"—areas in which advocates see men and boys as discriminated against or disadvantaged because of their gender. Brian is personally involved in the fight to end the practice of circumcision, which men's rights activists often refer to as "male genital mutilation." He fundraises for an "intactivist" group and occasionally writes for a men's rights website known for its virulent misogyny and male supremacist ideology.

Intuition, common sense, or, more simply, stereotypes might provide a picture of what the typical feminist man and the typical antifeminist man are like. We might envision Charlie, the feminist, to be a well-educated, well-off, married millennial. Our mental image of him might fit with terms like "hipster," "metrosexual," or "new man." On the other hand, popular culture would have us believe that Brian, the antifeminist, lives in his mother's basement. We might picture him as an unlucky-in-love loner who spends most of his time on Reddit or 4chan. While the specifics of our mental images for each man might vary, one thing is certain: we expect Charlie and Brian to be *different*.

But Charlie and Brian buck stereotypes about the men who associate with their respective social movements. While young men are often seen as more gender progressive than their older counterparts, Charlie, the feminist, is nearly thirty years older than Brian, the antifeminist. Charlie is divorced and never had children, whereas Brian is married with kids. Brian has a college degree; Charlie dropped out of college. While we might expect Brian's antifeminism to stem from religious or political conservatism, he is actually an atheist (as is Charlie) and considers himself a member of the Green Party. The two men also share important identities that have structured their life circumstances: they are both straight, white, working-class men living in the United States.

The feminist men and the men's rights activists I interviewed for this book had even more in common, much to my surprise. Across both groups, I found that men's pathways into gender activism were sparked by their desire to differentiate themselves from the "bad": from privilege, oppression, and guilt.

When I asked Charlie how he first came to identify as a feminist, he went back further, describing his deep sense of regret about how he acted when his college girlfriend became pregnant and sought an abortion. He said, "I didn't handle it well." He treated the pregnancy as if it were *her* problem, rather than *their* problem. His feminism, he explained, was part of a personal journey to become a better man. Decades later, he found himself in the same situation with another woman but chose a different response: "It was totally different. I was willing to support her in whatever her decision was. I was willing to discuss it with her. I was willing to pay for [an abortion] if she chose that. I was willing to step up and be a father if she chose that. Whatever she wanted to do."

In the intervening years, Charlie had worked on himself, and he was proud to be a different person than he had been in college. This second experience had confirmed his hard work, even if he still felt guilty about the first. Referring to the second woman, he told me, "After we split up, two years later she called me and wanted to just talk about how she appreciated how I handled it." Of his feminism, he said, "I want to be a better person than I was [then]."

When I asked Brian how he began to see himself as a men's rights activist, he described a controversy within the atheist community that revealed (what he saw as) bias against men. In what came to be known as Elevatorgate, atheist blogger Rebecca Watson criticized sexism within the community after she was propositioned in an elevator by a man and fellow World Atheist Convention attendee.[1] She faced a concerted harassment campaign for speaking out about her experience. Brian didn't believe Watson's version of the events, claiming that the man's request was innocent and that Watson couldn't have possibly been uncomfortable with it: "[The man] said, 'Oh, yeah, I'd really like to talk with you further. Would you like to come to my room'—this was in a hotel—'for some coffee?' She said no and then that was the end of it." According to Brian, when he made this case with other atheists online, he was attacked: "In discussing the dynamics between men and women, [others were] like, 'it was not okay for him to have done that!' . . . Just in my questioning, just to get people's perspectives about it, it seemed like because [I said] this guy did nothing really wrong, [they said,] 'You're a misogynist! You believe all these other things!'" Brian objected to feminists' understanding of power relations and, specifically, men as a privileged group. He said, "The whole context of [Elevatorgate] was framed in the 'patriarchy'—that there's an oppressor that is oppressing someone of an oppressed class." Brian thought this was not only untrue but also unfair to men. He discovered the men's rights movement at this time and wrote about Elevatorgate for a men's rights website, making the case that men are innocent victims of feminism. In summarizing his trajectory into the men's rights movement, he distinguished himself from those he saw as the bad guys: "I could no longer identify as a feminist, because I'm not like that."

Charlie and Brian *are* different. Their views on gender and their respective goals vis-à-vis gender equality are about as different as they come. This cannot be overstated. But in this book, I show that men like Charlie and men like Brian share something important in common: both wish to construct themselves as good *men* and to differentiate themselves from all that is bad. Charlie does this by distinguishing his current self from who he was before, highlighting how he has changed and how he now shows up for the women in his life. Brian does this by denying men's privilege and positioning himself and other men as unfairly demonized by feminists.

Men's desire to be and be seen as good people fundamentally, if subconsciously, motivates their gender activism. This is not to say that men gender activists are disingenuous about their commitments to their respective social movements. Rather, I argue their commitments arise out of their desire to be good men. I further argue that this subconscious motivation has meaningful consequences for the shape and effectiveness of their commitments to gender equality.

In defining "motivation," I draw on the dual-process model of culture.[2] In this model, cultural schemas can serve as both motivation and justification. The former refers to an automatic process that occurs below conscious awareness, while the latter describes how individuals deliberately and discursively make sense of their behaviors or decisions after the fact. In interviews, men gave a host of reasons for why they became feminists or men's rights activists, most of which boiled down to "because I care about equality." I don't wish to contradict interviewees' accounts of their own actions or, in particular, feminist men's intentions.[3] Instead, my goal is to reveal those automatic, subconscious, emotional, and cognitive processes that invested them in gender activism. By focusing on the patterns lurking beneath the surface of men's discursive accounts of their pathways into gender activism, I tap into what I refer to as their "motivation" or, more accurately, their "subconscious motivation."

From my interviews with feminist men and men who are men's rights activists emerges the deep story of their trajectories into gender activism.[4] Today, it is impossible for men not to have heard feminist claims that women are disadvantaged at home, at work, and in the street. These claims implicate men by naming them a privileged group. In response, the men I interviewed adopted what I call "privilege renegotiation strategies" to forge new and morally uncompromised identities. These strategies do not require men to confront gender inequality but enable them to maintain their moral sense of self in light of new information about the hierarchical social order and their place in it. Through privilege renegotiation strategies, men can absorb new knowledge about the disadvantages others face, adapt to changing cultural contexts that give greater voice to issues of social justice, find new and fulfilling communities, and portray themselves as egalitarian, all without altering the fundamental premise upon which their identities are built: supremacy. By leveraging privilege renegotiation strategies, men's greater awareness around gender inequality disrupts their understandings of themselves only temporarily. Men's performance of their "new" identities both obscures and reinforces gender inequality. While men's identification with feminism is a significant, positive development for the movement, their feminism would be more effective if it were not also (or primarily) a means for them to construct morally uncompromised identities.

I conceive of privilege renegotiation strategies as encompassing any course of action individuals take to navigate their high-status identities when confronted with inequality. Associating with social movements is one of many privilege renegotiation strategies, and, as I show, the men interviewed for this book use it to navigate their high-status racial and sexual identities in addition to their gender identities.

Feminism, Antifeminism, and the Men Who Love Them

The men interviewed for this book have different understandings of feminism. I use feminist scholar and activist bell hooks's definition of feminism as "the movement to end sexism, sexist exploitation, and oppression."[5] Feminism is commonly understood as a political movement that aims to secure equal rights, status, and outcomes for women. Its agenda stems from its foundational belief that women, as a group, are systematically disadvantaged by virtue of their gender. Feminism has roots in the Enlightenment and has changed in its focus and scope over time.[6] Historically, feminists have advocated for women's suffrage, property rights, right to work, and reproductive rights and engaged with issues such as domestic violence and sexual assault, among others.

Feminism is a global movement that is diverse in its strategies and ideologies; it is more accurate to talk of "feminisms."

Today, feminism enjoys mainstream popularity.[7] Social media in particular has contributed to feminism's visibility, and feminists have capitalized on digital networks to connect, organize, and reach new audiences.[8] Feminism is discussed in mainstream media outlets, incorporated into marketing campaigns, endorsed by celebrities and C-suite executives, and tweeted, retweeted, and shared.

Not all feminisms are equally popular, however. Neoliberal rationality, so central to the American economic, political, and cultural system, has produced a feminism that does not critique but rather complements neoliberalism.[9] Neoliberal feminism is commodified and depoliticized, but it is the most visible feminism in the United States today.[10] While this version recognizes inequality, it fails to identify or intervene in the conditions that create it.[11] Instead, as American and Canadian studies scholar Catherine Rottenberg writes, "the question of social justice is recast in personal, individualized terms."[12] Neoliberal feminism constructs a particular feminist subject who is both individualized and entrepreneurial in striking her own work-family balance through strategic calculation. Using self-care and self-love, she can achieve her ambitious professional and personal goals through sheer will. Neoliberal feminism's "interventions"—like efforts to include more women in the technology industry or to facilitate women's networking—illustrate its concern with the market and its focus on individual empowerment. In other words, neoliberal feminism has largely abandoned the idea of collective liberation.

The problems with neoliberal feminism notwithstanding, nearly 40 percent of American men identify as feminists.[13] This statistic was, at one time, unthinkable. Feminism's popularity is reflected in the stories of feminist men. Charlie, for example, described his journey into feminism as obvious. When I asked him whether he can imagine not being a feminist, he said that that would make him an "asshole," which is just "not [his] personality." A sizable and growing group of men find that feminism suits them. Their commitment to the cause of gender equality feels natural and almost inevitable, as it does for Charlie.

Charlie and his comrades' commitment to the movement is good news to feminists, who have long sought men's allyship because, as members of the dominant group, men disproportionately control the power and resources necessary for feminist change. Men can maneuver that power and those resources toward ending gender inequality, or not. As bell hooks writes, "Since men are the primary agents maintaining and supporting sexism and sexist oppression, they can only be successfully eradicated if men are compelled to assume responsibility for transforming their consciousness and the consciousness of society as a whole."[14]

Unfortunately, misogyny also seems as popular as ever.[15] While it is not exclusively the purview of men, men have largely been at the forefront of antifeminist organizing, and this remains true today. Because of feminism's newfound visibility and recent (though limited) successes, antifeminism has found new audiences by painting feminism as, at best, irrelevant in this more equal reality or, at worst, harmful to men. Online, antifeminism has transformed into a more toxic version, manifesting, for example, in concerted harassment campaigns against feminists and women who challenge the status quo.[16]

The idea that feminism has gone too far is the fundamental premise upon which the men's rights movement is built. The men's rights movement aims to improve men's position and outcomes based on its stance that men, as a group, are subjected to discrimination because of their gender. The movement defines itself in opposition to feminism and claims that feminism disadvantages men. Like feminism, the men's rights movement is active globally and is diverse in its tactics and activities.[17] The movement engages with a number of issues, including men's lower likelihood of receiving custody of children following divorce, men's obligation to support their ex-wives financially (i.e., alimony), the underreporting of domestic violence against men and lack of services for male victims, false rape accusations against men, and circumcision. In comparison to feminism, the men's rights movement has a much shorter history. Scholars typically date it to the 1970s, though views similar to those held by men's rights activists have existed for much longer.[18]

There is consensus among social scientists, including those that study the men's rights movement, that men do not experience gender-based discrimination. As one example, in *Men's Rights, Gender, and Social Media*, philosopher Christa Hodapp finds no evidence for two claims made by men's rights activists—that men are discriminated against in the family court system and experience domestic violence at rates equal to women.[19] To be sure, men face serious issues, but these are the costs of the high status of masculinity as compared to femininity, rather than gender-based discrimination.[20]

Instead, research characterizes the men's rights movement as an antifeminist and misogynist movement. Scholarship on the men's rights movement is an emerging field that has focused largely on the historical roots of the movement or has analyzed primary documents (e.g., books, websites) to catalog its claims. Scholars consistently find strong antifeminist themes among men's rights materials and websites and conclude that the movement constitutes organized antifeminism.[21] Men's rights activists use claims to victimhood as a strategy to obstruct feminist change efforts and strip women of hard-won protections. For example, men's rights groups used the equal protection clause to file a lawsuit to attempt to defund battered women's shelters in Minnesota.[22] The men's rights movement is male supremacist in nature, and its agenda, if successful, would lead to significantly worsened gender inequality.

Since its emergence, the men's rights movement has grown considerably, due in no small part to the internet, which allows men's rights activists to connect to one another and organize. Online, the men's rights movement has grown more extreme and spawned several related though distinct male supremacist movements, including involuntary celibates or incels, pickup artists, and men going their own way or MGTOW. These groups have been linked to terrorist violence. In 2020, for example, a lawyer and men's rights activist targeted a federal judge, whom he perceived as an opponent of men's rights, killing her twenty-year-old son and critically wounding her husband.[23]

Men's involvement in both feminism and the men's rights movement has a long history. American men's profeminism can be traced to the Revolutionary War.[24] The reasons for men's participation in feminism have varied over time, reflecting the cultural milieu, debates within feminism, and the movement's organizational structure.[25] Men's profeminism during the 1970s, for example, was shaped by the radical culture of the time and feminists' calls for accountability from within other social movements, like the peace movement. Existing research describes men's involvement in the men's rights movement as motivated by their desire to protect the status of their ingroup or the result of aggrieved entitlement, the feeling that their lived experiences do not match what they perceive they were promised as men.[26]

Research on men's involvement in feminism and the men's rights movement is limited. In regard to the former, research identifies the tensions within men's feminist activism but does not subject feminist men's accounts to a high level of scrutiny, often taking for granted that they are accurate representations of feminist men's motivations. While more critical work exists, research largely reflects the view that men's feminism is unproblematic and universally positive.[27] This reflects larger processes related to masculinity and gender inequality, specifically the tendency to praise men who exceed low expectations set for them vis-à-vis any sphere coded as feminine.[28] Men's feminist allyship is perceived by many as unexpected or selfless and thus deserving of more praise and credibility as compared to women's feminism.[29]

On the other hand, existing research largely dismisses men's accounts of their reasons for joining the men's rights movement as false consciousness. Sociologist Michael Kimmel, for instance, claims that men's rights activists misplace their discontent with traditional masculinity onto women and feminism.[30] While this is true, Kimmel does not seriously consider men's rights activists' own reasons for joining the movement or what their activism accomplishes for them personally. Besides Kimmel's work, there is very little research based on interviews with men's rights activists, likely because they are suspicious of academics, whom they see as feminists.[31] Until now, there has been no intimate account of men's rights activists' trajectories into the movement.

I take a critical eye to both groups in my examination of men's trajectories into feminism and the men's rights movement.

How Do Men Become Gender Activists?

Scholars describe the development of collective identity, or "an individual's cognitive, moral, and emotional connection with a broader community, category, practice, or institution," as a precursor to mobilization for social movements.[32] In this sense, people join social movements because doing so is congruent with "who they are."

But previous research on collective identity poses a puzzle when applied to the case of men's gender activism. High-status group identities, like masculinity and whiteness, are largely invisible to those who embody them.[33] They are the implicit norm to which other identities, like femininity and Blackness, are compared. They are neutral and unmarked and disappear into interactions, organizations, and institutional structures.[34] Privilege operates and is maintained through this invisibility. Moreover, privilege structures subjectivity such that high-status group members are less likely to recognize the kinds of inequality social movements aim to solve.[35] How then are high-status identities made visible so they can be leveraged by social movements? How are men's personal identities transformed into collective ones and mobilized for feminism and the men's rights movement?

While high-status group identities may typically be invisible, these identities still inform high-status group members' attitudes and behaviors, particularly those that defend their group's power and status. For example, they adopt policy preferences and voting behaviors that work in their group's favor and police the boundaries of their ingroup, especially in response to threats to their privilege.[36]

Social movements that work for high-status group interests, like the men's rights and white nationalist movements, should be understood as more extreme and organized forms of this backlash. However, activism is distinct from more mundane manifestations of backlash, which are based in rational self-interest and relatively cost-free. Because social movements require coordination among many people with no guarantee of success, activism is neither rational nor cost-free.[37] Mobilization requires more than self-interest, including, among other things, collective identity. But previous research on collective identity formation focuses almost entirely on low-status group members, whose identities, by virtue of their position in the status hierarchy, are more visible in everyday life. Previous research on backlash suggests that group threat and protection of privilege might motivate activism among high-status group members, but how are high-status, personal identities made into collective ones to be mobilized by progressive and right-wing social movements?

I untangle this puzzle by examining what gender activism accomplishes for men. When men have encounters that implicate their privilege, their high-status gender, racial, and sexual identities must be renegotiated to fit with their deeply held understandings of themselves as morally good people. They may use any number of privilege renegotiation strategies in pursuing this identity project, but the men I interviewed associated with feminism or the men's rights movement. In essence, the work men do for their personal identities invests them, almost incidentally, in gender activism. Thus, the personal becomes political.

At least it does for some. Resistance to structures of power, like gender, can take many forms, from the highly public, dramatic, and organized to the hidden, normalized, and individual.[38] Many of the men I interviewed—who volunteered for a study of feminists and men's rights activists—practice very little organized activism. As I describe later in this book, it seems few had put a great deal of thought into how they could practice what researchers describe as everyday resistance.[39] Instead, and consistent with their subconscious motivation, men's work is more focused on their own identity projects.

This is entirely compatible with neoliberal rationality broadly and with the neoliberal turn in feminism specifically. Within the logic of neoliberalism, there are no societies, only personally responsible individuals.[40] Individuals are responsible for their own self-realization and indeed must produce themselves. Said production happens through consumption. Thus, neoliberalism transforms feminism from an ideology and a practice into a personal lifestyle and aesthetic.[41] Feminist organizers seek men's support in the hopes that they will wield their power toward feminist ends, but the men I interviewed rarely do this. I find that men's relationship with feminism is largely one-sided: feminism serves *them* as a privilege renegotiation strategy. This has important consequences for the fight against gender inequality.

The Stalled Gender Revolution and the Limitations of Men's Gender Activism

The privilege renegotiation strategies the men interviewed for this book use reflect the sociohistorical conditions and cultural moment in which they are embedded. Specifically, they reflect the context of the stalled gender revolution.

In the United States, the so-called gender revolution of the past several decades brought sweeping changes to women's economic, legal, and relational circumstances.[42] The percentage of women in the labor force steadily increased from 34 percent in 1950 to 57 percent in 2015, making women nearly half of all workers.[43] College-going women entered traditionally male-dominated disciplines like business, and in 1982 women surpassed men in the proportion of college degrees awarded.[44] During that same time, women challenged various forms of discrimination, including at work and at school, and succeeded in securing legal protections and remedies.[45] Their increased economic power, the adoption of no-fault divorce laws, and the criminalization of domestic violence including marital rape altered women's relational contexts, giving them more power in their intimate relationships with men.[46] Over this period, Americans' attitudes about gender—for instance, their self-reported willingness to vote for a woman for president—became more egalitarian.[47] The conditions that shape women's lives changed dramatically in ways that reduced gender inequality, leading some to claim that "gender inequality has been fated for extinction."[48]

Such predictions proved to be premature. Several indicators show that this previously rapid progress has slowed, plateaued, or even reversed. For example, attitudes about gender roles have remained relatively consistent since the 1990s.[49] The desegregation of college majors has slowed.[50] Women and men are still concentrated in different industries, and in 2016 nearly half of women or men would have had to change jobs to eliminate gendered occupational segregation.[51] The percentage of mothers with children under eighteen who were out of the labor force steadily declined until 1999, but since then the trend has reversed, and they are now more likely to be out of the labor force than they were two decades ago.[52] This reversal was accelerated by the increased childcare demands of the COVID-19 pandemic.[53] And in 2022 the Supreme Court overturned nearly fifty years of precedent to end the constitutional right to abortion.[54] These developments have led scholars to conclude that there has been "a fundamental alteration in the momentum toward gender equality."[55] By some measures, the gender revolution has not just stalled but reversed.

This introduction began with a quote from Charlie, who paints a dire picture of gender inequality. Charlie is right; the gender revolution was interrupted at a moment when women and men are still decidedly unequal. The issue at the heart of the stalled gender revolution is that social structures and culture continue to value masculinity over femininity. Changes in the economy, like the growth of the service industry, and technical innovations, like the birth control pill, enabled and incentivized women to delay marriage and children, invest in education, and pursue careers.[56] While these conditions allowed for shifts in women's behaviors, behavioral change has happened largely in the absence of cultural and institutional change that would fundamentally alter the devaluation of femininity, denying women full economic, legal, and interpersonal equality.

At work, the gender pay gap exists in large part because women's work, by virtue of its association with women, is devalued.[57] As a result of the gender pay gap, the average full-time working woman will lose more than $400,000 over the course of her career.[58] If current trends continue, the gender pay gap will not close until 2058.[59] Despite women's entry into the labor force, most workplaces are still structured in a way that assumes workers prioritize paid labor and have few, if any, responsibilities at home.[60] In effect, the ideal worker is still a man. But at home women still spend more time doing unpaid labor, like housework and childcare, than do men, a pattern that was exacerbated by the COVID-19 pandemic.[61] Women's responsibilities at home, combined with aging and retirement, make it unlikely that they will ever make up half of the labor force in the United States.[62] To succeed at work, women are often encouraged to act more like men. In other words, they are told to work within sexist structures, advice that ignores gendered patterns in household labor and the sanctions women experience when they act too masculine.[63] Because men are more likely than women to be in corporate leadership positions, those with the power to change sexist structures benefit from maintaining them.[64] Moreover, women are the disproportionate targets of sexual harassment and violence. One American woman in five will be raped during her lifetime, and between one college-going woman in five and one in four will be raped during her college career.[65] In sum, positive changes for individual women have not been accompanied by, and perhaps have come at the expense of, larger structural and cultural changes. Even as particular conditions change and open opportunities for some women, the cultural and institutional devaluation of femininity persists and is reinscribed into new social forms.[66]

While men like Charlie are more comfortable calling themselves feminists today, men's everyday behaviors have changed very little over the course of the gender revolution. Unlike women, who stood to gain from engaging in the masculine, men have not been incentivized to engage in traditionally feminine behaviors because femininity is still low-status. While women's labor force participation has increased, men's labor force participation has not decreased to the same extent.[67] At the same time, women's increased hours of paid work have not been met with an equivalent increase in men's unpaid work in the home.[68] Research that indicates that progress toward gender equality has stalled, like the comparison of men and women's labor force participation, reflects the consistency in men's behaviors and priorities over the past half century. What is culturally permissible for men has not undergone the same dramatic transformation as what is culturally permissible for women precisely because of the gender status hierarchy. Men face negative social and material consequences for engaging in the feminine and also reap real benefits from continuing to engage in the masculine.

The question of why gender inequality persists is a complicated one, and scholars across disciplines have worked to tackle it from innumerable angles. One answer, which I have drawn on above, is that amid all of the progress of the so-called gender revolution, femininity's value in comparison to masculinity remains unchanged. While women are incentivized to engage in male-typed activities, the same is not true for men, putting an upper limit on the amount of progress we could make toward equality.[69] Another answer is that we use gender to coordinate interaction. In doing so, we draw on the same old gendered status beliefs, infusing inequality into even new and ostensibly gender-neutral situations.[70] Still another answer is that the successes of feminism and other social, economic, and technological changes have unmoored American men, stirring in them a potent desire to recapture male domination.[71] A powerful and well-organized Right has capitalized on men's sense of betrayal, manifesting, for example, in Donald Trump's success.[72]

I focus on one small but important piece of the larger puzzle of persistent gender inequality: men's feminism. Feminism's popularity among men has not, it seems, had the big effect feminist activists had hoped. The gender revolution has stalled or maybe reversed, and even as an unprecedented number of men join the movement, we have been unable to jumpstart it. Is men's feminism ineffectual? And if so, why?

The stalled gender revolution presents a sort of puzzle for the men interviewed for this book: on the one hand, men are still privileged, but on the other hand, men's lived experiences reflect their declining privilege over time. Some scholars describe this puzzle as the "crisis of masculinity." According to this body of work, masculinity is in crisis because, in addition to women's improved status and power, changes over the past several decades upended pathways through which men typically achieve masculinity.[73] Shifts in the structure of the U.S. economy, including the decline of manufacturing and the male wage and increased divorce rates, made primary breadwinning difficult for the average man.[74] Other traditional types of masculinity, like fighting for one's country, have been closed to the majority of men in the Global North. As social policy scholar Steven Roberts writes, "Fewer men than ever are able to connect the fabric of their lives to traditional archetypes of masculinity."[75]

The difficulty of achieving manhood for the average man has been compounded by women's adoption of traditionally masculine behaviors and entrance into male-dominated spaces. Masculinity is defined in opposition to femininity, and femininity is seen as "contaminating" masculinity.[76] This is evident in men's avoidance and denigration of behaviors that associate them with women, like being sexually attracted to other men or working in feminized occupations.[77] In a context in which femininity is still seen as contaminating masculinity but femininity is ever expanding by virtue of changes in women's behaviors, what is masculinity?

Scholars have posited two ways that men have reacted to this "crisis." The first is inclusive masculinity. Inclusive masculinity theory describes a culture's homophobia as a structuring characteristic of its masculinities.[78] In cultures that conflate men's femininity with homosexuality, homophobic attitudes regulate men's behaviors and encourage their performance of hypermasculinity. Inclusive masculinity theory predicts that as homophobia declines in a culture, men will be more inclusive of homosexuality and more likely to engage in the feminine. Importantly, the theory claims that multiple masculinities can exist outside of hierarchy and hegemony in the absence of homophobia. Research has documented the existence of inclusive masculinities online, in schools, in sports, and elsewhere.[79] Men's feminism can be understood as an example of inclusive masculinity. Today, more men are willing to engage in feminist activism—traditionally classified as "for women." Indeed, many of the feminist men I interviewed described their feminism as care work, a traditionally feminine act.

The work on inclusive masculinity conflicts with a second body of literature—work on hybrid masculinities—that describes how men respond to this crisis. Hybrid masculinities incorporate elements typically associated with femininity or marginalized masculinities. Most research indicates that such incorporation reinforces, rather than challenges, the gender order.[80] Hybrid masculinities discursively distance men from power and status and strategically associate them with subordinated groups even while they fortify boundaries between men and women and among men. Thus, research in hybrid masculinities refutes inclusive masculinity theory's claim that masculinities can exist without hierarchy. According to theory on hybrid masculinities, even broad-based changes in the practice of masculinity, like the apparent decrease in men's homophobia, have not challenged the gender order.[81] This work aligns with sociologist Raewyn Connell's conceptualization of hegemonic masculinity as the fluid pattern of practices that discursively justifies unequal gender relations.[82] Hegemonic masculinity is historically and socially contingent; it is adaptable to new contexts as old justifications for its high status become untenable. Hybrid masculinities, then, can be seen as hegemonic masculinity's answer to a particular historical and social context in which traditional masculinity—brashly insistent on its superiority—no longer holds water.

Works on inclusive masculinities, hybrid masculinities, and the crisis in masculinity share in common a focus on how masculinity is in a state of change. But the content of cultural gender beliefs and performances is less important than the work such beliefs and performances do in justifying unequal gender relations. Is masculinity in crisis? I argue it is not. Aspects of men's lives have changed, particularly their interpersonal relationships with women, but the fundamental relationship between femininity and masculinity persists. When scholars emphasize how economic, technological, and social conditions have changed the pathways available to men to perform masculinity, it obscures how masculinity adapts to counterbalance the effects those conditions might have on inequality. More simply, I argue that despite changes in style, the substance of masculinity is oriented toward the status quo. In this book, I return to Connell's conceptualization of hegemonic masculinity as temporally specific, flexible, and shifting, but instead of focusing on *how* masculine practices adapt, I emphasize *why*—as Connell writes, to provide "the currently accepted answer to the problem of the legitimacy of patriarchy."[83] I show how shifts in gender relations produce shifts in patterns of masculine practices, which restore the gender system to an equilibrium premised on inequality.

This book indicates that the literature on inclusive masculinity paints an overly rosy picture of contemporary masculinity by ignoring what inclusivity accomplishes for men individually and as a group. Feminist men are a quintessential example of so-called inclusive masculinity, but I show how most men's feminist allyship is oriented toward personal ends and is largely unconcerned with inclusivity. In fact, feminist men's masculinity is built upon exclusion—of men who are antifeminists, men who are apathetic to feminism, and femininity itself. I show how even a seemingly inclusive masculinity is in fact premised on status and hierarchy.

In constructing a masculinity around superiority to other men and women generally, feminist men reify masculinity's place in the gender hierarchy and so perform a hybrid masculinity. Moreover, they leverage a social movement meant to advance gender equality for their own purposes in ways that, I argue, hinder the movement from the inside.

The Approach and Organization of This Book

I compare the trajectories, perspectives, and sensemaking of feminist men and men who are men's rights activists. Feminists and men's rights activists represent the best- and worst-case scenarios, respectively, in terms of men's investment in ending gender inequality. Their variation on this dimension is useful in telling us what conditions facilitate men's mobilization into different forms of gender activism and how. More importantly, similarities across the two groups, despite their obvious differences, allow me to identify the processes that constrain men's feminism and make it less effective in challenging gendered power.

As extreme cases that likely involve more and stronger mechanisms, these two groups provide deeper knowledge about the attitudes, behaviors, and processes related to men's engagement with gender inequality compared to more middle-of-the-road men.[84] And yet I show throughout the book how the conditions that invest men in gender activism are common and likely at play in the lives of men who are unaffiliated with either movement. Additionally, research shows that beliefs associated with each movement are common among men more generally.[85] It's likely, then, that the processes I identify work outside the particular case I examine.

I chose to use interviews because I sought to understand the processes through which men join these movements and the meanings they associate with their activism, questions particularly suited to interview methods.[86] By engaging with feminist men and those who are men's rights activists directly through interviews, I am able to develop the deep story of men's gender activism:[87] How do men come to these movements? What does activism accomplish for them? And what can their activism accomplish (or not) for gender equality?

To qualify for the study, interviewees had to (1) identify as men, (2) identify as participants in either the feminist or men's rights movements, and (3) live in the United States.[88] I recruited interviewees through a variety of methods, including through cold emails, snowball sampling, fliers, and social media posts.

In general, men's rights activists are suspicious of researchers and women, who they assume are feminists ready to criticize their movement. Gaining access to this group for myself, as a woman researcher, was challenging. My recruitment was most successful when it was facilitated by an intermediary—a gatekeeper within the community. I built relationships with gatekeepers intentionally over several years in the lead-up to data collection. Even when potential interviewees heard about my study through other community members, we often corresponded by email or direct message over the course of several days, during which I would answer questions about myself and my project to build trust. I told participants that I was interested in their pathways into gender activism and their views on gender inequality and that I was committed to representing what they said fairly—a promise I believe I have kept. Sometimes I was successful in recruiting participants, sometimes I was not. In interviews, I found it no more difficult to build rapport with men's rights activists than with feminist men, and I used the same tactics for both groups (e.g., asking low-stakes, introductory questions first). Rather, the main challenge was building trust before men's rights activists agreed to be interviewed. On the other hand, feminist men were quick to trust me, but they were still difficult to find since the majority of individuals in feminist spaces do not identify as men. I discuss these and other challenges related to recruitment in the Appendix: Methods.

I deployed the aforementioned recruitment methods differently for each group of men and relied on them to varying degrees at different times throughout the data collection process.[89] My goal was to construct a sample of feminist men and a sample of men who are men's rights activists that matched on key variables through this purposive sampling process. The final samples had approximately the same average age (forty-five years old) and age distribution, geographic distribution across the United States, and distribution in terms of degree of movement involvement.[90] Ensuring that the two samples are similar on these variables facilitates their comparison.

I conducted sixty-two interviews—thirty-one with men who identify as feminists and thirty-one with men who identify as men's rights activists—from November 2016 through December 2017. Interviews lasted around two hours on average, and I followed a flexible interview protocol during each. To reach interviewees across the country, I conducted interviews over the phone. With two exceptions, I conducted interviews with men who lived in the greater San Francisco Bay Area in person. Interviews were recorded and transcribed verbatim. I used qualitative content analysis to analyze transcripts. My analysis was iterative and proceeded in three stages: (1) preliminary code generation, (2) a first round of transcript-by-transcript, line-by-line coding and memoing, and (3) detailed within-code analysis and comparison.[91]

In no uncertain terms, my structural position impacted this research, even beyond challenges in recruiting and building trust with men's rights activists. My gender and racial identities made interviews with both groups of men emotionally taxing. I am a biracial woman. It was difficult for me to listen to men's rights activists and feminist men express implicitly and explicitly misogynist and racist attitudes during interviews. In those moments, I worked hard to maintain my composure. As a sort of silver lining, the frequency with which I heard misogynist and racist viewpoints indicates that interviewees did not hold back out of fear of offending me. At the same time, interviewees assumed I knew very little about masculinity. Their presumption about my naïveté—rooted, I must assume, in my gender, race, and age—is reflected in the detailed answers they provided to my questions. I discuss how my standpoint and structural position impacted this research further in the Appendix: Methods.

I use this unique comparison case to illustrate how the strategies high-status individuals use to respond to inequality too often reproduce it by centering a certain kind of identity work. In chapter 1, I argue that feminist men and men who are men's rights activists do gender activism to prove their moral goodness. When they are confronted with information about the gender order and their privileged place in it, they search for ways to be and be seen as good men and to resolve the negative feelings evoked by their newfound awareness. Feminism allows men to see themselves as exceptions to the rule that men are privileged, whereas the men's rights movement allows men to portray all men as blameless victims.

Chapter 2 shows that men use feminism and the men's rights movement as a privilege renegotiation strategy to reconstruct not just their gender identities but other identities too. Interviewees who embodied multiple high-status group identities—straight, white, cis men—felt like they were seen as particularly privileged and thus particularly immoral. Men's multilayered subconscious motivation has important consequences for the shape of their activism. Namely, men's rights activists incorporate male supremacist, white supremacist, and homophobic beliefs into a cohesive guiding ideology, and feminist men's work centers the concerns of individuals with multiple forms of privilege like themselves.

Chapter 3 describes men's understandings of gender to show how such beliefs limit their imagination when it comes to solving inequality. While some men endorsed broad-based structural solutions to inequality, they more often saw inequality as unsolvable or solved only through narrow individual solutions. Because structural solutions are more effective than individual ones, it is essential that feminist men consider how they can work collectively in support of them.[92] Instead, men's beliefs serve their subconscious motivation by allowing them to see themselves as doing everything in their power to dismantle inequality.

Chapter 4 shows that, in keeping with their subconscious motivation, men define their activist identities through moral boundaries. They use masculine-typed traits, like agency and rationality, to position themselves as more moral than others. In doing so, they link together masculinity, morality, and superiority, reifying inequalities between masculinity and femininity and among masculinities.

Chapter 5 explains how men's social contexts shape the privilege renegotiation strategies they use to navigate their high-status group identities. Two dimensions that often coalesced at college—relationships with women and interactions with feminism—shaped men's orientations toward feminism. The former can facilitate men's deeper understanding of their own privilege and women's disadvantage and suppress feelings of moral identity threat. The latter can convince men of feminist frames and embed them in social networks that link them to activist opportunities.

In the conclusion, I explore how gender studies and similar academic programs, feminist organizations, universities, workplaces, and everyday people can recruit men as more effective allies for feminist change.

How, then, do men fit into the puzzle of persistent gender inequality? Men's trajectories into gender activism show that the gender revolution, though stalled, is felt by men. In particular, shifting cultural narratives demand that straight, white, cis men acknowledge their identities and their privilege. The work of redefining themselves commits men to specific courses of action vis-à-vis gender inequality: feminism and antifeminism. But it also invests them in other unintentional yet consequential behaviors, like boundary making, that reinforce gender inequality. Thus, even feminist men draw on the gendered narrative resources available to them as they undertake the work of redefining their identities, creating gender inequality anew. The accounts of men gender activists demonstrate that gender inequality is so persistent because it is written into our very identities. Without fully interrogating masculinity and disinvesting from old ways of defining the self, men's efforts to dismantle gender inequality will fall short.

1

Playing the Hero

I can imagine Gil and Craig—two men I interviewed for this book—getting along. Sit them down together and they would bond over growing up in New York. While Craig has since moved west, the two men would talk about the sweeping changes to the big city they call home. Turning to politics, they would lament the inability of the mainstream Democratic Party to address climate change, income inequality, and other pressing issues facing our nation. When their conversation turned to their political beginnings, they would discuss how the Vietnam War shaped their early political consciousness.

Undoubtedly, Gil and Craig share much in common. They are both cisgender, straight, white, and college educated and belong to the oldest cohort of men I interviewed. Despite the similarities in their demographics, political sensibilities, and childhoods, their conversation might take a different tone should it turn to gender politics. This is because Gil is a feminist and Craig is a men's rights activist; the two men sit at opposite ends of the men's gender activism spectrum. Their understandings of gender inequality, feminism, and feminists are antithetical.

In my interview with Gil, he told me that practicing feminism is an act of kindness he undertakes to build a more just world:

> My [seventy-odd] years has confirmed my belief that people are pretty consistent in their attitudes, and if you have a kind, generous, sensitive person, that person is probably going to be a feminist, whatever their politics, and the reverse is also the case. If you're an angry person, a selfish person, greedy, ambitious, . . . you probably treat not only women, but people in general badly.

In Gil's telling, a person's feminism is a natural extension of their inherent morality. Feminists are good people, and good people are feminists.

In contrast, Craig explained to me that feminists advance an antimen worldview for the sake of gaining power:

> You find somebody who is the scapegoat, and you scare people. You point the finger at Muslims or Mexicans, or, in the case of the feminist movement, men, and you make them the scapegoat. Then you say, "There's the boogeyman. Come join me because I'll protect you from the boogeyman." . . . Ultimately, it's political. It's, "we want power for our political movement, and this is how we can do it: we can scare people."

In Craig's view, feminists are bad people who secure power for themselves through fear mongering.

While the men interpret feminism very differently, these quotes provide an important clue about another, unexpected similarity Gil and Craig share. Above, both men discuss gender activism in deeply moral terms. Gil draws a stark, moral boundary between two types of people: feminists, who are "kind, generous, sensitive," and everyone else, whom he sees as "angry," "selfish," "greedy, ambitious." He imbues his description of feminists and nonfeminists with moral implications, using words that connote broader notions of "good" and "bad." Craig does the same, likening (what he sees as) feminists' demonization of men to racism and xenophobia directed toward Muslims and Mexicans. He even draws on the same understanding of what makes a person "bad" as Gil, describing feminists as greedy, selfish, and ambitious in their quest for power. While Gil and Craig disagree in no uncertain terms about whether feminists are good or bad, they both see gender politics and activism as suffused with moral meaning. For both men, being "good" or "bad" is what makes a person a gender activist or not.

In this chapter, I describe Gil's and Craig's pathways to feminism and the men's rights movement, respectively, to show how each man was motivated to become a gender activist to prove his moral goodness. Their stories show that men use gender activism as a way to feel like good people and resolve the uncomfortable feelings that arise from the moral identity threat of being privileged in an unequal world. As such, gender activism serves as a privilege renegotiation strategy, or a way for them to forge new and morally uncompromised identities in the context of social inequality.

Learning about Gender Privilege

Most of the men I interviewed—whether they identified as feminists or as men's rights activists—described a time in their lives when their gender was invisible to them. Men learned at a young age that others had gendered expectations of them. They described childhood (and adult) experiences being rewarded when they fulfilled these expectations and being penalized when they did not. Yet very few men recognized early experiences as gendered at the time. Instead, most men accepted these expectations and unconsciously incorporated them into their sense of self. This fits with the ideas that individuals "do gender" because it is routine and that the routine doing of gender makes it appear natural.[1] It also fits with a large body of literature that contends that identities can remain invisible to those with privilege because high-status identities are treated as normative and baked into institutional structures.[2] Men, as members of the dominant gender group, are not required to be as attentive as women to gendered structures and so are able to live "genderless" lives.[3]

Men's "genderblindness" was only temporary though. The men I interviewed described learning about gender inequality as the catalyst for their realization that they live gendered lives. Specifically, they encountered feminist cultural narratives that portray men as privileged, dominant, or oppressive. Such cultural narratives have become more prominent than they once were in mainstream discourse due to feminism's increased visibility online, in corporations, and in academia.[4] These narratives evoke a host of negative feelings in men—discomfort, anger, confusion—because the idea that men are privileged is incongruent with how they see themselves. The men I interviewed have diverse understandings of who they are, but before this moment they had not considered how their gender might bestow unearned advantage upon them. In this moment of confrontation, they were struck by a disconcerting realization: if they were privileged, they were bad people. Interviewees associated privilege with immorality and oppression with virtuousness, a connection made in the broader culture too.[5] As a result, feminist cultural narratives revealed how others might perceive men as bad people because of their gender privilege. Despite its invisibility in the early lives of the men I interviewed, gender is a primary way individuals make sense of and define the self.[6] These cultural narratives, which disturbed men's understandings of their gendered identities, were thus deeply unsettling.

Craig: Being Seen as the Bad Guy

When I asked Craig about how he first became involved in the men's rights movement, he told me about a series of events, beginning with early childhood, that shaped his gender consciousness:

> I think the first recollection I have of an awareness of any sort of gender issue was when I was about five years old. I remember sitting on the floor of our living room, and my mother was sitting on the couch and she said, "It's a man's world." I thought that was an interesting statement, and I said, "Why do you say that?" She said, "You'll understand when you get older."

Craig thought his mother's comment was "interesting" because it did not fit with what he himself had observed of his parents:

> It confused me because my experience was I saw my father . . . get up and leave really early to commute into the city. I never had the impression that he liked his job. He was doing it clearly to pay the mortgage and put food on the table. He would come back at night and he'd be exhausted. I didn't have a clear idea of what he did all day, other than—I got the impression he didn't particularly like it.

Craig contrasted this with the day-to-day experience of his mother, which he observed firsthand: "I saw what my mother did, and yes, she did housework, but she also got together with her friends for lunch. She could sit around and watch TV shows during the afternoon. She seemed to have a freedom in her life that I assumed my dad didn't have. That was like the first moment where I kind of went, 'something's going on here that I don't understand.'" Thus, Craig's first exposure to the idea that men are privileged did not make sense to him. Experience taught him that his father woke up early to commute to a job he did not like, while his mother enjoyed leisure time and the company of her friends. How, then, could he be living in "a man's world"?

Craig marks the beginning of his journey into the men's rights movement with his first moment of "awareness of any sort of gender issue." While he had previously taken notice of his parents' routines, he had not problematized the differences between them or attributed them to gender. Understandably, five-year-old Craig had not considered the impact of gender on his or others' lives. Craig didn't know what prompted his mother to say "it's a man's world," but this moment was incredibly impactful on him. It disrupted his genderblindness and caused him to reflect on the differences between his mother and father, his exemplars of "women" and "men." Despite her assurance that he would understand when he was older, her comment raised a question for Craig that remained unanswered until he discovered the men's rights movement later in life.

Before he would learn about the men's rights movement, however, Craig came into contact with more cultural narratives that claim men are privileged. Like other respondents of his age, Craig described the Vietnam War as an important influence throughout his childhood. He was consumed with the idea that he could be drafted: "I started to become aware that if you were a young man, you hit the age of eighteen, you could potentially be drafted and be sent off to fight and die in Vietnam. . . . I grew up having that sort of always in the back of my mind as I was growing up."

Yet Craig's sense of dread vis-à-vis the draft contrasted sharply with a narrative that was taking root in the broader culture:

> Around that time, I started to hear about feminism, and had a general perception that it was a good thing, although I also knew that there were some feminists who were out there who seemed very, very angry at men. It felt not good to me, basically, as a kid growing up. To feel as if as a male I have this responsibility [being drafted into military service], and I could get sent to die in a way, and somehow, I'm the bad guy. I think that was sort of my first perception that something was amiss and that I was seeing things that other people weren't seeing, or at least weren't talking about.

Like his early experience with his mother, Craig's exposure to feminism caused him confusion. Feminism's contention that men are privileged simply did not fit with his lived experience. Importantly, such a claim not only was incongruent with what he knew but also "felt not good" to him. This provides a sense of the discomfort Craig experienced when the meanings he associated with his ingroup—men—and a deeply held identity—gender—were questioned. Here, Craig describes himself as perceiving something others did not and the "feminists who were out there" as a sort of mysterious and looming antagonist. This foreshadows how Craig would ultimately resolve this identity threat: by recasting himself as a good man, uniquely astute in his observations of the gender order, and villainizing feminism.

The feminist narrative that men are privileged conflicted with another of Craig's childhood experiences. As a teenager and a "shy kid," Craig became frustrated with sexual scripts that put the onus on boys to initiate romantic relationships. He described feeling the pressure of this role and the obligation to pay for dates: "Even if she said yes, then you have to pay for it basically. All you're paying for is to spend time with her. It's not like the ball is ever in her court, like next time it's her turn to ask you out. It's like, no, it's still in your court and you have to ask again and again and again. It really didn't feel good to me." Once again, Craig perceived men were being both burdened, in this case to initiate romantic relationships, and blamed, and this created an emotional reaction ("it really didn't feel good to me"). Thus, Craig's experience—his understanding of his parents' roles and responsibilities, his fear of the military draft, and his frustration with sexual scripts—conflicted with the claim that men are privileged.

Craig's experiences, knowledge, and ways of knowing are situated, and so his retelling of these memories obscures alternative interpretations.[7] As one example, while Craig believes his mother had more "freedom" than his father, his description of her is consistent with "the problem that has no name," or stay-at-home mothers' feelings of dissatisfaction and loss of identity described by Betty Friedan in *The Feminine Mystique*.[8] Additionally, his mother's statement that "it's a man's world" might lead us to suspect that what Craig interprets as her "freedom" did not necessarily translate to power for her. Likewise, the dating scripts to which Craig objected strip women of sexual agency. My goal is not to contradict any of the men I interviewed but rather to analyze how they describe their experiences and the purposes their descriptions serve. In pointing out again and again how his lived experience conflicted with cultural narratives that portray men as privileged, Craig negotiated and minimized the negative feelings such narratives evoke for him throughout our interview, just as he does in his everyday life and through his activism.

Regardless, the idea that men are privileged created dissonance for Craig. As is clear from his statement that feminism makes him out to be "the bad guy," Craig equates privilege with immorality. This provides important insight into why the feminist claim that men are privileged is unintelligible to and uncomfortable for Craig. To understand men as privileged would require him to reconcile his understanding of himself with an understanding of his ingroup as unfairly advantaged and immoral. He would need to understand *himself* as privileged on account of his gender and therefore as "the bad guy." In other words, Craig's sense of self is incompatible with an understanding that men are privileged. Because gender is a deeply held identity and an important means of defining the self, this incongruence is not easily resolved.[9]

Craig's reaction is an outcome of processes described by a social psychological theory on identity formation and change: identity control theory. In part, identity control theory states that an individual in a social situation will engage in behaviors that reflect her identity standard, or the meanings she ascribes to her identity.[10] She receives feedback from others that indicate the meanings they attribute to her identity. She will compare her identity standard to the feedback she receives from others, and if she detects a discrepancy between the two, she will experience negative emotions.

Put in terms of identity control theory, Craig's identity standard does not include an understanding of himself as privileged. Craig understands himself as a moral person who has not benefited from systems of oppression. Yet his mother's statement that "it's a man's world" and feminists' anger with men provide him with new feedback: that others perceive him as privileged and thus immoral. There is a discrepancy between this feedback and how he sees himself, which produces feelings of discomfort. These feelings are highlighted throughout Craig's narrative when he says, for example, "it really didn't feel good." We cannot know whether Craig's mother and the feminists "who were out there" really did think he was a bad person because of his gender, and it is worth noting that feminist theory does not equate structural privilege with personal wrongdoing. What matters, though, is Craig's *interpretation* of his mother's and feminists' claims. He *felt* that they were calling him "the bad guy."

Gil: Reckoning with the Past

Immediately after Gil graduated from college he moved to the South, where he became the only civil rights worker in the county. He described his decision to become a civil rights worker as a natural consequence of his upbringing: "I was brought up in a Baptist family, and we were taught by example more than words that every person is born equal and it doesn't matter what race or gender or religion, national origin [they] are, you treat people according to who they are. . . . I grew up with that and I was taught if there's something not right, you should do something about it." During his time in the South, Gil lived with a Black family and had so little contact with white people that "I would look in the mirror in the morning and flinch because I saw a white person looking at me." Gil spent two years as a civil rights worker and describes the experience as having a deep impact on him. He told me that racism will always be "palpable" to him because of it.

Gil's civil rights work eventually brought him into contact with feminism and the idea that men are privileged. When I asked Gil when he first started thinking of himself as a feminist, he replied,

> Well, I can tell you my first confrontation—encounter with feminism which was when I was in the South in [the 1960s], I guess it was. I went up to [a national civil rights conference] and there was . . . an announcement that a group was meeting on feminism, and so I went. And these women were talking, and quite angrily, about the treatment of women and they just set me back, and I was thinking about what they were saying, and saying, "Wow, I never understood this before. I've always tried to treat women as equals, but there's something else going on here." I certainly sympathized with what they were saying, but I didn't quite get it at the time.

Like Craig, Gil answered my question about the origin of his activism by referring to one of the first times he was exposed to a gendered way of thinking about the world. Interestingly, Gil describes his first experience with feminism as a "confrontation." Though Gil's emotional reaction ("I certainly sympathized") is substantively different from Craig's ("it really didn't feel good"), he was likewise "set back" by feminists' anger and their claims about the treatment of women. Like Craig, Gil was also confused. Gil describes himself as having "always tried to treat women as equals," yet he admits to not fully understanding the grievances the women articulated. He had not fully considered, by this point, how he and others experience the world in gendered ways.

Gil continued his civil rights and peace movement work. The spheres of these social movements overlapped with feminism, which again brought him into contact with the claim that men are privileged. He became more familiar with feminism through "articles in various places and political magazines." He told me,

> I never found anything objectionable until there was a period in the late sixties, I guess, when there was this radical feminist movement . . . that was hostile to men, and I . . . thought of it as a little crazy. For example, there was a group of these radical feminist women . . . [who] were invited to go up to Montreal to meet a delegation from the National Liberation Front to Vietnam—women from the NLF. They went up and said to these NLF women, "Are you gay?" And the women, of course, they just didn't know how to respond. It was totally beyond this thing, and that to me just seemed funny.

While Gil had become more familiar with and accepting of feminist writing, he found radical feminism to be "a little crazy" and used this story about what seems to be a lesbian feminist group as an example of how such groups were "objectionable." Importantly, he perceived this sect of the movement as being "hostile to men."

Gil referred to being a feminist as "a constant learning process" and remarked, "I [still] don't know if I have the full picture." In my conversation with Gil, it became clear that some of his initial difficulty in understanding the "anger" and "hostility" of feminists was that their claims—that women are subjected to sexism—required him to reckon with his sense of self. They required him to reflect on how he might have the upper hand in his interactions with women or might have mistreated women in the past. Directly after attending the feminist meeting at the civil rights conference, he remembered asking himself, "Hey, I open doors for women. Should I be doing that or is that not treating them as equals?" Later on, he reflected on more troubling instances of male power and privilege that implicated his moral character:

> When I was in college, I heard about this incident thirdhand where this fellow ... had decided that two freshmen [men] whom I knew, only peripherally, should have a sexual experience, and he got this woman drunk and they had sex with her, supposedly. Again, I don't know that it actually occurred, but I know for sure that if it occurred now, it would be considered rape, without question. But in that case, I didn't do anything to follow it up and to verify its veracity, its truth, and I certainly didn't report it. At the time I found it offensive, but it didn't really register to me what the effect on the woman was. I think I felt more that it was wrong, that you don't take advantage of people in that kind of situation.

Gil's newfound gender consciousness required him to reflect on his past behaviors, ranging from the inconsequential—opening doors for women—to the profound—his inaction following the supposed sexual assault of a fellow student. Feminism forces Gil to reckon with what his past behaviors mean about him: do they make him a bad person? Gil's reluctant reflection, activated by his exposure to feminism, illuminated how his experiences, behaviors, and interactions were gendered and privileged, which had largely been invisible to him until that point.

Feelings of regret from behaviors dating back to before he identified as a feminist came up several times in my interview with Gil. At the end of every interview, I asked respondents if they could recommend any additional questions I should ask interviewees. Gil suggested that I ask my feminist respondents whether they had engaged in behaviors that they felt were wrong in retrospect. When I asked him how he would answer that question, he responded,

> Well, there are a couple of incidents, and I feel that certainly if I had to do them over again, I would not have behaved the way I did. And it wasn't because I didn't know any better at the time. I did. But I'd had too much to drink, or whatever, and I was engaged in what was then culturally appropriate behavior ... but I knew at the time that it was wrong. It was not, in any case, anything terrible, but I just feel I shouldn't have behaved that way and I would expect that my son never has and never would. So, in that sense I think society has improved. But in general, I mean, certainly in relation to, say, sex, that there's been a solitary change in the culture that men are much more conscious of women's sexual desires, as in both

men and women are more open to discussion about sexual issues. That change occurred only about five to ten years too late for me, so there's a limit to how much I can beat myself up for that for being on the wrong side of the cultural transformation. I'm happy that things are better now in that particular sense.

While Gil recognizes the culture has changed and believes he cannot "beat himself up" too much for earlier mistakes, he still feels regret and sorrow in regard to his past behaviors. These feelings stem from his participation in "culturally appropriate behavior" for men. Gil regrets not only his treatment of women in early sexual encounters but also and more specifically his automatic engagement in masculine norms of behavior he sees as "wrong." Put another way, he regrets his earlier unreflexive and problematic gender performance in light of the gender consciousness he has since developed.

Gil's story is similar in many ways to Craig's and illustrates a common theme among the feminists and men's rights activists I interviewed: coming into contact with feminism for the first time required them to grapple with their gender identity, privilege, and morality. Feminism provided both Craig and Gil with new information about their place in the social order, which was deeply unsettling to their sense of self. Like Craig, Gil's immediate reaction upon hearing feminist women's experiences with sexism is to perceive them as "angry" and to assure himself that he has "always tried to treat women as equals." Even when he became more familiar with feminism, he believed more radical groups to be "a little crazy" and "hostile to men." Gil described his own confusion with feminism as stemming from his sense that he had treated women fairly in the past. In other words, feminist claims conflicted with Gil's understanding of himself as a good person.

Even though, as a white civil rights worker, Gil may have considered the idea that he was privileged before his first encounter with feminism, he did not consider himself a wrongdoer. In fact, in his own words, his identity was built upon treating people equally, no matter their "race or gender or religion [or] national origin," and fixing it "if there's something not right." He had sacrificed his physical safety to live out this identity as a civil rights worker. In encountering feminism, Gil was forced to grapple with the idea that he may not be fulfilling these values. Like

Craig, then, Gil experienced discomfort resulting from the discrepancy between how he felt about himself—a moral person who treats people equally—and how he suspected others might see him—as a man who mistreats women and benefits from male privilege.

Dealing with Discomfort

Following confrontations with feminist cultural narratives that pointed out men's privilege, the men I interviewed sought ways to prove themselves as good men. Once again, this fits with identity control theory, which predicts that when others' perceptions of an individual do not align with her own identity standard, she is motivated to act in a way that reduces this discrepancy and the negative emotions that accompany it.[11] When feminist cultural narratives raised tricky questions about their moral goodness, men looked for ways to remake themselves as good men. Gender activism offered them a solution. Contributing to what they believed was a moral cause was a means of securing their identities as morally good men.

Craig: Diving Headfirst into the Men's Rights Movement

Craig's initial experiences with feminism confused him. Yet by the time he arrived at college, he was open to learning more about it:

> When I was in college, I started reading more about feminism, and this was like back in the seventies. The feminist movement at that time was—there were a lot of what I would call "even-handed moderates" who were really very much in power in that movement. Women like Betty Friedan, for example, who said famously, "Men are not the enemy. They are the other victim." Karen DeCrow, I think was head of [the] National Organization for Women at that time—a very even-handed feminist. I thought of them as natural allies, because they were poking at the whole rigid gender system, and pointing out that it didn't really match real human beings, that we were being kind of pigeonholed. Their focus was of course mostly on [the] pigeonholing [of] women into a rigid gender role, but certainly writers like Betty Friedan acknowledged the same thing was going on for men.

Craig described being "delighted" when he first read feminist literature recommended to him by friends. During our conversation, he reiterated to me that he "originally thought of [feminists] entirely as allies." Because the feminism Craig first came into contact with was "moderate" and "even-handed," he was able to draw parallels between feminist issues—like strict gender roles for women—and his experiences as a man. As a result, Craig supported a feminist organization: "Then when I graduated college, and I started making enough money that I could support organizations that I believed in, I became a member of the National Organization for Women [NOW]. I was a card-carrying member of NOW for years, because I didn't see any inconsistency at all."

Craig's initial support for feminism was predicated on its expression of moderate views—that is, its recognition that men too are constrained by the gender system in ways equal to women. Craig saw his personal experience (like his sense that his father had few "freedoms" because of the masculine role he embodied) as consistent with the claims of these more moderate feminists. Initial conditional support of feminism, so long as it recognized how men are also constrained, was common among the men's rights activists I interviewed. Indeed, early men's rights groups can be traced to the men's liberation movement, which initially painted a false sense of symmetry between "women's oppression" and "men's oppression."[12] This understanding of the gender order portrayed men and women as equals in their discontent and ignored matters of power and status. Moderate feminism's positioning of men as "the other victim," rather than a privileged group, absolved men like Craig from feelings of guilt and so posed no identity threat to them. Indeed, Craig implies that his support of a feminist organization made him virtuous: he sacrificed what little money was available to him to fight for a good cause he "believed in."

Broader changes within the feminist movement eventually made Craig's initial privilege renegotiation strategy—supporting feminism while continuing to recognize men as blameless victims of the gender system—unsustainable. In the early 1970s, critics began to argue that such understandings of gender were not adequately relational or political.[13] They objected to the portrayal of men and women as equally constrained by gender and the failure to identify men as beneficiaries of women's oppression. As some men's consciousness groups adopted this more politicized framework, more moderate men splintered from men's liberation, forming the first men's rights groups. As time went on, men's rights groups too abandoned the idea of sex roles as equally oppressive and instead emphasized the costs of masculinity.

The adoption of a more politicized framework that included an analysis of power had real effects among men who identified as feminists at the time. Craig's description of receiving literature from NOW over the course of the 1970s is illustrative:

> At some point I started to notice the tone changing of the literature. At some point it started to get increasingly hateful. After a couple years of that, I started looking at, why am I supporting this organization? Because they're sending me hate literature basically, that's what it feels like, and I'm the subject of it actually, yet I'm sending them dues every year. That's when . . . I basically ended my membership and I stopped supporting them.

Craig interpreted the more political language of feminist literature as "hateful." Specifically, he perceived that he, as a man, was the subject of feminists' hate. Emotions played an important role in Craig's rejection of feminism: it *felt* like he was receiving hate literature directed at him because of his gender.

Craig felt like this shift toward blaming men was happening in discourses beyond explicitly feminist ones too:

> There were a few key people on [large newspaper] staff who were very ardent feminists, who wanted to make sure that their viewpoint was expressed, not only on the editorial page, but in the news. There was an increasing tone, I thought, of anti-male. Sometimes it was explicit, sometimes it was implied. Whenever a gender issue was suggested, there was always kind of a dig at men in there. I noticed it . . . listening to National Public Radio. I started thinking, "Am I the only one seeing this stuff? Because it doesn't feel balanced to me, and it feels like half the viewpoint is being left out. The whole other viewpoint is being left out, and it's in the name of supporting women. It sounds like we're really dumping on men."

Craig believed men were being demonized by feminists, whose views had infiltrated mainstream news sources. The more politicized language of a new wave of feminists clashed with Craig's belief that men are not responsible for women's oppression but, like women, are victims. His strategy of supporting feminism to bolster his claim that men are constrained but blameless became untenable because feminism had rejected that claim.

When I asked him why he thought this shift in the tone of feminist writing and mainstream media had occurred, he explained it as a political technique, repeating that feminists use men as "an effective boogeyman" to become more powerful. Individuals are motivated to have a positive conception of their ingroup, particularly in terms of its morality.[14] Here, we can see this process in action. Craig abandons feminism and claims feminists demonize men as a political strategy, which allows him to ignore the claim that men are the beneficiaries of women's oppression and sustain his belief that men are good.

Craig found a new strategy to cope with his feelings of discomfort and prove his and his ingroup's morality despite feminists' claims: the men's rights movement. This community allowed Craig to maintain that men are victimized and thus moral. Referring to a popular book written by men's rights leader Warren Farrell, he told me, "That's when I actually ran across Warren's *Myth of Male Power*. It totally blew my mind, because it was saying all these things that I had been thinking, but was actually documenting it with like fifty pages worth of footnotes." As its title suggests, *The Myth of Male Power* attempts to discredit feminist claims that men are privileged.[15] In it, Craig found support for the idea that men are neither oppressive nor immoral, which was immediately attractive and comforting to him.

Upon discovering the movement, he threw himself into it:

> There was one page at the back of *Myth of Male Power*, called "Resources," and it listed all these different organizations around the country, all these different newsletters and magazines. . . . I sat down and went down that list, item by item, and if there was a phone number, I called it. If there was an email address, I sent an email. If there was a snail mail address, I wrote something and said, "Who are you? I want to connect with you." Within a few months I was networked with basi-

cally... everything that existed of the men's rights movement across the board. Within a few months after that I actually started writing articles, because there were things I was seeing in the news that I didn't see being addressed even in the men's rights publications, so I started writing stuff and sending it in. I was being published in a whole bunch of different tiny men's magazines.

The men's rights movement resolved Craig's discomfort with feminist claims that men are the recipients of unearned privilege by discounting those claims. Craig's hunger for a strategy to portray men as he saw them—virtuous—caused him to become quickly and deeply involved in men's rights activism. As a result of his personal identity project, Craig also engaged in constructing a collective identity among men predicated on victimhood. For example, through his activist writing, Craig contributed to a growing body of men's rights literature that identified common grievances and interests among men. Craig's effort to resolve a personal identity threat, then, invested him in a collective identity and a social movement.

Craig's narrative reveals a consistent motivation for his activism: making himself feel like and be seen as a good man. Craig experienced feelings of discomfort as a result of the discrepancy between the way he saw himself—a moral person—and the way he thought feminists saw him—a man who has unfairly benefited from women's disadvantage. While he initially resolved this discomfort by reconciling the idea that women are disadvantaged with his belief that men are *not* advantaged, changes in feminist frameworks made this strategy insupportable. Instead, he reduced his discomfort by immersing himself in a community that claimed men are blameless victims of the gender system. The men's rights movement's assertion that men are disadvantaged and thus virtuous fit Craig's identity standard, thereby reducing his feelings of discomfort. Surrounded by the men's rights community, Craig is able to feel like a hero rather than a villain.

As a privilege renegotiation strategy, engagement with the men's rights movement allows Craig to reconfigure his identity in light of feminist claims about men's privilege. Importantly, men's rights activism does not force Craig to confront or challenge inequality, or even to understand his own identity in a new, more nuanced way. Rather, the essential premise of the movement—that *men* are oppressed—simply denies the existence of real inequality. Like other privilege renegotiation strategies, Craig's participation in the men's rights movement allows him to sidestep new knowledge about gender inequality. He is able to portray himself as a good man, even progressive in his advocacy for the little guy, and surround himself with a fulfilling community based on his "new" identity.

Gil: Becoming a Better Man

Unlike Craig, who threw himself into activism after first learning of the men's rights movement, Gil only rarely participates in feminist activism. He told me, "I go on marches. I contribute money." Yet his identification with feminism accomplished the same task as Craig's involvement in men's rights: Gil was able to realign how he believed others saw him with his sense of himself as a moral person. Specifically, Gil believed his identification with feminism made him different from other men who he suggests are neither as enlightened nor as moral as he. Returning to the quote that opened this chapter, Gil sees feminists as "kind, generous, sensitive." Gil believes his association with the movement indicates to others that these qualities describe him too. In other words, identifying as a feminist makes him an exception to the rule that men are the bad guys.

One of the ways Gil portrayed himself as exceptional was by comparing himself to other men in terms of how much household work and childcare he completes. For example, Gil described the division of labor in his childhood home, differentiating himself from his father by saying,

> One interesting incident that happened to me when I was old, probably in my fifties, I remember my mother saying . . . that "when you were young, [your] father had made speeches about women's equality." But [if he were alive today] I would say to him, "You make these speeches, but you don't practice it in the home at all." It was the wife—my mother—and then us children who would do the dishes. My mother would do all the housework. My father never did any at all, but I didn't notice that as a child. I noticed he often wasn't there and if I needed something I would ask my mother. Sometimes on a Saturday he would take me or my older brother

and sister out with him while he went shopping or something. He did do some of the grocery shopping, I'll say that. But in general, it was just assumed that my mother would do all the housework and all the childcare.

Gil described his father's actions as hypocritical. Despite supporting women's rights, his father undertook very little of the housework and childcare. Gil and his siblings "were told that men and women were equal, just like Blacks and whites are equal" even though this was not the case in their own home. Again, this quote reflects men's relative lack of awareness of gendered dynamics: Gil did not realize this until adulthood, after he had developed a gender consciousness. Still, Gil says he would have called out his father on his hypocrisy had he still been alive.

In describing his behaviors as a husband and father, Gil drew a stark contrast between himself and his own father:

> I probably did more closer to half [of the housework and childcare]. But there was always the expectation that my desire to do half, including half the cooking, taking care [of the kids], picking up the kids, whenever. And I had, at that point, a flexible job where I had to get the work done but I didn't have to go into an office nine to five, which made it much easier. And then, actually, when my daughter was an infant, my wife had gotten a job . . . and those days they used to have an all-night shift, almost all-night, on Friday nights, and I would come up on the subway so she could nurse my daughter. Otherwise, I was the one doing the housework and the childcare then. And the same with our son, I took care of him at least as much she did, I would say.

Gil describes himself as not only doing half of the housework and childcare but having the "desire" to do so. While he does not explicitly compare himself to anyone in this quote, there is nonetheless an implied comparison, both to the average man and to his own father. In describing himself as doing and wanting to do half of the childcare and housework, Gil draws boundaries between himself and other men. He portrays himself as a true feminist, unlike his father, whom he describes as all talk and no action. Gil is able to distance himself from the kinds of men feminists describe—that is, from men who treat women poorly and reap the benefits of their membership in a privileged group. Put another way, in distancing himself from other men, Gil achieved a moral sense of self at the expense of the morality of his ingroup. At the same time, his identity project invests him in a new collective identity he shares with other feminist men. This suggests how men's incorporation of feminism into their performance of masculinity constitutes a hybrid masculinity that they use to differentiate themselves from other, "lesser" men.

Part of feminist men's strategy for feeling like morally good men was engaging in a form of personal activism to lessen the disadvantages their women partners and friends face. They considered this an extension of their feminism. This fits with the literature on everyday resistance, or "individual or small-group resistance practices that are guided by specific situations (and individual creativity) but done regularly in a way that is (sub)culturally patterned and that are not recognized as 'political' by mainstream society."[16] According to this literature, resistance does not have to be recognized as such, nor does it have to be intentional to challenge domination and power.[17] Nevertheless, feminist men described intentional forms of everyday resistance that they practiced. Discursively, they used these practices as evidence that they were good men and as a way to distance themselves from other, bad men.

For instance, Gil's ownership over childcare facilitated his wife's career. As another example, when I asked Gil how being a feminist affects his day-to-day life, he said, "Well, certainly I've always encouraged my daughter as much as my son. I've never treated them differently. I don't treat—to the best of my ability, certainly by intention—I don't treat women differently from men." Recall that Gil's first exposure to feminism was during a feminist group's meeting at a civil rights conference. The women present described mistreatment and sexism, and Gil was "set back" by their anger. By actively trying to treat women the same as men, Gil distances himself from the kinds of men those feminists described. He claims to put his identity standard—as a good man who treats people fairly—into practice through his interactions with the women in his life. It is worth noting that men's rights activists also maintained they treated people the same regardless of their gender. Craig, for example, told me, "I have frequently spoken up when I see anything that is unfair to—that I perceive as being unfair to either women, or to men, or to gay people, or to. . . . To me it's always been just wanting everybody to be treated with respect."

It's worth noting that feminists and men's rights activists' descriptions of their practice of everyday resistance were sometimes vague. Gil's ownership over childcare was specific and without a doubt made a real impact on his wife's ability to pursue a career. In contrast, he did not elaborate on his statement that he always tries to encourage his daughter as much as his son. How did he achieve that? Other men likewise said they tried to treat everyone equally but did not point to specific examples or strategies. For instance, when I asked Ari, a straight, white, cis man in his seventies, whether he does any activities he would call feminist, he said simply, "I guess, in my social interaction," before turning to describe some of the more involved activism he did around same-sex marriage. Other men were more specific. When I asked him how his feminism translates to his daily life, Noah, a queer, white, cis man in his twenties, said,

> I think it can be a number of ways. It's important how I interact with men and women. I think with men, and some women, when they say something that is kind of sexist or maybe a little bit blind to a feminist side of an issue, I try to actually speak up and say what my feminist point of view would be on that issue. If it's with women who are talking about some sort of problem that I've been fortunate enough to be shielded from because I'm a man, I try to actually listen to them, instead of talking over them and trying to act like I'm the expert on an issue that I don't encounter personally.

I contend that when interviewees were more specific about the strategies they used to treat the people they interact with well and equally, it indicates that they had put more thought into how they might engage in everyday practices of resistance.

From our interview, a consistent story of how Gil became a feminist emerged. Gil's first exposure to feminism made it clear that he might be perceived as mistreating women. This was troubling to him because he had built an identity—and, indeed, a career as a civil rights worker—on advocating on behalf of the disadvantaged. There was a discrepancy between the way Gil saw himself—his identity standard—and the feedback he received from others. Engaging in certain behaviors, like childcare and housework, distancing himself from other men, and identifying as a feminist allowed Gil to realign how others perceive him with his identity standard, reducing his feelings of unease. The same basic psychological need—the desire to feel like a morally good person—subconsciously motivated both Craig and Gil to engage in gender activism as a privilege renegotiation strategy.

Privilege Renegotiation Strategies

The strategies Craig and Gil employed to resolve negative feelings evoked by feminist cultural narratives were exemplary of the strategies other interviewees used. Men's rights activists denied their privilege, insisted men are virtuous and victimized, and worked on men's behalf, which provided them with a positive conception of themselves, because of both their own "victimization" and their protection of a "marginalized" group. Feminist men, on the other hand, recognized their privilege but claimed to use it to reduce women's disadvantage. They thus sustained a positive self-concept even while recognizing the privilege of their gender ingroup. While they engaged in different movements, both feminists and men's rights activists became gender activists to transform themselves into good men in their own and others' eyes and to immunize themselves against aspersions cast upon their moral character. Both groups of men use gender activism as a privilege renegotiation strategy—a way to recoup their moral sense of self in light of new information about their privileged place in the social order.

This identity problem—the mismatch between men's sense of self and the implications of feminist cultural narratives—presumably can be resolved in several ways: men can (1) engage in behaviors to change others' perceptions so they better align with their identity standard, (2) reshuffle the importance they assign to their various identities to render the discrepancy irrelevant, or (3) change their identity standard to bring it in alignment with others' perceptions.

Craig, like many of the other men's rights activists I interviewed, opted for the first route. The cultural agenda of the men's rights movement—promoting the belief that men are disadvantaged—would, if successful, resolve this identity problem by changing others' perceptions of men. While the men's rights movement has not had widespread public success, on a personal level and within the men's rights community, Craig's participation allows him to feel and present himself as a good person. On the other hand, feminists like Gil often opted for a combination of the first and second strategies. Gil distanced himself from other men (and thus his gender identity) by emphasizing his feminist identity when he described how much housework and childcare he did. In doing so, he sent a signal to others about who he is (a good person), prioritized his identity as a feminist over his identity as a man, and resolved this identity problem. Put another way, Craig attempted to develop a positive conception of his *ingroup* (men), while Gil distanced himself from his ingroup to maintain a positive *self-concept*. Gil's strategy requires men to reject their ingroup to some extent. This could suggest that an individual man's choice of strategy may be related to the centrality of his gender identity. It may be that men whose gender identities are more salient to them are more likely to deploy strategies that maintain a positive conception of men as a group in the face of identity threat, as men's rights activists do. Men whose gender identities are less central to them may be more willing to distance themselves from other men, as feminist men do.

Still, some feminist men used a strategy that was similar to Craig's. That is, some feminist men tried to redefine masculinity itself so it is not associated with privilege and thus immorality. For example, Matthew, a straight, white, cis feminist in his forties, told me,

> In mainstream culture, it seems like what men are holding onto—all they seem to have left is all the bad masculine stuff. So, well, "We like to break things! And we like to get drunk and scratch ourselves!" All the low-end masculine culture stuff. . . . Masculinity is being redefined because femininity is being redefined. But if you're not actively redefining what masculinity can be, you're going to be left with the dregs of what nobody wants.

Matthew believes that contemporary culture largely defines masculinity negatively. He thinks these definitions are unfortunately true: he says that these are, in fact, the definitions men are holding onto. His strategy for coping with this identity problem is to try to redefine what it means to be a man through his own actions. Matthew does this by being a "caretaker" for his wife, who has a prestigious career and is the breadwinner for their family. His approach is more similar to Craig's than Gil's; he does not distance himself from his ingroup but attempts to change what defines his ingroup by performing a personal, moral masculinity.

None of the men I interviewed opted for the third strategy to resolve this identity problem—that is, none of them came to see themselves as immoral. While feminist men subsumed feminist claims about male privilege into their understandings of masculinity, they didn't see *themselves* as bad by virtue of their gender. They skirt this issue by creating a new collective identity—as feminist men—to project to others that they are morally good. They position themselves as exceptions to the rule that men are privileged and immoral.

It is possible that other men I did not interview, including nonactivists, come to see themselves as immoral when confronted with feminist cultural narratives to resolve this identity problem, but I doubt it. Interviewees' abiding desire to be and be seen as morally good people speaks to the implausibility of such a strategy for most people, as do interviewees' attempts to distance themselves from privilege at nearly every opportunity. Gil's narrative—his discomfort reckoning with his past "wrong" behaviors and his positioning of himself as an exceptional man—illustrates how tenuous men's moral identities are and how much discursive work they do to maintain their moral sense of self.

Identity control theory broadly describes how the meanings people assign to their identity routinely shape their behavior.[18] As a concept, privilege renegotiation strategies are useful in understanding one particular but ever more common situation in which identity meanings are contested—that is, when the structural location of an identity becomes visible. Identity control theory recognizes how behaviors that verify social identities maintain group boundaries and the group's position within the social structure. Privilege renegotiation strategies show us how this can be the primary function of such behaviors rather than a byproduct of them. When men use privilege renegotiation strategies, they make their privilege invisible once again by claiming (for men's rights activists) it does not exist or (for feminists) that they use it for good. When men's identity work obscures male privilege, it makes it more difficult to name and dismantle.[19] Thus, recognizing identity processes as privilege renegotiation strategies can reveal how they discursively shore up privilege and hierarchy.

The specific case of men gender activists also shows how individuals can adopt new identities to resolve discrepancies related to old identities—something not yet explored by work on identity control theory. Privilege renegotiation strategies are useful in understanding how this happens. Men's primary focus is on fortifying their gender identities. In pursuit of this goal, they adopt new identities as feminists and men's rights activists. These activist identities come with new meanings, which bolster the identity standards they associate with their gender identities.

With its roots in symbolic interactionism, identity control theory focuses on how identities are verified (or not) in interaction, and the symbols, signs, and resources individuals use to control meaning within interaction.[20] The case of men gender activists extends our understanding of what might pose a threat to an individual's identity beyond face-to-face contexts. Men can perceive a disconnect between how they understand their own identity and how others see them when they are exposed to narratives about male privilege that are circulating in the culture. In other words, discrepancies can be produced outside of interaction. We can see this in both accounts detailed in this chapter: Craig when he read "hate mail" from NOW and Gil when he read about a lesbian feminist group in the newspaper. The men I interviewed described multiple sources of threat to their identities as morally good men, including sexual harassment trainings, affirmative action programs, online feminist activism like #YesAllWomen and #MeToo, and even words like "patriarchy."

This last point in particular illustrates the wide applicability of privilege renegotiation strategies as a concept. Craig and Gil belong to the oldest generation of men I interviewed for this book, but the processes may be amplified for younger men. Because more radical strains of feminism are easily accessible today via the internet, the identity threat younger men experience might be even stronger than the identity threat Craig and Gil experienced in the 1960s and 1970s.[21] Moreover, feminism's prominence in social, commercial, and broadcast media means that all men (activists and nonactivists alike) are exposed to claims about male privilege. More visible forms of feminism, like corporate and celebrity feminism, may be less threatening to men than radical feminisms, providing opportunities for men to affiliate themselves with the movement, if only to support their moral self-concepts.

Even nonactivist men are likely to experience this sort of identity threat at work, at home, and in the media. Men may resolve these identity threats in diverse ways, like sharing housework or childcare with their women partners, resisting gender diversity initiatives in their workplaces, harassing feminists online, or making misogynist jokes, all without identifying as feminists or men's rights activists. Given the near universality of the threats described by interviewees, most men, whether they are activists or not, have had to grapple with these same questions and find privilege renegotiation strategies that work for them. The process I describe may thus explain the motivation underlying the behaviors of many men. Indeed, I have described only two possibilities—identifying with feminism or the men's rights movement—of what are surely many strategies men employ for dealing with identity threat and privilege. Importantly, some of these strategies are better than others in terms of their consequences for gender inequality.

* * *

When I asked Travis, a bisexual, white, cis man in his twenties, why he engages in men's rights activism, he shared,

> As for why I continue? I continue because it's the right thing to do. If I didn't do it. . . . It got to the point where I would hear somebody make a remarkable comment about men or even dogpiles [gang up on someone] for suggesting that men should have better services for proceedings for false allegations [of sexual assault]. I [would] feel wrong for not trying to rectify that somehow.

Tyler, a gay, white, cis, feminist man in his thirties, offered,

> Manhood, for me personally, just means that if I'm having this position and privilege that I have within my life, that I was born into, I didn't ask for it, but making sure I use that for whatever good I can do within the world. It's all about showing up, and being a force for good, and making sure that, at the end of the day, after every busy night that . . . I go to bed knowing that I've done as much as I can to make the world a better place that day.

Travis and Tyler see the world fundamentally differently: Travis believes men are structurally disadvantaged, while Tyler believes they are systematically privileged. Yet their activism has the same causes and consequences vis-à-vis their self-concepts. First, they see their activism as moral work. Travis describes his work lobbying politicians on behalf of men's rights groups as "the right thing to do," and Tyler says his work as the president of a women's organization makes "the world a better place." Second, their activism fits with their identities. Travis says he would "feel wrong" if he didn't do anything to help men, and Tyler describes his feminism as defining his "manhood." For feminists and men's rights activists alike, gender activism is a means to express their identities as good men living in an unequal world.

That feminist men and men who are men's rights activists are motivated through the same process is surprising. After all, feminism and the men's rights movement each frame the other as an antagonist. Feminists claim women have and continue to face structural and cultural disadvantage, which men's rights activists ardently dispute. Their agendas have diametrically opposed goals and, when successful, radically different consequences for the state of gender inequality. Yet the accounts of Craig and Gil and the other men I interviewed illustrate how men's involvement in right-wing and progressive gender activism is motivated by the same processes related to emotion and identity.

"Moral emotions" are often described as underlying participants' involvement in social movements.[22] In constructing narratives about the causes of social problems and their potential solutions, movement organizers appeal to moral emotions, like indignation and compassion, to motivate participation. Likewise, collective identity is seen as a necessary precursor for micromobilization because collective grievances and interests emerge from it.[23] Collective identity is associated with persistence in social movement participation, bonding to organizations, networks, and leadership, and increased commitment and solidarity.[24] Collective identity is not preformed but must be constructed. One way individuals build solidarity and thus collective identity is through emotional investments, since they promote a sense of shared fate with others.

In the case of men gender activists, however, men's investment in their activism is an outcome of their *personal* identity projects. In naming men as beneficiaries of the gender system, feminist cultural narratives threaten men's moral sense of self. While such cultural narratives describe men as a group, the problem interviewees face is one of personal identity: such narratives do not fit with their idea of themselves—as individuals—as good people. The negative emotions that interviewees first experience are not moral emotions per se. They are not, for example, feelings of indignation about some injustice. Instead, they are emotions like embarrassment and anger that result from the mismatch between their personal identity standard and the way they feel they are being portrayed by feminists. Men's motivation to resolve these emotions and this identity threat invests them, almost incidentally, in gender activism because identifying with feminism and identifying with the men's rights movement are two solutions to the problem of needing to feel like and be seen as a good person. This is not to say that men gender activists do not care about the social problems championed by their respective social movements. They do. But their accounts indicate that their emotional investments in and their identification with their social movements follow from their personal identity projects. In a sense, men fall into gender activism on account of their more deliberate, personal identity work. In this way, the personal is transformed into the political.

Whether the world needs feminism, and indeed whether feminism itself is a force for good or evil, has become an increasingly contentious question as postfeminism and antifeminism have found more popularity on- and offline. Craig's and Gil's narratives help us understand why: identity work invests men in different orientations toward feminism and gender inequality. Men may cling particularly firmly to their ideas about feminism—either positive or negative—because their personal identities are implicated by feminism. Both Craig and Gil described being unbothered (and so unthreatened) by moderate feminists because they recognized the costs of patriarchy to men or tempered their claims about men's place in the gender order. When feminists named patriarchy or displayed their anger, however, both men questioned what a feminist worldview meant about *them*. By rejecting feminism or committing to it, each man was able to resolve this question. Reopening it would mean subjecting themselves again to a sort of existential angst, so both men became deeply invested in the strategy they selected. And so their orientations toward feminism and gender inequality became integrated into their very sense of self. This was true for all the men I interviewed.

George, a straight, Black, cis man in his sixties, told me being a feminist is "part of [his] DNA"; Frank, a straight, white, cis men's rights activist also in his sixties, told me he would have to be a "complete zombie" not to see the disadvantages men face.

This gives us one explanation, then, for why gender inequality is so persistent: *it is written into our very identities*. Individuals derive comfort from their gender because it provides a sense of identity—a sense of "who we are." Craig and Gil show us that gender's influence on "who we are" also invests us in specific strategies or courses of action vis-à-vis gender inequality. The particular identity projects we pursue commit us to behaviors that ultimately shape the state of inequality. Identity projects lead some men, like Gil, to deliberately engage in behaviors that ameliorate inequality and other men, like Craig, to deliberately engage in behaviors that worsen it. As I describe in chapter 4, these identity projects also invest men in unintentional behaviors, like moral boundary making, that have complex and contradictory consequences for gender inequality. Gil's story illustrates this: in focusing on framing himself as a good man, often by differentiating himself from his father and other men, Gil elevates his own version of masculinity above others.

It is worth noting here that the privilege renegotiation strategies Craig and Gil use do not compel them to address inequality. Craig's strategy allows him to deny it altogether. Gil's strategy means that he must recognize that gender inequality exists, but simply associating with feminism's moral framework could be enough to resolve his identity threat and the negative emotions that accompany it. Gil's sense that, through feminism, he is better and more progressive than other men may provide him with an excuse not to do the work, so to speak.[25] If men can reconstruct themselves as good, moral people simply by calling themselves feminists, they can continue to unreflexively reap the benefits of male privilege without engaging in organized activism or practices of everyday resistance. In other words, feminism as a privilege renegotiation strategy could get in the way of feminism the movement.

2

Straight, White, Cis Men at the Intersection of Privilege

Matthew spent his twenties and thirties working a series of blue-collar jobs and raising his child, whom he had at a young age, as a single parent. He eventually returned to school to earn bachelor's and master's degrees. For his wife's job he moved to rural New England, where he now teaches as adjunct faculty and does freelance work. Matthew describes himself as a "caretaker" and does the majority of the couple's household labor, while his wife is the primary breadwinner. He didn't see this as special though: "I don't see anything extraordinary about that. I like cooking. Cleaning—I don't like it, but I also don't like living in a dirty place."

Matthew did, however, recognize that his and his wife's arrangement is rare. He explained that common stereotypes about men—that they don't help around the house, for instance—reflected poorly on him: "I'm just like, 'Guys! Just get with the program!' Because every time I see an article like, 'Men aren't doing this!' or every time I see something where men are screwing up, I'm like, 'You're making me look bad.'" Matthew was frustrated with how other men's bad behaviors defined masculinity and, in the eyes of others, himself.

Matthew's masculinity was not often top of mind for him. Like most men interviewed for this book, the invisibility of his gender identity was disrupted when these negative stereotypes became salient. When I asked him when he is most often aware of his gender, he responded, "For instance, if it's, say, dark outside, I will be very cognizant of who is around me. I will cross a street to avoid walking behind a woman for too long, because I don't want her to think that I'm stalking her. Those sorts of things. I'm trying to be very aware of the ways in which men make women uncomfortable, and I try not to do that." As was true of all the feminist men I interviewed, Matthew's intentions were altruistic: he didn't want to "contribute to [the] feeling of menace" women experience when walking alone at night, so he took steps to avoid doing so. But he also had a more self-centered, subconscious motivation for engaging in such practices. He told me, "It's not because I'm a danger. It's other men making me look bad." To avoid looking bad, Matthew avoided behaviors that might associate him with other, more ill-intentioned men.

The idea that men pose a danger to women evoked feelings of discomfort for Matthew:

> I remember when I first started becoming aware of these things, when I would have my female friends talk about experiences where somebody follows them for two blocks, or whatever, and they felt really uncomfortable. And I'd be like, "Well, that's not me." It was very close to a "not all men" argument that I would catch myself initially thinking, and then I was like, "Well, no, it's just, that's their lived reality."

The idea that men follow and intimidate women on the street sparked a question for Matthew: what did that mean about *him*? He was eventually able to answer this question through his feminism. Feminism allows Matthew to recognize women's "lived reality" and still feel good about himself. Despite his explicit rebuke of "not all men" arguments in this quote, as a privilege renegotiation strategy, feminism allows Matthew to feel like and be seen as not that kind of man.

The questions I asked Matthew were all oriented around gender—how he felt as a man, how he thought he was perceived as a man, what he felt expected to do and be like as a man. But Matthew's responses also turned to matters of race. He continued,

> If having to be aware of the fact that men, especially at night, near a woman, can be menacing, if that's the way I'm being stereotyped, okay. Other groups have had to be stereotyped. And yeah, it's uncomfortable, and I don't like it. The best advice I ever got from somebody was like, "Well, when you feel like that, sit with it. Sit with that discomfort, because that's how it is. A lot of other groups feel that kind of discomfort all the time." I've had Black people tell me, "Yeah, walk into a store, and feel how uncomfortable you feel when people start watching you, thinking you're going to steal something." Or, "If you think you're uncomfortable being stereotyped as a man at night, too close to a woman, imagine how that woman feels, knowing that every man out there could be the poison Skittle in the bowl," to use that analogy.[1]

Matthew compared his experience being stereotyped as threatening because of his gender to Black people's experience being stereotyped as criminals and to women's fear when on the street at night. He drew a connection between these experiences, even as he downplayed the significance of his own as more infrequent ("A lot of other groups feel that kind of discomfort *all the time*") and less pernicious ("If you think *you're* uncomfortable").

Throughout our interview and unprompted by me, Matthew drew connections between gender, race, and sexuality. He understood these identities, and the processes that governed them, as inextricably linked because his own experience had taught him so. As a straight, white, cisgender man, Matthew's high-status gender, racial, and sexual identities were linked together. For much of his life they had been invisible, but recently they had come under more scrutiny in the broader culture:

> Women have to be representative of all women. Black people have to be representative of all Black people. People get stereotyped all the time, but men, especially straight, white men, have been normal for so long, with all this attention and all of a sudden. . . . It gets back to the defining point. Suddenly "whiteness" is being defined. "Maleness" is being defined. "Straightness" is being defined as things, as categories, and we've never really had to deal with that before.

Matthew recognized the visibility of his high-status identities as a new phenomenon, brought on by recent cultural shifts that elevated feminist, anticisexist, antiracist, and antiheterosexist claims and narratives. Here, he implied that masculinity, whiteness, and straightness are being defined by these countercultural narratives as oppressive and privileged—as bad.

Matthew identified this newfound visibility as an issue for straight, white, cis men, explaining that it sparked feelings of exclusion and aggrieved entitlement:[2]

> I think there's a lot of men who feel left behind, because they're seeing people talk about Black people being important, gay people being important, trans people being important, women being important. And men aren't hearing that [about themselves]. They look at the books, and they

say, "Well, hate crime laws. . . . Well now, if you want the smallest punishment for beating up somebody, go beat up a white guy. You'll get the smallest punishment for it. Everyone else is protected." They don't see that all those protections are there in order to level the playing field. They're not there to hurt white—like I said before, if your masculinity can be taken away, you're manning wrong. Nobody's taking anything away from you. It's not a zero-sum game, and I think most men don't realize that.

In this quote, Matthew is responding to my question about what the biggest issues are facing *men*. He answered by identifying an issue that impacts *straight, white, cis men* in particular, even as he referred to this group with the general term "men." In a statement that foreshadowed many of the arguments I make in this book, Matthew summed up this group's reaction to their feelings of discomfort: "So, either there's a lack of reflection going on, or there's this backlash reaction to seeing other people being forefronted. Whereas they're [straight, white, cis men are] just used to being forefronted, like they were normal."

The activism of feminist men and men who are men's rights activists is motivated by identity processes related not only to their gender but also to their race and sexuality. High-status group identities—masculinity, cisness, whiteness, and straightness—are interconnected because they are subject to the same infrequent unveiling, and these disruptions to their invisibility evoke the same feelings of discomfort that must be rectified. Gender activism serves as a privilege renegotiation strategy for feminist men and men who are men's rights activists, allowing them to navigate these feelings and construct new and moral gender, racial, and sexual identities. This was the case for Matthew, who saw his experience being stereotyped as just—an opportunity to atone for his multiplex privilege: "That's [being stereotyped] fair. It would be great if we lived in a world where nobody had to be uncomfortable, or stereotyped, and maybe one day we'll get there. But in the meantime, I'm taking my punishment like a good boy, I guess." Matthew's acceptance of the ways he is stereotyped as a straight, white, cis man and his feminism more broadly are strategies he uses to be and be seen as "a good boy," as he put it.

The centrality of these identities to interviewees' behaviors and the way they understand their experience make sense. Both gender and race are primary frames in the United States, meaning we use them as systems of difference to coordinate our action.³ Upon meeting someone, we automatically categorize their gender and race (or try to), and this categorization conjures the complex system of cultural beliefs we have constructed around these axes of difference. Some of these beliefs are status beliefs because they identify certain groups as more competent, respected, and worthy. Even when we don't explicitly endorse these beliefs, they shape how many and what kinds of opportunities we receive and give others in interaction. Moreover, both gender and race are diffuse status characteristics, meaning they have corresponding status beliefs that apply far beyond contexts we might see as immediately and directly relevant to them. In other words, gender and race play in the background and subtly impact the participation, influence, and prestige of individuals across social contexts. While sexuality is not a primary frame, it is similar to gender and race in important ways and emerges prominently in interviewees' narratives, though not as often as gender and race.

Gender, race, sexuality, and other identities interact with one another to shape experience. My analysis in this chapter is informed by intersectionality, a theoretical, methodological, and analytical approach that recognizes how stereotypes, status, power, resources, and lived experience are shaped by mutually constituted and complexly interacting systems of oppression.⁴ A common limitation of even feminist and antiracist work is reifying the normativity of high-status group identities by, for instance, treating *white* women as representative of women or Black *men* as representative of Black people.⁵ In response, Black feminist scholars developed intersectionality to understand how the disadvantages faced by individuals who embody multiple low-status group identities (particularly Black women) were not simply additive. Instead, the theory envisions groups as situated at the intersection of multiple axes of oppression. Legal scholar Kimberlé Crenshaw, for instance, argued that this new framework was needed to understand Black women's experiences with discrimination and violence.⁶

Through intersectionality, it is clear that many of the men I interviewed experience privilege on account of multiple high-status group identities. Of the sixty-two men I interviewed, fifty-five were white, fifty were straight, and forty-four were both white and straight; only one identified as transgender and one as genderqueer.⁷ Privilege, like oppression, is not additive. Instead, interviewees experience and perceive the world as straight men or white men or straight, white men. These particular combinations of identities associate them with positive status beliefs that convey upon them resources and opportunities not afforded to others.[8] In an essay that lays bare the connections between masculinity and whiteness (and likewise applies to straightness), feminist and antiracist scholar Peggy McIntosh describes privilege as "an invisible package of unearned assets that [high-status individuals] can count on cashing in each day, but about which [they are] 'meant' to remain oblivious."[9] Those with privilege on account of their membership in high-status groups are made to "think of their lives as morally neutral, normative, and average, and also ideal."[10] Straight, white, cis men in particular are treated as the neutral and implicit standard by which other groups are measured. Importantly, if they cannot see their privilege, high-status group members cannot relinquish it.

This chapter focuses on two straight, white, cis men—Theo and Alex—and their trajectories into feminism and the men's rights movement, respectively. First, I describe how their high-status group identities are made visible by the same processes, producing feelings of discomfort. Then I show how both Theo and Alex resolve negative feelings about their multiple high-status group identities through gender activism, which provides them with opportunities to perform moral whiteness and straightness in addition to moral cismasculinity.

When Invisible Identities Become Visible

Theo: A Slap in the Face

I interviewed Theo, a feminist who works in higher education, at his work. Theo is married and in his thirties. He's good-looking and has an ease and sincerity that I guessed would allow him to connect easily with students. When we met, he was wearing two small wooden hoop earrings and a trendy brown wool sweater with a shawl collar over a crisp button-up shirt. He greeted me with a handshake and, after leading me to the room where we would do our interview, proceeded to make us coffee while asking me politely about my project.

Over the course of our interview, Theo expressed his interest in matters of social justice related to gender and beyond it. His passion project—a program that provides opportunities for men students to reflect on masculinity and privilege—is centrally focused on gender, but his previous work was not. For instance, as a K–12 teacher, Theo earned a master's degree and conducted research investigating how students talk about race in a multiracial classroom.

His racial identity formation and racial awareness began as a child, however:

> When I was doing my thesis defense, my mom came and watched and decided to chime in which was adorable and embarrassing. She was like, "I remember this story." She started telling stories about my own racial awareness that I had forgotten about, one of which was—we lived in [the Midwest] when I was in the fifth grade. They had a multicultural week or whatever and they brought in this woman who was an African storyteller and we had this schoolwide assembly and she was doing this oral storytelling. Apparently, I went home that day and I said to my mom, "I looked around the gym and realized that she was the only nonwhite person in the building and we had to import her from Africa to tell us stories." She was like, "Yeah, we live in [the] rural [Midwest]. What did you think?" I grew up [on the West Coast] and I was a little more accustomed to seeing some visible diversity. Moving there, it was the first time that it became really apparent to me how white that community was.

Theo had lived in a more racially diverse community prior to moving to the Midwest, but said that this moment was significant for his "racial awareness." In the Midwest, he witnessed acute difference in a context that was otherwise especially homogeneous, which highlighted his own identity as a member of the racial majority. Importantly, Theo brought up this topic himself after I asked him about how he became involved in feminist activism. To explain his awareness around *gender*, he described how he first came to see his and others' *race*.

Theo described recognizing his privilege as an ongoing process. He recounted several times when he had failed to notice how his high-status group identities shaped his experience or the situation. For instance, when conducting his master's research, a student, Jessica, told him her mother would not allow her to participate in his study. Jessica wanted to participate and asked Theo to call her mother:

> I called her mom and I said, "Jessica is really excited about participating. Just wondering if you could share with me your point of view about why you'd rather she'd not." She said, "I'm sure that you're great and all but there are just a lot of really well-intentioned white people studying Black and Brown kids and I don't really need mine to be one of them." That was the first time in the design of my study that it had occurred to me that being white might have some influence over the way that my students talk to me about race. My thesis advisor was a white man—straight, white man. The professor for the thesis design class was a white woman. It had never occurred to any of us that my racial identity would have an influence on my study. It was this moment of feeling completely embarrassed and mortified that that had been so invisible to me—that my lack of racial awareness would have anything to do with my students' racial awareness. That was a very obvious moment of failure.

Theo's whiteness was invisible to him (and his advisor and professor), even as he designed a study explicitly about race in the classroom. He felt "completely embarrassed and mortified" when the student's mother identified racial dynamics—the position of power he inhabited on account of his race—as the determining factor in her decision to prohibit her daughter from participating in his research. This story speaks to the normativity of high-status group identities like whiteness. As a rule, such identities are invisible, even when they are directly relevant to the situation at hand. Even when they are named, they are able to disappear back into the background in between those rare moments. Importantly, their naming provokes intensely negative feelings—in Theo's case, humiliation.

Sometime after this experience, Theo returned to the Midwest. As before, the setting illuminated his racial identity in a way that was deeply uncomfortable for him:

> It was this extremely white—not just white community, but that it was culturally white too. The things that people did. The restaurants. The community fairs. Everything was just a really white experience. I felt my whiteness in a way I hadn't really ever before. That was an uncomfortable experience for me in a way that being in a more visibly diverse place never felt uncomfortable.

Theo found living in a culturally white community uncomfortable, embarrassing even. He seemed to feel that unchecked and unreflexive whiteness was shameful. He identified this overwhelming whiteness as an important spark for his racial identity formation, which preceded his feminist identity formation: "I think [living in the Midwest] was really helpful and educational in terms of me becoming more aware of how [race] manifests itself in social privilege and in the workforce and in these ways, that I'm now trying to do that same level of education with myself around gender." Theo's recognition of white privilege was a precursor to his recognition of male privilege. He continued to "educate" himself around gender through his project with students on masculinity and by taking cues from his wife, who often shares with him her experience working in a male-dominated field.

Theo's time in the Midwest also allowed him to observe his privilege as a straight man. As a K–12 teacher, Theo worked with a principal whom he described as an "old boy." The principal chose Theo and another straight man to advise the Gay Straight Alliance (GSA) at their school:

> I think a big part of why he chose the two of us is that he felt more comfortable with straight men leading that organization because there's no way we could be accused of having some agenda. That we weren't trying to convert kids or whatever. I think that was an environment where I could really clearly see the way that my identity was allowing me to be an ally to a community that otherwise wouldn't be supported institutionally. It was a place where my queer colleagues were not comfortable outing themselves publicly in a way that being the advisor to the GSA would do.

This experience illustrated to Theo how he, as a straight man, had privilege in a heteronormative and homophobic context. Unlike his queer colleagues, Theo neither had to hide his sexual identity nor risk anything when disclosing it. His experience as a straight person was one of comfort and normativity, even in proximity to queerness. Moreover, this experience allowed Theo to see how the privilege associated with his high-status group identity allowed him to navigate heteronormative institutions in a way that was closed off to his queer colleagues. He suggested that, without straight advisors, the club would not have had institutional support.

Theo referenced his multiple high-status group identities throughout our interview. He described himself several times with multiple signifiers, for instance, "straight, cisgender, able-bodied, white man." In doing so, Theo indicated that these identities were connected, first, because they all shape his experience. Second, together, they make him particularly privileged in his view. For instance, he saw his racial and gender identities as providing him with access to and inclusion in multiple, exclusive spaces in higher education:

> I also get the benefit of being able to occupy hegemonic spaces without question. That I show up to an all-male group, I show up to an all-white group, and I deserve to be there. I don't have to justify my presence. It's a benefit obviously but it's also an invisible benefit that folks who enjoy those spaces, those privileges, don't often notice in a way that colleagues of color or women or whoever do notice.

To Theo, his high-status group identities are linked because they provide him with similar kinds of benefits. He pointed out that such privileges remain invisible to most who have them.

Theo's recognition of these dynamics—of the status hierarchy and his place in it—presents a tension for him and others that live with privilege: Do you continue to use your privilege for good or for personal gain, or do you divest yourself from it? He shared,

> If you're a man who claims to want to be an ally to nonmale peers in the workplace, what does that physically look like in practice? Does that mean pulling a Jerry Maguire and grabbing papers and throwing it in the air and saying, "I don't work here"? Does it mean making your presence there a daily positive reminder of what it means to have an inclusive community? Is it turning down incentives that might otherwise come your way if you're willing to be part of the old boys' club?

Theo explained that a person can navigate their privilege in several ways: opting out of the environment ("pulling a Jerry Maguire"), refusing to benefit from privilege when provided an opportunity to do so ("turning down incentives"), or working toward inclusion (being "a daily positive reminder").

Theo suggested that once a person sees their privilege, it requires a response. Why? While Theo did not describe his feelings in as explicit of terms as Craig or Gil in the previous chapter, it is clear that his privilege, when visible, is uncomfortable for him. This is evident in Theo's retelling of the "African storyteller" experience. As a child, the presence of someone who was an "other" illuminated Theo's (and his school's) whiteness and privilege, so much so that he needed to tell his mother and seek an explanation from her after school. Theo's return to the Midwest as an adult provoked the same feelings of discomfort: in his own words, it "slapped [him] in the face." Throughout our interview, Theo indicated that he believed living with and among privilege is deeply uncomfortable and almost shameful. Just as with Craig and Gil, the visibility of high-status group identities—masculinity, whiteness, and straightness— provoked negative feelings for Theo that he sought to resolve. In not so many words, Theo explained that high-status group members must seek out strategies to feel better when confronted with their privilege.

What to do about privilege arose again and again in our interview, including related to axes of inequality besides gender. For example, when I asked him how he navigates tension around his own privilege, he replied,

> Where do you create that balance? Do you do more good by staying in that environment and exerting a positive influence over the long term or do you do more good by opting out entirely? . . . I definitely opt in. I have been fortunate to never find myself in a work environment where I felt like it was that explicitly sexist or explicitly racist or homophobic. I've never had to confront my own conflict around that in a really overt way. Certainly I will talk to colleagues of color, queer colleagues, or female colleagues who see things that I don't see.

Again, Theo implied that a person will necessarily find strategies to navigate their privilege once they recognize it. In this quote, he referred to sexism, racism, and homophobia, and his privilege specifically as a straight, white man. Theo had chosen to "opt in," to stay in unequal environments where he might make a difference for marginalized people.

In "opting in," Theo had chosen a broad strategy, which includes feminism, for remaking himself when confronted with his own privilege. Importantly, Theo explained that recognizing his privilege was an ongoing process, requiring assistance from people of color, queer people, and women. I return to Theo's reliance on the work others do to make him cognizant of his and others' privilege later in the chapter. Here, I will note that Theo's subjectivity may prevent him from recognizing when his work environment is sexist, racist, or homophobic, explicitly or implicitly. It seems, for instance, that Theo's queer colleagues may have felt their workplace was homophobic if they could not come out publicly and advise the GSA.

Alex: No Seat at the Party

Like Theo, Alex is a straight, white, cis man in his thirties. Unlike Theo, Alex is a men's rights activist. He lives in the western United States, where he supports himself by doing a variety of odd jobs, like delivery and graphic design. I interviewed Alex over the phone, and though our conversation initially focused on Alex's experience as a man, it quickly turned to his experience as a person who embodies multiple high-status group identities.

Alex's pathway into the men's rights movement was sparked by his discomfort with feminist claims. He began our interview by explaining that feminists ignore issues pertinent to men:

> There's a lot of different stuff out there that did seem unfair to me that men were facing. Looking at the statistics and everything like that, crime victimization even, I felt that there were a lot of issues that the feminist narratives that I was seeing weren't touching on. Like I've heard a lot of lip service that "we [feminists] care about everyone's stuff," but I see everything couched in terms like "toxic masculinity" and the like that I don't think are entirely fair.

Alex explained that despite claiming to "care" about "everyone," feminists fail to pay sufficient attention to issues that disproportionately affect men. Alex said that when they do discuss men's issues, feminists use terms that he feels are unfair: "What I really think is that we have an overall culture that disadvantages people in different ways, but I'm also uncomfortable with terms like 'the patriarchy' and other similar terms because I feel like there's a lot of blame that's placed on men, somewhat unfairly, and I think that we all contribute to the upholding of current cultural norms." Alex argued that terms like "toxic masculinity" and "patriarchy" are inaccurate for two reasons. For one, he believes that all people, regardless of their gender, face disadvantages in their own way. Second, he believes that all people, not just men, reinforce social norms that might be considered toxic.

As was the case for Craig in the previous chapter, Alex's disagreement with feminism was not borne out of cold rationality or simple logic. He believes that feminist narratives are not just untrue but also *unfair*. Terms like "toxic masculinity" and "patriarchy" evoke discomfort in Alex because he perceives them as assigning "blame" to men. Alex's reaction to feminist narratives was exemplary of the majority of men (feminists and men's rights activists alike) I interviewed: as a man, he worried what such narratives meant about himself. The idea that he could be seen as toxic or privileged sparked negative feelings for Alex, which he sought to quiet. Like his involvement in the men's rights movement more generally, the rhetorical moves he used above are privilege renegotiation strategies that allow him to reckon with his privilege, to both deny men's advantage and to diffuse responsibility for gender inequality beyond his own gender ingroup.

Alex explained that, online and in the liberal city where he lives, feminism and other movements for social justice are prominent and that he often finds himself arguing with people about it:

> Feminism and social justice is a very big thing. . . . I try to point out what I believe are logical fallacies in the way that people are thinking. When I bring up, for instance, [that] many of the actual statistical disadvantages that are faced by one sex or another are faced by men rather than this kind of ambiguous, vague, "patriarchal oppression" that I hear a lot about . . . I hear that blamed on patriarchy too. That somehow, for instance, the heavier sentences for men in courts which are over twice as long on average, or something like that, are somehow actually a disadvantage to women because of the way that they're viewed. I try to bring up the idea that speculating [about] people's motives for doing something is a lot less

important than saying, "Hey, we both committed the same crime and I got twice the sentence you did." That's just a disadvantage and I don't see why we should frame that in a female-centered paradigm when it is men who are obviously and evidently, materially, disadvantaged by that.

Alex rejects particular explanations for gender differences in criminal sentencing—for instance, that judges engage in benevolent sexism when they hand down lighter sentences to women.[11] He interprets such explanations as missing the point by emphasizing intent over impact. Alex objects to interpreting patterns in sentencing through a "female-centered paradigm" at all. In Matthew's words, part of Alex's discontent with feminism is that it "forefronts" women rather than men. What is more, feminist narratives and claims make his own gender visible while simultaneously centering women's issues, needs, and disadvantages.

Alex said that he often debated others on topics beyond feminism. He told me that, lately, he had been focusing on "the whole electiony stuff." I interviewed Alex just one week after the 2016 presidential election, and it was at the top of his mind. When I asked him what those conversations consisted of, he responded,

> People are putting out a lot of articles or news stories these days about how people are having, say, graffiti put on their walls that's racist or people are supposedly getting their hijabs pulled off. Although that actually didn't happen. I chime in and I try and show these instances that have already been occurring of people getting attacked, one way or another, for being a Trump supporter or something like that. . . . I'm not a supporter of Trump, but I think that modern discourse is just so full of hate and venom and really inconsistent ethics, and people calling speech "violence," which I think is an incredibly dangerous way to think about these sorts of things.

While Alex said he did not support Donald Trump in the 2016 election, he doubted reports of hate crimes against people of color and Muslim women that occurred in the lead-up to and wake of the election.[12] Instead, he claimed that Trump supporters had been "attacked" for their political views. He implied that he expected to see more attacks on Trump supporters ("have *already* been occurring") but that "modern discourse" is unlikely to recognize such attacks as violence because of "inconsistent ethics." Alex perceived mainstream culture as minimizing violence against Trump supporters and instead exaggerating hate speech as equivalent with violence, but only when directed toward people of color and religious minorities. What remains unspoken in this quote is that Trump supporters are likely to be white. Even while Alex talked about his perception of racial dynamics, he used "Trump supporters" as a stand-in for "whites." This speaks to his discomfort with making whiteness explicit and visible and also to his white racial politics.

But whiteness did not remain implicit for long. In describing what he saw as a double standard, Alex explicitly compared the treatment of Black men to white men. He continued,

> I've been hearing that sort of thing out of feminist circles for a while. That certain kinds of speech are themselves considered violent, and that they therefore will justify violence in return. I've been trying to push the point here that, no, it's not okay to do this. It's no more okay to talk about how white people or white men are pieces of shit than it is to say that Black men are pieces of shit or are violent thugs or anything like that.

Fifteen minutes into what began as a conversation about his experience as a man, Alex described how he believes feminists openly ridicule *white* men specifically. Alex perceives feminists as objecting to stereotypes of Black men as criminals but endorsing stereotypes of white men as privileged and toxic. He described this as the inconsistency of feminism and other progressive movements: "If you want to engage in a discourse to say these sorts of things are unfair you need to be consistent with it or you're not going to convince anybody. You're just going to make people feel attacked. That's the big thing."

While Alex often spoke in general rather than personal terms (e.g., "you're just going to make *people* feel attacked"), it is clear that he himself experiences discomfort and negative feelings when his privilege is named. *He* feels attacked. He admitted as much during our interview when I asked him why it is important to him to continue having such conversations, even when they often turn contentious:

> I think a lot of what propels a person like Trump into office is the fact that people were feeling silenced. People were listening to terms like "mansplaining" and stuff like that, and "check your privilege." I think those are all profoundly silencing ways of talking to people. . . . Honestly, part of it too is because I can see what happens to me, that feeling of anger and defensiveness that I get. I think that there's something profoundly dangerous about this narrative that you are a member of an oppressed class in this oppressive system, kind of thing. It makes people feel like they live in a hostile place. When people feel that they're in a hostile place, they themselves become more hostile. I don't think it's helpful, even to the degree that it's true. I don't think that it's a useful way to think about it.

Alex's claims—about how other people feel when they hear terms like "mansplaining" or why Trump was elected—are all based on his own experiences. He himself feels like the target of progressive movements and spaces that insist he "check [his] privilege" on account of his high-status gender and racial identities. *He* feels silenced. Moreover, he perceives feminist and other similar movements as sorting individuals into two classes: oppressed and oppressors. While it is evident that being perceived as an oppressor is deeply uncomfortable to him personally, Alex also insists that it is an unhelpful way of looking at the world for oppressed people, even when it is "true." He attributes the "hostility" of minoritized group members—women, people of color—toward white men like himself to this black-and-white worldview. A clear picture of Alex's gender and racial ideology emerges from this quote. He pursues a genderblind and colorblind vision of the world because it allows his high-status group identities to disappear into the background. His insistence that identities and power should remain invisible and unnamed serves both his own privilege and his feelings.

I did not ask Alex about his race at all. Our conversation organically—and quickly—turned to race as Alex made connections between how feminism makes him feel as a man and how non–Trump supporters make him feel as a *white* man. Alex's feelings are the through line linking his gender and racial identities. He feels that he is seen in a particular way—as especially privileged or toxic or deserving of disdain—because he is both white and a man. It is worth noting that Alex is reporting about his *perception* of feminists and progressives, rather than their intentions or, even, their actual behaviors. What matters to Alex's trajectory into the men's rights movement is not what feminists, antiracists, Democrats, or progressives do but Alex's interpretation of their actions and his feelings.

The election was an epiphany of sorts for Alex because he felt "a lot of these people have been feeling fairly content to speak in generalities about people who look like me, or have my genitals, or sexual preferences, or something like that." In other words, Alex felt targeted as a straight, white, cis man. As this quote indicates, Alex also saw his straightness as relevant to the way he is viewed and treated. For both Theo and Alex, the visibility of their straightness required them to reckon with the privilege it bestowed upon them. As before, Alex did this by insisting that sexual identities did not matter and should remain invisible:

> You see the "Victim Olympics" and these people, these identities are so important. These labels. All of these different labels people are putting on themselves and each other. "Queer" is one that I see as almost . . . it's so amorphous that it's basically just a membership card. It's a declaration of which side you're on because it doesn't necessarily mean anything in particular. It could mean that you like wearing eyeshadow and you're a dude or it can mean that you are gay. A lot of things. But there is this club kind of mentality. Kind of congregation of the oppressed looking out at oppressors, and the only people who don't get a seat at that party are straight, white men because we're just not a valid identity group.

Alex objects to labels generally, and to "queer" specifically. He claimed that queer is an empty signifier because people with different sexualities and gender performances can all identify with the term. Yet Alex also noted that the word is highly significant in one way: in his words, it specifies "which side you're on." Alex sees the function of "queer" as separating the moral—"the oppressed"—from the immoral—"oppressors."

The visibility of queerness and, by contrast, straightness made Alex uncomfortable, just as "female-centered paradigms" and attention to hate crimes against people of color and Muslims did. In this quote, Alex once again raised a social distinction besides gender—queer versus nonqueer—without my prompting because they are linked in his mind.

He generalized his belief—that being a "victim" makes one moral in public perception—across multiple social categories—gender, race, and sexuality. Importantly, this means that straight, white men, as the group seen as most privileged, are seen as most immoral and excluded from making the same claims as others. According to Alex, the broader culture does not allow straight, white, cis men to participate in the "Victim Olympics." In other words, straight, white, cis men cannot make claims to victimhood and thus morality. He described straight, white, cis men as excluded from a "club" or "party." He evoked a picture of straight, white, cis men being judged by those who can engage in identity politics (a "congregation of the oppressed looking out at oppressors").

In the next section, I turn to how Alex resolved the negative feelings prompted by feminist, antiracist, and antiheterosexist narratives through his activism. But, as I have already noted, Alex used other privilege renegotiation strategies to manage his feelings. In particular, he insisted that identity labels are unimportant:

> I hate labels. I think that they are stupid. I think racial labels are stupid, gender labels are stupid. It is trying to boil down ineffable human character into this. . . . We're all individuals, and we're actually unique, and nobody really knows what it's like to be a man, or a woman, or a white guy, or a Black guy, or whatever. . . . I think that when we label ourselves and we label each other we simplify that. We make ourselves into a caricature.

Alex's insistence that gender, race, and sexuality are unhelpful in understanding lived experience ignores the fact that they are important axes of social difference because they shape access to resources, power, and status. The privilege Alex is afforded and his belief that identities do not matter sustain one another: his privilege allows his identities to remain invisible and neutral (for the most part), and his worldview that identities should be invisible maintains his privilege. Importantly, his perspective is based on the discomfort he experiences when the labels that mark him as privileged and, as he perceives it, immoral are made visible.

Theo's and Alex's narratives indicate that acknowledging one's multiplex privilege is an uncomfortable process. This was common throughout the sample. As a young boy, feminist Sam felt bombarded by news coverage of the AIDS epidemic: "They were in the news constantly. It was homosexual rights: 'Homosexuals are protesting, and blah, blah, blah, blah, blah.'" Despite later deciding that being gay was "okay," Sam's rather flippant language suggests he had some initially negative feelings toward the media coverage of the AIDS crisis, possibly because the focus on a disease that disproportionately impacted gay men revealed his own, typically invisible, straightness. Now, he described this media coverage as essential to his pathway into activism. Likewise, media coverage of protests against the Dakota Access Pipeline made it impossible for men's rights activist Luke's whiteness to remain invisible. In regard to Black Lives Matter, Luke perceived the media as "pushing an agenda" because they publicize only the incidents "where there's a difference in color." News coverage drew attention to white cops' violence against Black civilians, thus drawing attention to Luke's own whiteness.

There are subtle and important differences in Theo's and Alex's narratives though. While both men experienced negative emotions when their high-status group identities were named, their feelings were different. Theo described himself as feeling mortified and ashamed, while Alex described himself as defensive and angry. Additionally, while both had experienced moments when their masculinity, whiteness, and straightness had become visible, Theo's and Alex's descriptions of how often such moments occurred were vastly different. Theo could point to specific instances when his high-status group identities were revealed, which he contrasted with his more frequent experience of invisibility and normativity, for instance by saying that he is able to enjoy majority-white or majority-men spaces without thinking about it or isn't cognizant of microaggressions that his marginalized colleagues are. Alex, on the other hand, described himself as fielding a constant barrage of attacks from social justice advocates who can't seem to help throwing their oppression and his privilege in his face. His description of a "congregation of the oppressed looking out at oppressors" and his sense that identity labels are "a declaration of which side you're on" reflect his feeling that he is constantly under siege.

Some of these differences likely preceded Theo's and Alex's trajectories into gender activism, reflecting, for example, their childhood socialization, their role-taking abilities, and the diversity of their networks. Yet they also likely reflect differences in the norms of the feminist and men's rights communities. As Theo and Alex committed to feminism and the men's rights movement as privilege renegotiation strategies for navigating their place in the gender, racial, and sexual order, they were socialized to adopt the perspectives and language of those spaces.

Performing Moral Identities through Gender Activism

How did Theo and Alex recoup the feeling that they are good people when their privilege was made visible and morality threatened? Each man employed a broad range of strategies—informal and formal, rhetorical and practical—to navigate their high-status group identities and privilege. Ultimately, they both used gender activism as a privilege renegotiation strategy to resolve feelings related to their masculinity, whiteness, and straightness. Theo's feminist activism and Alex's men's rights activism differ in important ways, primarily in that the former aims to reduce real gender inequality while the latter exacerbates it. This is an essential and important difference, and by pointing out the similarities in Theo's and Alex's subconscious motivations, shortcomings, and behaviors below, I do not mean to minimize it. Still, the similarities in their activism illustrate how feminist men's conscious intentions are complicated by the subconscious identity processes underlying them.

Theo: Divesting from or Living with Privilege?

Theo's recognition of the interconnectedness of his high-status group identities means that he tries to practice intersectional feminism. He defined feminism as

> a way of seeing the world that accounts for the way that social identities are privileged or progressed by systems of power. Gender is certainly one of those bits. It's gender identity, sexual orientation, race, social class, ability. . . . I like the much more inclusive and encompassing definition [of feminism] because you can't be just a woman and not also a woman of color or a white woman or an able-bodied woman or a straight woman. I can't be a man without also being all those other identities. It feels artificial to say that we're talking about gender without talking about all those other things.

An intersectional approach to feminism allows Theo to recognize how he is privileged on account of multiple identities.

Importantly, Theo's intersectional feminism allows him to perform a particular white masculinity that is attuned to how feminism historically and currently excludes people of color: "I think the younger generation of feminists that I talk to see all of that intersectionality as part of feminism in a way that I think earlier waves of feminism didn't include. . . . It's why I understand that folks of color might have been disenfranchised by that ideology in a way that hopefully the more modern way of thinking about it has shifted." Theo's interactions with a younger generation of feminists—the students he works with—exposed him to an intersectional feminism that is more inclusive. Reimagining feminism to be more attuned to the problems of people besides upper-class, able-bodied, straight, white, cisgender women is an important goal, and progress has been hard-won by those most marginalized in feminist organizations and spaces. According to many activists, the success and continued relevance of feminism is dependent on its ability to tackle issues that affect people marginalized by multiple axes of oppression.[13] But beyond any altruistic motivations, Theo's adherence to intersectional feminism accomplishes something else for him personally: it allows him to perform a particularly moral straight, white cismasculinity. He juxtaposes himself not just with nonfeminist, straight, white men but with *feminists* who are not attuned to matters of race, sexuality, class, gender identity, and more. This allows Theo to portray himself as an especially empathetic and compassionate person. In his attentiveness to the exclusion of others from certain forms of feminism, he is able to negotiate some of the discomfort he feels because of his own multiplex privilege.

As part of his gender activism, Theo established a program for men students at his university: "The grand, pie-in-the-sky goal is to help men-identified students understand their conceptions of manhood and masculinity better in order to make campus safer and more supportive for all the students, of all genders." Theo and his cofacilitator have collaborated with other groups on campus toward this goal. For example, they hosted an event on "locker-room talk" with their university's athletics department, the women's center, and Greek organizations following publicity around a 2005 taped conversation in which Donald

Trump bragged about groping and kissing women without their consent. Trump, who was the Republican nominee for the 2016 presidential election at the time of the tape's release, dismissed the remarks as "locker-room banter."[14]

Following the success of that event, they hosted additional programming for a men's allyship program organized by a campus group for women in business. Their conversation with the men in the program centered on what it means to be an ally in practice:

> What does [allyship] look like? And asking the guys there to take a really critical look at that. For most of them, their concern was about in the immediate future. "I'm going to be in this entry-level position where I don't have a lot of capital. I can't push too hard on my superiors even if they say things that I find morally abhorrent." The example one of them gave was being in an internship last summer and his supervisor tried to build camaraderie with him by talking about, "Which of the female interns do you want to have sex with?" This kid is like, "I can't turn around and tell my boss he's a pig but I don't feel good participating in this." Where does he find the balance for himself so that he can reconcile wanting to be employed with wanting to feel like he's making a positive influence?

Theo's description of this young man's dilemma is sensitive to issues of power that so often make changing toxic work environments difficult. The student wondered what he could do in a sexist encounter with his boss when he lacked "capital" as an intern.

Theo and his students' interest in learning to be allies to women is a positive development. It signifies that cultural norms around masculinity are changing, opening opportunities for men to challenge patriarchy and their own privilege. Discussions such as the one Theo recounted can be an important first step toward action that will effect wider change. Yet Theo's discussion of the student's dilemma is exemplary of a serious limitation in his approach to feminism and the approach of many of the feminist men I interviewed: it centers *men's* feelings, challenges, and opportunities vis-à-vis feminism. For the student to have done nothing is at once both understandable—because of his position as a subordinate—and morally objectionable—because of the egregiousness of the encounter. The student's decision to prioritize his own comfort and his "camaraderie" with his new boss does nothing to dismantle a work culture that favors straight, white, cis men. While I do not wish to minimize the consequences for men who speak out against patriarchal systems, what Theo codes as the student's desire to balance having "a positive influence" and being "employed" is also the student's desire to feel as though women are included while he continues to benefit from masculine bonding rituals. What is missing from Theo's description of his conversation with these students is an acknowledgment that men must give up privilege to end women's disadvantage.

Stating this in such black-and-white terms would be discordant with Theo's practice of feminism because he aims to "meet [his] students where they are." Through our conversation, it became clear that this meant validating men's fears about losing privilege:

> A lot of the conversations we were having was about the tension that the men were feeling about, "Yeah, I want to be an ally, but there's also a really powerful disincentive to speak up in environments like that." Where do you create that balance? Do you do more good by staying in that environment and exerting a positive influence over the long term or do you do more good by opting out entirely? That's the kind of stuff that we've been working on this year.

Theo's work focused on this tension for the largely straight, white, cis men with whom he works with, it seems, little acknowledgment of how their paralysis in morally reprehensible situations reinforces toxic work environments that harm women, trans men, nonbinary people, people of color, and queer people. As Theo and others slowly and thoughtfully reflect on this question and the personal tension they occupy as self-identified allies, inequality remains the status quo.

In centering cis men, Theo centers not only their concerns but also their sensibilities:

> When we did this with the allies thing a few weeks ago, the word "feminism" I don't think came up, although what we were doing was a very profeminist activity. . . . I think as an educator, I have to be thoughtful

about the target audience. Are they going to find that [language] threatening? Are they going to write it off because they don't identify with that language?

Theo's own experience has taught him how uncomfortable it is for men when they are "threatened" by feminist language and claims that make their privilege visible. There are pedagogical reasons for avoiding jargon with an audience new to any subject, but I contend that there are benefits to teaching men feminist vocabulary. For one, teaching men that terms like "male privilege" are not a personal, moral indictment but a description of social structure could allay the feelings of threat so often described by the men I interviewed. Moreover, feminist language allows men to truly understand their position in the gender hierarchy. In focusing so exclusively on men's issues and feelings—a focus that reflects his own motivation for becoming a feminist—Theo and his students miss this opportunity.

Moreover, while Theo's intersectional definition of feminism allows him to resolve feelings related to his whiteness and straightness in addition to his masculinity, in practice his feminism is fairly narrow. Theo works at an elite, historically white university, and so the programming he plans necessarily has a majority white audience. But Theo also caters his programming to a particularly white and masculinized space: fraternities. Theo stressed how Greek life at his university is different from Greek life on other campuses:

> Greek life on this campus is pretty different from most places. . . . These are not necessarily men who associate with traditional notions of masculinity in a really overt way. They're pretty open to talking about gender socialization and allyship to women and queer folks and talking about being traditionally white organizations and how do they create space for people of color in their membership and trans people in their membership and things like that. We work a lot with Greek life but they are also really open to having us. It's not like we have to try really hard to get in that community.

Besides being exclusively male spaces by definition, fraternities on Theo's campus are decidedly white organizations. While the fraternities he works with are often exemplars of white masculinity, Theo discursively distances them from "traditional notions of masculinity" by describing them as surprisingly open to conversations about diversity and inclusion. In fitting with his approach to meet men where they are, he sees these comparatively progressive fraternity brothers as natural partners and a receptive audience.

But there is disagreement on Theo's campus about whether the cultural and structural issues that are so deeply embedded within Greek life can be reformed. Previous research would suggest that fraternity brothers' openness to *talking* about diversity and inclusion might be a hybrid masculinity that allows them to justify their continued presence on campus to the administration and the student body while maintaining their fundamentally exclusive nature.[15] Theo's approach centers the feelings and challenges of high-status group members like himself—straight, white, cis men—and gives them an opportunity to perform inclusivity without giving up the privileges—relative autonomy, exclusive housing, and social status—they enjoy on campus.

Importantly, talking with fraternity men about how they may be more attentive to matters of gender and race helps Theo navigate his own feelings around his gender and racial privilege. In his day-to-day life, Theo said being a feminist "means trying to live a life that models the values that I think matter to a just society. . . . [It means] creating spaces where I can meet people where they are and try to help them see what they might not be able to see." Theo's feminism resolves his discomfort around his multiplex privilege because it allows him to "model" particular, moral "values" for others, like the fraternity men he works with. It allows him to both be a moral person and be seen as a moral person.

At the same time, Theo described his discomfort with being praised for any social justice work he does, including for the programming he plans for men on campus:

> I feel like I get unearned praise a lot because I work in such a progressive environment. I get applauded just for showing up I think a lot of the time, which makes me really uncomfortable. I don't even have to do anything and people are like, "Man, you did such great work." I'm really not doing

much of anything. I think I probably spend 5 percent of my time thinking and working on the [program].

Theo described a similar dynamic around racial justice:

> The last couple of years on campus, there have been a number of student protest actions particularly around racial justice. I will go to those things and often I'm one of very few of my white colleagues present. My colleagues of color will pat me on the back for being there and I get invited into the conversation, like, "Did you see who wasn't there? So-and-so didn't show up and so-and-so didn't show up." I get to be part of the "in" club in those moments that I feel like I haven't really—I just went and stood at a protest for half an hour. I don't deserve an award.

Theo sees the praise he receives for his interest in and work for social justice as unearned and "[un]deserve[d]," and it makes him uncomfortable. His discomfort stems from his understanding that the praise is the result of his high-status group identities. Theo engages in activism to resolve negative feelings related to his privilege, but this praise is a reminder of his privilege and initiates the same moral identity threat.

In response, Theo tries to be conscious of his own privilege in social justice spaces. He told me that being a feminist also means being "attentive to the space I take up and trying to be aware of how I experience privilege and how I can dismantle that when I have the opportunity to." This extended to the "space" he takes up within feminism itself. For example, he did not ask the women's center to sponsor his program, saying that he worried their presence in a space intended for women would be "invasive." (The women's center later offered to sponsor the program, which Theo agreed to.) Likewise, he said, "I have definitely had moments in my career where I've seen people who were carrying a lot of privilege in positions of authority speak on behalf of marginalized folks. I think that makes me feel pretty icky. I want to be in a position where I can create space but not take up too much space."

The dynamics Theo describes are well documented by activists, who often ask allies to "pass the mic" rather than to speak on behalf of marginalized people.[16] But Theo does not entirely manage to avoid replicating his privilege in his social justice work. For one, the systems within which Theo works are designed to hand him the mic over and over again, so to speak. This is evident, for example, in his "old boy" principal asking him to lead their school's Gay Straight Alliance.

Second, Theo has acted on his desire to avoid "invading" spaces for marginalized people by creating new, exclusive spaces for straight, white, cis men to work on the problem of social justice without the input or leadership of marginalized people. While Theo hopes his programming makes his campus safer for students of all genders, it must be noted that his work centers the feelings and challenges of those with privilege. It focuses on the tension of social justice for *allies*, rather than its imperative for marginalized people. As a result, his work does not decenter high-status group members and does not necessarily challenge his or his audience's privilege but rather may provide them an opportunity to prove their morality. As Theo told me,

> When I talk to men about being allies like this allies thing that we did, there's some disincentive to speak up against people who have supervisors like the guy who was talking about his female interns. There's also a lot of people who applaud progressive mindedness as long as it doesn't affect them personally. You can also get a lot of positive incentive out of showing up and claiming to be an ally and not having to do anything. I think there's that piece too that's a challenge to reconcile.

At the same time, Theo relies on his marginalized colleagues to raise his own consciousness around issues of social justice: "They will help me to understand why I'm not seeing [some things] in terms of the privilege that I get in those spaces of having my voice heard and having my presence invited and welcomed and being allowed to take up space and airtime." He was particularly thankful to his boss:

> My direct supervisor is a woman of color and we will often walk out of a meeting together and she'll be like, "Did you hear what so-and-so said?" I was like, "Oh. Yeah, I heard it but it didn't register that that was problematic, but now that I'm hearing it through your ears or your interpretation, I'm realizing I could see why that's not cool." That happens to me pretty regularly.

Likewise, he described his wife as continuing to support his social justice education: "[She] has to point out to me all the time things that I don't realize I'm doing or things that she experiences that I wouldn't have noticed. It's really humbling to be reminded pretty regularly. I feel like I'm pretty woke and I have a lot of learning to do."

My impression of Theo is that he is an earnest and caring person. I believe his relationships with his colleagues and his wife are good ones built on mutual respect. But the particular dynamic Theo describes is problematic. Theo recognized this himself:

> [My colleagues] are really generous about pointing it out for me. I try not to do my learning on their backs but sometimes that's how it happens. I think again, it's like I try to invest in those relationships in a way that it's not one-sided. It's reciprocal. If I'm learning from their experience, I'm also showing up in a way that provides support and love and compassion and being accountable to when I'm the one who says or does the thing that unintentionally impacts somebody else.

Theo tries to ensure his relationships are reciprocal, but he also knows that marginalized people often do the work of educating him when he or others commit microaggressions or something more egregious. When low-status group members teach high-status group members about the latter's own privilege, their status position requires them to manage their own emotions as well as the emotions of their audience. It is a sensitive operation that requires considerable time and effort and, in the workplace, disadvantages marginalized people by distracting them from their work.[17]

I believe Theo intends, through intersectional feminism, to better himself, to make the spaces he inhabits more inclusive, and to forge mutually beneficial relationships. But I must also note that Theo's activism may not have the impact he intends. This decoupling stems, in part, from his subconscious motivation: to feel like and be seen as a good person. Because the tension he experiences around masculinity and other high-status group identities is central to his trajectory into activism, his activism centers that same tension. Despite what he may intend, Theo extracts knowledge about injustice from those who experience it—his wife and his marginalized colleagues—and takes said knowledge back to high-status audiences—the largely upper-class, straight, white, cis men students with whom he works—so they can navigate their complicated feelings about their own privilege. Of course, high-status group members must play a role in making the world more equitable and inclusive. Theo's sympathetic and unchallenging approach and the fact that privileged people often do benefit from performative allyship suggest that the type of programming Theo organizes will not effect change. Instead of learning how to *divest* themselves of privilege, Theo and his students instead learn how to *live with* their privilege.

Alex: Feeling Attacked, Alone, and Bullied

While Theo intends to reduce the disadvantages faced by women, trans men, nonbinary people, people of color, queer people, and others social scientists understand to be low-status group members, Alex believes that straight, white, cis men are disadvantaged and intends to advance their group position. Perhaps it goes without saying that this is an important difference between how the two men interpret the threat to their group position and how they react to it. Theo's activism has unintended consequences that limit his ability to effectively challenge patriarchy and its intersecting oppressions. In contrast, while he wouldn't put it this way, Alex's activism outright reinforces cisheteropatriarchy and straight, white, cis men's dominant group position.

Alex told me that the majority of his activism consists of debating feminists and other social justice advocates: "I basically argue with people is what it is." As a resident of a liberal city, most of Alex's advocacy deals with providing friends and acquaintances with "counterpoints" to the arguments of "feminism and social justice." Additionally, Alex has written a handful of articles for a well-known, virulently misogynist website.

Alex sees his viewpoints across a variety of subjects—feminism, antiracism, Trump, and more—as tied together by "consistency, principle, [and] logic." But his narrative points to his desire to quiet the negative feelings he experiences when his multiplex privilege is named and challenged as the subconscious motivation for his multifaceted activism:

> I feel like they treat me like an enemy. It's really hard when somebody treats you—talks about you like the enemy, like you're a villain, to not emotively go into that role, to not seek out your own identity grouping to feel like you're at least included somewhere, like you're a part of something. Because right now over here you're excluded. You feel alone and you see people being inconsistent with the way that they talk about you. They're like, "No, if you're not the one who's like this—who's doing this, then this isn't about you." [I say,] "Yeah, but all you said is 'white men.' You didn't say 'some white men.' Why do you have to bring up that they were white men in the first place?"

Alex described white men as particularly singled out by the culture as immoral and responsible for some (here, unnamed) crime. He explicitly described his activism—engaging in online debates with others—as a response to cultural narratives that call out white men's complicity in and responsibility for others' disadvantage. As a result of these threats to his racial and gender identities, he "seek[s] out [his] own identity grouping" and defends white men. By dismissing the claim that white men are all privileged and immoral and arguing that white men are the victims of a culture of identity politics, Alex is able to reconcile the negative feelings these identity threats produce. While different in intent, impact, and form, Alex's activism is reminiscent of Theo's in that both center the concerns of white men.

As is evident in several of the quotes above, Alex claims to use "reason" and "logic" when debating. In addition to being a technique to dismiss claims that evoke negative feelings vis-à-vis Alex's masculinity, whiteness, and straightness, this privilege renegotiation strategy covers up real harm and disadvantage experienced by low-status group members. Alex declared,

> I've even seen articles from some writers talking about how the use of reason and fact is basically elitist, talking about wanting to respect lived experiences when it's like, well I can hear that you went through something shitty. A lot of times it's not even really provable that it's because of some kind of bigotry. It's just like, "I was treated badly by this person and I just know it was because I was a woman, or because I was Black, or

whatever." I'm like, "Well, how do you know that? They didn't say that. They didn't call you a name."

Alex objected to the critique by feminist and other critical researchers that the methods scientists refer to as "objective" are actually not but instead privilege white men's experiences and perspectives. These researchers have created new epistemologies and methodologies for accessing women's and other marginalized people's experiences and perspectives, with the goal of better illuminating oppressive social structures.[18] Alex misrepresented feminist standpoint theory and other similar approaches meant to reveal explicit and covert instances of oppression. In the face of claims-making about oppression, he provided a simple response steeped in the positivism that feminist researchers critique: "How do you know that?" He said, "I think we need to strongly embrace reason. . . . I see an almost anti-intellectual strain, a very ideological strain in these things, an emphasis on lived experiences instead of statistics, on feelings instead of facts." Yet Alex uses "reason" when it is convenient to him. For example, Alex's argument here contrasts with the quote earlier when he discussed sentencing disparities. Then, Alex insisted researchers studying sentencing should analyze impact over intent; here, he questioned intent in order to downplay impact.

Alex deployed this strategy in relation to gender. For instance, he described his disagreement with rape culture this way:

> People frame it as very much an aspect of toxic masculinity and stuff like that, and to me I think the fact that rapes do happen in the numbers that they do, and people disagree on exactly what those numbers are, but that they do and with the [gender] disparity that there is, I honestly think it comes down more to physiological differences and also just an overall asshole culture. . . . I don't think that women are virtuous and men are bad. I just think that everybody's kind of amoral or we have different abilities.

Alex recognized that men are more likely to be perpetrators and women victims when it comes to rape (though he added a caveat by noting "people disagree" about the size of the disparity). But he misrepresented feminist claims ("women are virtuous and men are bad") and argued that the disparity could not be explained by toxic masculinity. He diffused responsibility for rape by describing it as "an extreme manifestation" of "an overall asshole culture." In our interview, he likened raping someone to buying chocolate when it is "actually grown by literal slaves in Africa" and to buying a new phone despite "the horrific working conditions of people in China who are building the new electronics." Of course, unethical consumption under capitalism and rape are fundamentally different, but comparing them allows Alex to put the onus for rape on the broader society rather than on the men who perpetrate it or any cultural norms specific to masculinity. He also claimed that men's disproportionate perpetration of rape has everything to do with their biology: "If women were more physiologically capable [then] female on male rape . . . wouldn't be nearly as disparate as it is." By insisting that the cultural causes of rape are universal and that men just happen to have the physiological ability to do it, Alex created a seemingly rational explanation for why men are more likely to be perpetrators than women. Alex was not saying that men are blameless per se but rather that boys will be boys—even while he refused to implicate boyhood (or masculinity) at all.

Alex also applied a "hyperrational" approach to race. In keeping with his discomfort with identity labels, Alex disliked the Black Lives Matter movement:

> The disparity between Black and white in terms of police shootings, say with the Black Lives Matter thing, is way, way less than the disparity between men and women for police shootings, including for unarmed shootings of people. As a matter of fact, an unarmed Black woman is way, way less likely to be shot by a policeman than an unarmed Black man or white man—than any man. I put out there a little while ago that I feel like if you . . . really wanted to focus on the most affected group, you would go with Black Men's Lives Matter rather than just Black Lives Matter because Black women aren't being killed by cops, or at least not in any kind of real statistically significant sense compared to the other ones.

Contrary to his assertion, Black women (including trans women) are disproportionately subjected to police violence, yet, reflective of the larger problem of Black women's invisibility, are often left out of media narratives.[19] Black women's experiences with state violence are shaped by both patriarchy and white supremacism, a fact that Alex would be unwilling to acknowledge. Denying state violence against Black women supports Alex's perspective that women are not victims. Furthermore, his critique distracts from the imperative that police violence against Black people, including women, must be stopped. While Alex seemed to admit here that the Black Lives Matter movement is responding to a real problem (at least when it comes to Black *men*), he still took issue with it: "I really do believe in the colorblind ideal. I feel like because to me those things really are not important, and I feel like if you insist on them being important that's just a bad thing. You're dividing people up."

Alex's "just the facts, ma'am" approach contrasts sharply with the way of knowing he himself most often relied upon throughout our interview: his experiences and feelings. He said,

> I feel attacked, kind of alone. . . . I feel bullied. That's a big thing for me. I see people acting like bullies. I don't know if you're familiar with an incident that happened, I think it was at a California school somewhat recently, where this Black woman was accosting this white kid with dreadlocks on his head and giving him shit about the cultural appropriation of hair, kind of thing. Just the smugness, the smirks and stuff like that that I see with these things. It feels very bullying to me. It makes it very, very hard to want to be sympathetic. I understand that there are real issues and everything like that, but . . . I don't know.

Here, Alex stated that his feelings make it difficult for him to sympathize with the problems faced by people different from himself. In essence, he admitted that his own feelings are more convincing as an epistemology for informing his opinion about social issues he recognizes to be "real." Despite relying on his own feelings as a way of knowing, Alex rejected other people's feelings as an invalid and subjective epistemology.

While Alex's emotions limit his sympathy for low-status group members, his emphasis on logic and reason pose another problem when it comes to combating inequality: it limits his imagination in regard to solutions. He said,

I'm not sure that every problem is actually solvable.... People, whenever they see a problem, they're like, "We have to fix this. We have to fix this." I'm not sure that's always a good idea because whenever you try and impose this large-scale societal solution to a problem, there's always, always fallout. The drug war's a great example. People are getting hurt by drugs, and now that they started the drug war, really more people are being hurt by drugs. The same thing happened with the original prohibition.

Even for those inequalities Alex recognizes as real, like the gender wage gap and police violence against Black men, he questions the relative benefits and costs of ending them. This perspective, disguised as simple pragmatism, is another privilege renegotiation strategy. By claiming that any effort to reduce inequality will have unintended consequences, Alex is able to justify policy preferences that protect his own privilege.

* * *

That men's pathways into gender activism were motivated by their whiteness and straightness, in addition to their masculinity, was common throughout the broader sample. Like Theo, many feminist men saw themselves as especially privileged because of the multiple high-status group identities they embodied, which evoked negative feelings for them. We see this in Matthew's story that opened the chapter. His subconscious motivations related to his other high-status group identities show up in his gender activism. For instance, he described how he tries to amplify the voices of feminists of color because they are "more marginalized" in the movement. When I asked Peter, a straight, white feminist in his thirties, when his gender is most salient to him, he answered when others give him some preferential treatment:

> I think that people absolutely take [you] more serious if you're a man—I think your credibility, especially if you're a white man.... I think most of the time white men, at least in America for this generation, are getting the benefit of the doubt in a lot of different areas or seen positively in a lot of different areas that other people aren't. That could be with police, white men versus minorities.... If we're going for a job or something like

that and that job has a type of leadership component, I think that men are perceived for whatever reason to have that [compared to women].

Peter linked his gender and race as conveying to him special privileges. To avoid being seen as one of the bad guys, he told me, he tries to treat women and people of color with respect in his day-to-day life: "How people perceive you can be one way, and I don't want to be perceived as somebody who's trying to take advantage of situations purely because I'm a white male. . . . Generally, I try to treat everybody in the most positive manner I possibly can to make sure everybody's experience is as good as possible." Part of the way he accomplishes this is through his feminism.

Sam, a straight, white feminist in his thirties, answered my question about whether he ever receives any advantages as a man this way:

Oh, of course, I assume every day. . . . I mean, my God, I drive a taxicab. I'm alone with passengers all the time. I know a coworker, on her Facebook page said something about like, "Yeah, I like being a cab driver, except for the constant sexual harassment." . . . And I assume men benefit one way or another almost every moment of our lives. It's just the same with being white in this country, or being wealthy, or whatever—social hierarchies.

Sam described the everyday privilege of being a man as identical to the everyday privilege of being white and wealthy. And he recognized that seeing one's privilege is uncomfortable, adding, "People don't like to think about how the opportunities that they have are not due as much to their own effort as they are to having won the lottery at birth, and to the disadvantages of others." Sam negotiates his own feelings around his multiplex privilege by advocating for a feminism that incorporates antiracism and labor concerns.

Like Alex, many men's rights activists believed that others saw them as especially privileged because they embodied multiple high-status group identities. They claimed they were victims to negotiate the negative feelings that this realization evoked. Ken, a straight, white, cis man, is both a men's rights activist and a white nationalist. He described white men as disadvantaged by affirmative action and not given their due credit, which he hoped to rectify through his activism. Of Black Americans' and women's suffrage, Ken said,

> According to history, they [white men] were so kind that they voted to allow other groups to have rights to vote and so forth because they have a history of altruism and nobility. And that's actually, to be really honest, that's the main reason that women around the world have the rights they do today. . . . Of course, they [Black Americans] marched, or whatever they did, it didn't really matter. None of it mattered unless the white males voted for them to have rights.

Both men's rights activists and white nationalists co-opt a victim identity to obscure their privilege.[20] As I argue, this also allows them to reconcile the negative feelings the idea of their own privilege conjures in them.

Ken is unique in the sample in having disclosed that he is also a white nationalist. But the views he expressed about white men's victimization were far from unique. For instance, Ralph, a straight, white, cis man in his fifties, told me about a video game set during World War II that includes a white woman and Black man character:

> Look, I get it's a video game, but they talk about being realistic—there were no females in Normandy. There were no Black men on Normandy Beach, taking the beach. Now, did Black men contribute to World War II? Yeah, they did. Should they be included in the narrative? Yeah, but another thing is and you're going to be seeing a bunch of Filipino, Chinese women storm the beach at Normandy, and the white men weren't even there.

According to Ken, Ralph, and other men's rights activists, straight, white, cis men are not given the recognition they deserve because they are seen as especially privileged. They are being made invisible as, in Matthew's words, the culture has shifted to "forefront" more marginalized people. These men attempt to resolve their complex feelings related to their masculinity, whiteness, and straightness through their claims to victimhood and their men's rights activism.

If men are seeking privilege renegotiation strategies related to their masculinity, whiteness, and straightness, why *gender* activism? For many of the feminist men I interviewed, feminism complemented their engagement in other movements for social justice. Many talked about marching in gay pride parades or, like Theo, attending antiracism events. I found participation in other social movements to be less common among men's rights activists. It may be that men's rights activists do engage in other supremacist movements but felt uncomfortable telling me. I believe it more likely that they chose to engage in men's rights activism over the alternatives, like white nationalism, because doing so presents a clearer if still muddy signal of their morality. The argument that men are biologically different from and superior to women still has considerable purchase among Americans, and while similar arguments are often made about race, they are less publicly acceptable.[21] In the United States, a general prohibition against talking about race might persuade men's rights activists not to engage in organized white supremacism. Even Ken was happy to talk openly about "women" and "feminists" but referred obliquely to Jews as "people wearing yarmulkes" and Black Americans as "a certain ethnic minority." While white supremacist beliefs were common among men's rights activists, they felt more comfortable talking about gender than about race and likely saw men's rights activism as a more desirable privilege renegotiation strategy than white nationalism. In focusing largely on the concerns of *white* men, the men's rights movement helps interviewees navigate their multiplex privilege without explicitly organizing around race.[22]

As is clear from Theo's and Alex's stories, the fact that men gender activists are motivated by processes related to their masculinity, whiteness, and straightness has important consequences for their activism and inequality. Men's rights activists like Alex fold together male and white supremacist and heterosexist beliefs. They subvert social scientific understandings of power and status to undermine feminist, antiracist, and queer organizing. In doing so, they draw on and reinforce supremacist narratives that straight, white, cis men are victims. They advance a cultural, social, and political agenda that benefits straight, white, cis men. In sum, they exacerbate existing inequality.

While the feminist men I interviewed consciously intend to dismantle inequality and privilege, I find that their subconscious motivation impairs them. Their motivation is self-centered: they seek to mollify their negative feelings related to their privilege and prove they are good people. Often, this meant that what they believe—that people like them need to listen, follow, and decenter themselves—was disconnected from what they do—engaging in activism that centers themselves, people like them, and their own identity work. This contradiction is evident throughout Theo's story and in the stories of other feminist men I interviewed, and I explore this more in chapter 4. Often, feminist men were too focused on learning to live with their privilege to figure out how they could decenter themselves and work more effectively toward dismantling their privilege. By pointing out these limitations, I do not mean to ignore the symbolic, cultural, and material importance of men's profeminism for feminist goals. Instead, I aim to illustrate how men's subconscious motivations make it more difficult for them to achieve what they consciously intend. Activists working for the betterment of low-status groups have called for high-status group members to recognize and divest from their privilege. This chapter revealed that high-status group members have heard them. But high-status group members' response can end up inadvertently reifying straight, white, cis men's multiplex privilege.

I believe that high-status group members who become initially interested in activism through this self-centered process can learn to put aside their own identity work and prioritize social justice. They would need to find peace with their complicated feelings, follow the leadership and knowledge of low-status group members, and follow through by sacrificing their comfort and the other benefits of their privilege. While it is possible, it was uncommon among the sample of feminist men I interviewed. In the conclusion of this book, I return to lessons learned from feminist men who were able to achieve this. As is clear here, encouraging men to engage more effectively in feminist activism will require a new approach.

3

Making Inequality Unsolvable

James first started identifying as a feminist when he was studying theology in college. He wrote a paper about when—not if, he insisted—women would become Catholic priests. In an understatement characteristic of James, he said he "got a little feedback on that." He told me, "I got called a 'feminist' by one of the other theology students, and he was using it as a derogatory remark. He said, 'Well, you must be just one of those feminist people,' and I said, 'I guess, thank you.' Because that kind of crystallized a lot of what was going on." James worked as a youth minister for a few years but was eventually asked to leave because he "wasn't allowed to teach that stuff to kids."

James has progressive beliefs about masculinity and gender, particularly for a person of his background—a Catholic, straight, white, cis man in his fifties. This often placed him at odds with the people who surrounded him. For instance, as a young man, when James began thinking about marrying his then-girlfriend, his friends told him that women should be subservient to men in marriage. He challenged them, saying,

> No, men are to be equal to and treat the woman in their life as an equal. If we go to the symbology of Adam and Eve, Eve didn't come from the foot. She came from the side. You know, she came from the rib. Side-by-side. And there's a lot of symbolism with that, in terms of the rib cage, what holds in the lungs, which holds in the air we breathe, and you can't get along without air, so the spirit is self-contained by the feminine in some ways.

In our interview, James distinguished between sex and gender and recognized genders beyond the binary. He spoke about honoring the traits within himself and others that some might perceive as inconsistent with their gender and questioned such categorization: "They don't have to have a masculine or feminine label put on them." He also described how socialization trains boys and girls to be men and women.

But James combined his understanding of gender as socialized and socially constructed with an understanding of gender as biological: "In terms of physical strength, men have got better upper body strength, and women are physically designed to have lower body strength. That's something I can't change, because that's part of the genetic structure of who we are." As is clear from this quote, James conceived of gender as fundamental and unchangeable in some ways, and he understood men and women to be different. When James explained the origin of Eve, he reified gender differences by juxtaposing femininity and masculinity: he described them as complementary, but *different*. As another example, James talked for some time about how women are more collaborative and men are more competitive and individualistic. He explained this through biology and sex-specific evolution: "Men and women went out to hunt. But I think it's because, by the nature of women having babies, they stick around the babies, and so men were more free to move around, I guess, and hunt."

James's contradictory beliefs about gender informed his understanding about what he could contribute to the fight against inequality. Because he believed some inequalities were natural and biological, he saw them as things he couldn't change. The solutions he could imagine were small. He told me, "As a feminist, as a male feminist, I take what I know, or what I'm learning—because I'm still learning, oh God, am I learning. I take what I know, and try to stand and talk to guys." He envisioned his contribution to feminism narrowly: as having small conversations with men about topics like marriage and Monday Night Football.

James's understanding of men's and women's "natures" conflicts with consensus among sociologists and feminists that gender is not internal but structural, performed, and compulsory and thus produces gender differences and inequalities by constraining interaction and individual personality, behavior, and agency.[1] While I don't expect James to be up-to-date with the sociological literature, it is somewhat surprising that his views contrast with those of most feminists—a group with whom he happily identifies. This speaks perhaps to James's relative isolation from feminism as a middle-aged religious man living in the Midwest. Yet it also speaks to the function his beliefs serve: they relieve him from greater responsibility for solving inequality.

This chapter zeroes in on the gender beliefs of men gender activists because beliefs are an important mechanism of persistent gender inequality. For one, cultural beliefs about gender provide meaning for individual behavior. Gender beliefs entail prescriptive and proscriptive stereotypes that limit individual personality and behavior. At the same time, they are resources upon which people can draw to perform gender in their everyday lives, as they are compelled to do.[2] As a result, cultural beliefs about how men and women are, should be, and shouldn't be produce and reinforce gender inequality, like men's higher rate of participation in paid labor and women's higher number of hours of unpaid labor in the home.[3]

Moreover, "folk norms" about the nature of gender and gender difference shape what, if anything, people believe should be done about gender inequality.[4] In previous work, sociologist Amy Johnson and I theorized gender beliefs on a spectrum between the individual lens and the structural lens.[5] Through the individual lens, gender is understood as an individual attribute, existing within people rather than within social structure, culture, and interaction. One common manifestation of the individual lens is gender essentialism, or the idea that men and women are basically different from one another.[6] Essentialist beliefs describe gender inequality as the outcome of gender differences in men's and women's personalities, skills, choices, or behaviors. In other words, they locate the cause of inequality in men and women themselves. For example, one might explain women's exit from the labor force after childbirth by stating that women have an inherently greater desire to care for children compared to men. The individual lens and gender essentialism often leverage pseudoscience as evidence but can also deploy the language of social science. In this example, genetics, evolution, or even socialization could be used to explain why women are better or more interested caregivers than men. No matter the particular evidence employed for the individual lens, such beliefs describe gender as something that is internal and gender inequality as the aggregate of the personal choices and actions of individual men and women.

On the other hand, the structural lens conceptualizes gender as existing in the ongoing relationships between individuals, organizations, and institutions. The structural lens describes gender not as an individual attribute but as embedded in structures and culture, which in turn shape individual action and produce the gender differences and inequalities we observe. Through the structural lens, mothers' exit from the labor force can be seen as the outcome of cultural schemas that hold women (but not men) to norms of intensive mothering and the lack of structural support—from employers and the state—for mothers trying to invest in the paid labor force.

These two lenses have different implications for social change. The individual lens attributes gender inequality to immutable differences between men and women, so eliminating gender inequality would entail asking individuals (namely, women) to make different choices and to engage in different behaviors—ones that do not come "naturally," whether because of biology or something else. For instance, the individual lens would put the onus on women to "choose" to return to work after giving birth despite their or their families' desires or needs. Within the individual lens, then, there are few viable solutions for gender inequality, and those that do exist blame the victim or are available only to a privileged few (like those who can afford childcare). In contrast, the structural lens implies that strategies for eliminating gender inequality must change structures and cultures. Within the structural lens, solutions for mothers' exit from the labor force include making childcare more affordable and providing paid parental leave to all.

Structural solutions are more effective than individual ones because they change the conditions under which all individuals make decisions and take action, regardless of financial means, for instance.[7] Yet they are difficult to implement because they nearly always require buy-in from decision makers who may be hesitant to use resources—money, time, labor—for such solutions, particularly when public support for them is mixed. And support for structural solutions is mixed because the individual lens holds such a prominent place in the public imagination when it comes to sensemaking around gender and other inequalities. While it provides a woefully incomplete picture of inequality, the individual lens gives people a sense of agency that they can overcome (what are, in reality) structural obstacles by making better choices.[8] In contrast, the structural lens shows that individuals *as individuals* have little power to fight inequality, which may lead to feelings of disempowerment. But the structural lens also shows that collective action—social movement campaigns and collective bargaining—can be leveraged toward structural solutions.

Sociologists of gender and feminist organizers have increasingly used the structural lens to understand gender inequality since the late 1980s, but public understandings have been slow to change.[9] Even young people, who are often thought of as more progressive, consistently prioritize the individual lens in their approach to gender inequality and change.[10] The majority of Americans believe men and women are different. While many Americans attribute gender differences to biology, men are more likely to do so.[11] These common, biologically essentialist beliefs fit squarely within the individual lens. They may discourage Americans (and men in particular) from seeing gender inequality as a problem at all and encourage them to see it as something natural. Importantly, they limit public support for broader, creative, and more effective solutions for gender inequality.

Why is the individual lens so often the default and intuitive way to understand gender and gender inequality? A host of psychological and cultural factors encourage people to make sense of the world through the individual lens.[12] People tend to attribute others' behaviors to personality rather than the situation at hand and infer trait characteristics from behaviors that could be better explained by contextual factors.[13] These cognitive biases prevent people from seeing agency as constrained. In the United States, where neoliberalism is inextricably woven into the culture, meritocracy and individualism are dominant cultural ideologies that pervade modern institutions and influence individual thought and action.[14] All of these factors combine to produce the widely held cultural belief that individuals can overcome structural barriers through strategic decisions and behaviors—what Johnson and I referred to as "the agency myth."[15] By focusing so narrowly on the individual agent, the agency myth ensures that the individual lens is the default explanation for gender inequality and approach to change.

Still, we might expect feminist men to use the structural lens when discussing gender, gender difference, and gender inequality. In fact, the feminist men I interviewed were more likely to describe gender as structural compared to men who were men's rights activists, who were more likely to describe gender as an individual attribute. Yet there was variation within each group, and feminists and men's rights activists deployed both the individual and structural lenses. As the quotes from James that opened this chapter show, men gender activists often had contradictory explanations for gender and gender inequality. Moreover, even men who used the structural lens described gender inequality as unsolvable or endorsed ineffective individual-level solutions. Such views allow men's rights activists to dismiss women's disadvantage altogether. Unfortunately, they also relieve feminist men from committing more meaningfully to doing something about gender inequality, even though they recognize it as a problem.

In this chapter, I detail the beliefs of Rick, a men's rights activist, and Harrison, a feminist, who exemplify the individual lens and the structural lens, respectively. Then, I provide examples from additional feminist men and men who are men's rights activists to show how both groups of gender activists combine the two lenses to explain gender inequality. I show how men gender activists construct gender inequality as unsolvable or solved in only certain (ineffective) ways, preventing them from thinking more deeply about the role they could play in dismantling it.

The Individual Lens

Rick is a straight, white, cis man in his fifties who earns a living by managing his wife's business and investing in real estate. I interviewed him in his office where, from behind a large wooden desk, he answered my questions with a sly smile. We spoke just two days after the 2016 presidential election and together watched as students from the local high school marched past the window in protest of Donald Trump's victory. The city is nearly one-third Hispanic, and there was a spattering of Mexican flags waving in the crowd. Rick remarked,

> You know, this is the United States of America, and several people are carrying the Mexican flag. This is the kind of thing that creates Trump voters. My secretary is from Mexico, all of my employees are from Mexico. I love their work ethic, I love the culture, but it's still America. My secretary got naturalized because she loves this country. She wanted to integrate into the country. But this kind of shit, that's what the cucks are doing.

Despite not voting for Trump ("I voted for Hillary, by the way. I think Donald Trump's a complete lunatic"), Rick confessed to understanding

Trump's appeal: "I think the anger generated by the excesses of the Left caused him to be elected." We were momentarily distracted by the noise of the rally and paused our interview to watch the students march by.

His comment about the protestors encapsulated much of what I came to learn about Rick. Like the other men's rights activists I interviewed, Rick was propelled into the movement by a desire to make visible identities, like the protestors' Mexican heritage, invisible once more. He failed to understand how Donald Trump—who launched his campaign by calling Mexican immigrants criminals, drug traffickers, and rapists—spearheaded a broader cultural attack on these students' ethnic identities and that the Mexican flags they carried were symbolic of their resistance.[16]

Rick's views on gender and masculinity are exemplary of the individual lens and, more specifically, biological essentialism. Rick constructed men and women as fundamentally different from one another and saw biology as the cause of these differences. For instance, Rick explained feminism's lack of appeal in "less developed countries" in this way:

> In most countries, labor is physical labor. If they were to start a feminist movement in the Middle East, for example—the poor countries—and women decided to reject the patriarchy, so to speak, they would have no means of support because if your job is building a road or lifting stones all day, you're going to hire a man for that, because physically, there is a big advantage. Okay? You can't sell feminism to a culture where physical labor is so important to that culture.

Rick describes women as incapable of or poorly suited to physical labor. He ignores how cultural and social factors shape men's and women's bodies and intervene in who seeks or is hired for jobs involving physical labor.[17] Instead, he sees men's engagement in such jobs (and women's lack thereof) as a straightforward reflection of their natural physical capabilities. The individual lens allows Rick to dismiss feminist demands for equality as delusional, resolving the threat feminist claims pose to his sense of self.

Rick's adamant use of the individual lens meant that he flatly rejected structural or social explanations of gender. When I asked Rick what most people think it means to be a man, he said,

> I think this is the wrong question. When you're talking about what it is to be a man versus what it is to be a woman, or masculinity versus femininity, I don't see this as a subjective subject. I think there's a right and a wrong answer. The reason is, is you cannot separate sex from reproduction. That's the purpose of it, that's why it exists. In the world of biology, you measure masculinity and femininity based on reproductive success, based on how many descendants you leave. That's the right answer.

Rick refused to answer my question, which asked him to reflect on what he perceives to be social definitions of masculinity. Instead, he described a purely biological definition: masculinity is measured through reproductive success. Rick's perspective conflates sex and gender. It erases the gendered experiences of men (including trans men) who cannot or choose not to have children and pathologizes people who do not fit within the gender binary. By rebuking me for my question, he also implied there are no socially derived definitions of manhood or, at least, none that are correct. In other words, Rick believes social constructionist understandings of gender are objectively wrong and disregards the structural lens.

Through this narrow biological perspective, Rick saw men as relentlessly pursuing sexual reproduction by any means necessary and portrayed this desire as a fundamental and natural characteristic of men. He referred to his own strategy to achieve reproduction as "traditional pair bonding":

> My strategy has been pretty traditional: to get together with one woman, be married, never divorced, provide financial support, raise our child and so on and so forth. As far as what it means to be a man, it's to be responsible, not leave my family, you know, things of that nature. That is a successful strategy. That's the reason why it's considered by many to be a respectable way to be a male.

Rick described how social expectations of men—what most people think men should do or be like—are actually based on sexual reproduction. In Rick's view, because it makes sense biologically for men to invest in monogamous relationships, that lifestyle has become socially common and approved. He believes that the relationship between biology and the social is entirely one-way: biology structures and determines the social. If there are any social definitions of masculinity, they evolved from masculinity's biological basis.

Rick recognized that there are multiple ways of being a man, but by this he meant multiple strategies for obtaining manhood through sexual reproduction. According to Rick, his personal strategy is one of several men can take to be men. He contrasted his own strategy with another, sinister one:

> If you take a man like Genghis Khan, who's well-known for being the biggest rapist in history, he would tell you if he was sitting here right now, that to be a man is to rape and pillage, is to conquer, is to subjugate both man and woman, but as far as women, having his children as many times as possible. If you were to look at his descendants, and they have—genetically, he has millions of them. That is the right answer, okay?

In reducing gender to something purely biological, Rick characterizes rape as a possible avenue for achieving manhood because reproduction is a possible outcome of rape. He continued,

> Now, it's the wrong answer on an individual level, because obviously, these are heinous crimes and he murdered an untold number of people, but in a strictly biological sense, that is the right answer. . . . Obviously, I'm not advocating rape. Don't ever quote a men's rights advocate saying they're advocating rape. I'm just saying on a purely biological level, that is a strategy.

Despite his disclaimer—and his recommendation to me to never portray a men's rights activist as supportive of rape—Rick described rape as an understandable outcome of men's natural desire to sexually reproduce and characterized impregnating women as a way to "subjugate" them.

Rick's steadfast commitment to the individual lens is supported by his belief in evolutionary psychology. He told me, "[Evolution is] the real driver of human behavior." Evolutionary psychology has gained traction in the broader culture and among male supremacists in particular by offering what women's studies scholar Stevi Jackson and sociologist Amanda Rees call "campfire tales" about the causes of human nature.[18] It advances a reductionist and revisionist theory of culture and society; its use of "the standard narrative," as professor of critical theory and gender and sexuality Mari Ruti calls it, lends it a simplicity and appeal despite its questionable methods and conclusions.[19] Through a straightforward narrative structure linking a clear cause—humans' innate desire to mate—with a diverse array of effects, evolutionary psychology proposes appealing, though incorrect, theories of human behavior. Rick explained human behavior through evolutionary psychology and, despite not finishing his bachelor's degree in biology, presented himself as an authority on the subject. As is clear, part of the danger of evolutionary psychology is in how it naturalizes harmful human behaviors, like rape and war.[20]

Importantly, evolutionary psychology locates the cause of gender differences within individuals—at the level of their sexual organs, hormones, and genes—which has important ramifications for how those who subscribe to it understand gender inequality and social change. In explaining rape as a function of men's natural sexual needs, rape is expected and even inevitable. In contrast, understanding rape as gendered violence reveals that rape is not natural but both a cause and outcome of gender inequality, gendered power, and gendered entitlement.[21] Seen through this lens, a world without rape is possible but only if gender inequality were to be systematically dismantled. A sociological view of rape implicates men and the privilege they enjoy within the gender system. Rick advances a biological view of rape that allows him to defend his understanding of himself as moral rather than connected with systems of oppression. The individual lens, biological essentialism, and evolutionary psychology are thus privilege renegotiation strategies Rick can deploy.

Proponents of evolutionary psychology often problematize technological and social change. They believe the supposed mismatch between such change and humans' basic, unchanging instincts creates widespread unhappiness and even more catastrophic problems.[22] This was reflected in Rick's concerns. He saw many of the changes that accompanied second-wave feminism in the United States as counterproductive to a functioning society because they intervened in natural, biological processes—that is, sexual reproduction. He discussed declining fertility—a concern that has white supremacist roots—as evidence of the dysfunction of modern masculinity and femininity:[23]

Americans, as of today, have a declining population, just like Japan. The only reason our population is increasing is people are immigrating from mostly South America and Asia, Central [America]—I guess Mexico's technically North America, duh. We have a lot of influx of foreigners, which means our population continues to grow. Looking at it from the way I do, from a biological standpoint, we're broken, as masculinity/femininity is broken.

Rick calls American society "broken" because birth rates are below replacement levels. According to Rick, declining fertility rates are a problem because they might "send your race into extinction" and limit available care for the elderly, but also because fertility is the objective measure of successful masculinity and femininity.

By constructing low fertility as a problem that runs counter to human biology and evolution, Rick could oppose long-established, commonsense laws and policies that reduce gender inequality. For example, he said a simple "contract" had long sustained the traditional pair bond: "The contract between a man and a woman is she will give him sex, and ultimately, children. He will give her material support, and feed her, and keep her safe, and this is the contract which has kept the pair bond intact in the human species." In Rick's view, this contract had been perverted by alimony and marital rape laws:

> We have a society now where the man's material support is forced by law, almost forever, in many cases forever. Her obligation is treated as completely irrelevant. If she doesn't want to even have sex with him within the marriage, she doesn't have to. If she wants to leave him and still get money, she can do that, okay? This is an abomination to our basic human biology. This was never the way it was supposed to be. We didn't evolve with any of this.

Using the individual lens, Rick essentialized men's providership and need for sex and women's caretaking and need for material support. He claimed that social changes have pushed women away from their natures but have not altered men's. He problematized two hugely important feminist gains of the past half century—no-fault divorce and the criminalization of marital rape—and once again implied that rape is natural. The policy implications of Rick's perspective would renew men's control over women through marriage and would be hugely detrimental. Moreover, his worldview constructs men as the victims of women's entitlement and dereliction of duty, refuting feminist claims that men are privileged.

Rick attributed low birthrates, the deterioration of the marital contract, and the broader dysfunction of modern masculinity and femininity to a conspiracy led by feminists and elites. He said that the solution was to return to "1950s culture": "[Women] would have to, once again, embrace the role of the caretaker, the homemaker, and the men would have to be the ones going to work every day and earning a living and taking care of the children, in a way. You return to that, and then I think things would be fixed." He continued,

> I think the reason both men and women have to work today, to get ahead, whereas in the 1950s, it just took one wage-earner, I think that's by design. I think the world aristocracy, they want everybody working, okay? They can pay individuals less, they can get more production, they can accumulate more wealth, if that's the case.... I think culture has sold women on this idea that they can have it all, but they can't. That's a lie. You sacrifice. If you were going to make it to the top and be the CEO, which is a big feminist goal, you have to sacrifice your family.

In Rick's view, feminists and "the world aristocracy" have created a problem that is "very bad for our society, very bad for marriage, [and] very bad for culture." He claimed that the social has interfered with the biological. He described this as an unnatural reversal of the true relationship between the social and biological and thus constructed low fertility and women's economic independence as problems.

While Rick saw returning to the male-breadwinner / female-homemaker model as the solution to these problems, he did not see it as a real possibility:

> I don't want to sound like if I were emperor, I would force women back in that role. I think choice is a good thing. I'm just saying, the way things are now, they're broken.... If we're going to get back on track, then a lot of women are going to have to voluntarily go back to the role of homemaker

and child bearer. . . . I don't know if it's even possible. I think there's too many obstacles.

While returning to the 1950s would be an effective solution, it was unlikely because, according to Rick, "you can't put the genie back in the bottle." Change would require women to "voluntarily" forgo careers and dedicate themselves to biological reproduction and caretaking. Note how Rick's view is clearly linked to neoliberal rationality in two ways: in framing (1) individual people as responsible for fixing the problem and (2) individual choice as essential. This quote exemplifies how the individual lens envisions social change as the outcome of individual choice and action, absent changes in the structural conditions and cultural climate. Likewise, when Rick claimed women will inevitably "sacrifice [their] family" if they want to become CEOs, he illustrated his lack of imagination vis-à-vis structural changes to work and family that could make sacrificing either unnecessary. Within Rick's worldview, feminists and elites duped women into pursuing paid labor against their nature, and it was up to women to course correct. This reveals another way in which the individual lens can serve as a privilege renegotiation strategy: it relieves men of any responsibility over solving gender inequality.

In keeping with his view that biology is fundamental, Rick foresaw that biology would naturally and inevitably triumph over the social. For one, he predicted human biology would outsmart birth control in countries like the United States: "In the First World, the way things correct are things like biological resistance to the birth control pill. That's something nobody ever talks about, but it's guaranteed to happen, just like antibiotic resistance, you know?" While there is no scientific evidence of Rick's claim, biological resistance to the birth control pill is a no-brainer if the assumptions of evolutionary psychology are taken as true.

Rick also predicted that poor and working-class people in the "First World" would become predominantly responsible for reproducing the human species:

> More promiscuity at a younger age, maturing at an earlier and earlier age, which has been measured. People talk about it all the time. They don't talk about why. People blame crap like hormones in the milk and all this other stuff. It's very simple. I mean, if you start having sex at age fourteen,

and you get pregnant, like they do in a lot of states—they have teen pregnancy problems—you're going to turn over a generation every fourteen years. You're going to outperform by order of magnitude somebody who waits until thirty, which is the upper-middle-class to upper-class way of doing it, okay? This is much more successful, and so, in the long term, evolution is going to fix all this. It may not be in a way people like, but it's going to happen.

In Rick's mind, women who had invested in careers and delayed childbearing—women who had been duped by feminism and the world aristocracy—had disrupted their own natural desires, but not all women act so unnaturally. He predicted that poor and working-class women would disproportionately populate the world. His class analysis fails to interrogate why middle- and upper-class women delay childbirth more than their poor and working-class counterparts. The reasons for demographic differences in birth rates have everything to do with the social structure—education, jobs, access to reproductive health services and other opportunities, and resources that are gained through different forms of capital and determine social mobility—which would upset Rick's understanding of biology as the be-all and end-all.[24]

According to Rick, women's financial independence and educational achievements have made them pickier about selecting a mate, leaving a large swath of the male population unable to "fulfill their biological imperative." Male supremacists commonly use this line of reasoning—what they call "hypergamy"—to construct men who have difficulty finding romantic partners as victims of women's entitlement.[25] While Rick believed that a majority of men cannot find a mate today because of women's unreasonable standards for their potential partners' physical attractiveness and income, he again predicted that biology would win out:

> [Men] won't put up with that. No species will put up with that. . . . They will, again, fulfill their biological imperative to reproduce, and they will adjust, and they will do what's necessary. . . . You're going to see more and more violence. You're going to see more and more aggressiveness. . . . You have large segments of men, who now cannot get married or date or have women around. What do you tell them? You tell them, "Well, you're not allowed to have sex now, because you don't measure up." Well, on a so-

cietal basis, that might work. On an individual basis, you know, the men are going to say, "Screw this." They're going to get together, they're going to form gangs. I have a good friend I talked to about this. He is predicting actual rape gangs. Not now, maybe fifty years in the future, but he thinks that's where we're headed. He might be right.

Rick's point here—that "rape gangs" of men are an understandable and expected outcome of women's higher standards for romantic partners—was the culmination of the rhetorical moves he made throughout our interview. He laid the groundwork for this argument by claiming that sex is purely biological, human behavior is a direct outcome of the desire to mate, and feminism and other social changes upend human biology and evolution. This line of reasoning not only condemns women's greater standards for romantic partners but also insists that women provoke sexual violence by acting against their biological instincts. As before, Rick's perspective allowed him to entirely dismiss the idea that men are privileged. Instead, he constructed men as victims and women as entitled. His apparent obsession with rape is a testament to the threat the idea of rape poses to his moral identity as a man; the arguments he made throughout our interview alleviate that threat. Thus, his understanding of gender and gender inequality is a privilege renegotiation strategy. By naturalizing gender inequality, Rick can dismiss any effort to reduce inequality. Like for Rick, for many men who used the individual lens gender inequality was natural, not worth solving, and, in reality, unsolvable.

The Structural Lens

Harrison walked into my office wearing a cranberry-colored wool sweater, khakis, and boat shoes. He is tall, with effortless blond hair, and at the outset of our interview he presented himself as having what many men at elite colleges strive to achieve: popularity, intelligence, and ease. Yet during our interview Harrison unraveled this persona, layer by layer, to reveal an anxious young man. Throughout our interview he reflected on his parents' traditional relationship, the unfairness of it, and how his father does not view his mother as a true equal. When I asked him whether he ever thinks about how the same dynamics might shape his own relationship were he to get married, he said, "Yeah. Like, relentlessly." Right before he left my office, he asked me whether I thought two people could really be happy in such a marriage.

Harrison is straight, white, cisgender, and in his twenties. When I asked him what the biggest issues are that men face today, he explained how men might feel "threatened" when their privilege is made visible:

> I think one big issue that men face in the U.S. as a whole is coming to terms with a lot of these advantages, which I think can be hard and kind of threatening. And there's often this feeling of you know, "I worked hard. What are you saying? I earned this stuff." And I think developing that kind of nuance of understanding, which I myself am trying to work toward, of being proud of accomplishments and being proud of hard work. I worked really hard to get the grades I get. But still, feeling that pride and yet also recognizing some of the advantages that you've had. I think that's going to be a big problem, a big thing for men across the country to wrestle with and deal with.

Harrison believed that men are struggling to negotiate their sense of self in light of feminist claims about male privilege. He based this on his own experience, admitting that he still grapples with being secure in his identity as a hardworking student because, he believes, he receives certain benefits as a man in the classroom. Like the other men I've discussed so far, Harrison's trajectory into gender activism was catalyzed by the disconnect between feminist claims and his sense of self, and the negative feelings this disconnect produced. Through feminism, he can feel proud of his accomplishments despite his privilege, knowing that he has a more "nuance[d]" understanding of privilege than most men.

The classroom had proved an important site for Harrison's burgeoning feminist consciousness:

> You know, it's funny, I never noticed this actually until, I'm embarrassed to say, quite recently. But I remember in class, I always felt super comfortable speaking in class and these people . . . don't say a single word for the entire class. What a waste of. . . . It's a little bit judgmental, like, "What are you doing?" And then recently talking to this female Asian friend of mine

who was like, "You know, people listen to you as a tall, white man with a deep voice." And she said it's a lot scarier [for her] to speak up.

Harrison was "embarrassed" to realize only recently that he is perceived in a particular way in the classroom on account of his whiteness and masculinity, which makes his classmates and instructor more likely to take his contribution to class discussion seriously. His friend's comment pointed out to him that people unlike him may reap a smaller payoff for speaking up in class because they are not given the same respect. Harrison admitted to having judged his peers harshly before, perceiving them as squandering their expensive and prestigious education. His realization of the processes underlying their silence produced feelings of embarrassment that recall the shame Theo described feeling in chapter 2.

This example illustrates how Harrison conceptualized gender and gender inequality through the structural lens. After talking with his friend, he attributed his peers' silence during class discussion to how they expected they would be received, not to their personality or some other inherent characteristic. While Rick might have explained the same phenomenon through sex-specific evolution that makes men and women students fundamentally and internally different, Harrison implicates students' surroundings—that is, the structure and culture in which they are embedded.

In keeping with the structural lens, Harrison described gender inequality and male privilege as operating through how others expect men to act, how others treat men, and the opportunities men receive:

> I think there's so much evidence to show how much better it is [to be a man than a woman], in terms of how you're treated, and paid, and opportunities are given [to you], expectations around just how much you succeed, in housework, et cetera, et cetera. So, from a national level, I think it's pretty hard to argue with the fact that there's privilege for being a man.

He underscored his understanding of gender as socially constructed by explaining that what it means to be a man has changed over time: "I think that, in some ways, you could argue that it's . . . the worst time to be a man because I think there's been progress in making it more equal between men and women." Harrison went on to explain that he believes this line of reasoning is faulty because women's liberation is good for men too. In any case, he recognized that what it means to be a man is not static, which differs hugely from Rick's understanding of masculinity. Unlike Rick, Harrison located the cause of gender inequality in the structures, cultures, and relationships in which people are embedded. Such a lens does not naturalize inequality or problematize interventions because it reveals inequality to be constructed.

Harrison sees himself not as separate from the gender system but rather as operating within it. When I asked him whether he has ever felt that being a man has been an advantage to him personally, he said, "definitely," then proceeded to describe the three contexts—work, romance, and school—in which he had noticed that was true. At work, "it's a huge advantage. Almost everyone I interviewed with [for a job] has been a man and I can attach to them faster. And then all my mentors that I've connected with at companies that I've worked for have been men. And I've connected with them probably because I'm a male." Harrison referred to how homophily is an advantage to him in elite labor markets—in his case, the technology industry. Because these industries are dominated by men, men applying for jobs and seeking mentorship are able to connect with interviewers and mentors more easily than women. He described forging instant connections with men over sports, for example. Despite not being a sports fan, Harrison had learned how to perform masculinity by engaging in sports talk. Unlike Rick, Harrison did not attribute men's success in certain jobs to their inherent capabilities (e.g., their physical strength). He explained it through social processes: men occupy higher status positions in particular industries, and their preference for people culturally like them replicates this structure.

In the context of romantic relationships, Harrison said, "It's way better [to be a man] because then I get to choose. Because the initiative is generally on guys to make the first move, I get to kind of make the first move with somebody I'm interested in rather than waiting. And unfortunately, there's already a power imbalance and that works to my advantage." Harrison drew on different explanations to explain men's advantage in romantic relationships. First, he believes the social expectations of men and women in romantic relationships are different. Men are expected to initiate the relationship, whereas women are expected to "wait." In other words, men are positioned as agents and women as objects. For Harrison, this meant being able to "choose" whom to pursue and when to act. Unlike Rick, Harrison saw this as an expectation (it "is . . . on" men to initiate) rather than a natural inclination.

Second, Harrison perceived a "power imbalance" between men and women in romantic relationships. He saw the macro-level structure bestowing power onto men, which men bring to their individual interactions with women: "The man is the one that not only talks and introduces himself and meets the girl or whatever—this is obviously hetero stuff—but then prompts them saying, 'Do you want to go back to my room?' And then the man hosts the thing, asks her back [to his room] generally." Harrison described men's power in relationships as stemming from and enacted through their control over the initiation of romantic encounters.

What is more, he saw men's control over physical space in the university as an important aspect of their power:

> In terms of the Greek experience, the frats always invite the sororities over to their house. So, there's a power imbalance there. . . . We've tried many times to get sororities to host more stuff. Most are not allowed to by their national organization and some have just hosted a few anyway. But it's a big risk because if [their national organization] found out they would strip them of their charter. And then [the university] would take their house away.

Here, Harrison provided an excellent example of the structural lens and more specifically how macro-level policies impact small-scale interactions. The national organizations that charter and oversee local chapters enforce a policy that sororities cannot host events with alcohol. This policy not only is out of touch with current campus culture and the desires of sorority members but also makes sororities dependent on fraternities, which are not held to the same rule.[26] As Harrison explained, sororities can face severe consequences if they break this rule; instead, they are resigned to relying on fraternities to host—and control—one of the most important social spaces on campus.

In addition to his understanding that men's contributions in the classroom are valued more than women's, Harrison believed he experienced other academic benefits as a man:

> I just never really doubted that I belong in engineering classes. And all these things I've talked to female friends about, who are in [computer science] classes with me, [they] are like, "I don't belong here. I'm not good enough. I'm not smart enough." I sometimes have those doubts in the sense that I'm not good enough to be an engineer because I haven't been coding since I was young, but it's never . . . because of my gender. It's never like, "Oh, I'm a guy so I can't really do this." Everyone I see doing this well is a guy that looks like me.

Harrison sees the macro-level structure of his academic field as relevant to his personal experience in it. In the academy and in industry, computer science is dominated by men. Men's success in the field legitimizes Harrison's presence in it, to himself and to others. In contrast, his women friends question their abilities because they don't "look like" the people at the top.

Much of my interview with Harrison focused on how men are expected to behave. He defined masculinity through socially constructed gender norms: "I think there are certain gender norms, which men feel pressure to conform to, I felt pressure to conform to at times." He continued, "I think it's things like dominating men a little bit through sports events. . . . It's like being wealthy and the breadwinner. And it's being wealthy in terms of dominating others with money, but also being the one to support the family. And then I think third would be sexually dominating. So, you know, a true man is a player." Power is central to Harrison's understanding of masculinity: men seek to dominate others. Rick too saw "real men" as being sexually dominating, particularly through rape. The difference in their perspectives lies in their understanding of why. Whereas Rick insisted that biology acted from inside men to direct their actions and desires, Harrison described how social expectations constrain men from the outside. Harrison saw gender norms as being enforced through relationships with others. While he didn't think his peers at his relatively progressive university would "be mean" to men who did not perform traditional masculinity, he thought there would be social consequences: "You'll just have a slightly harder time maybe connecting to some of the other guys." Given many young people's social goals during college, this is quite a consequence indeed.

Additionally, he described socialization as a primary way gender norms become incorporated into men's and women's personalities. Harrison saw normative gender norms represented in "the media" and other "things you've been exposed to growing up," even if the demands they place on men and women are not "explicit." He also saw the family as a primary site of socialization. When his own family gets together, "the men and the women in my family like to separate for a little bit. And the men will go do something athletic, and the women will do something less athletic. And there's all this pride in being competitive and winning as a male in my family and all this pride for being strong. A lot of the time it's all positive but it's still steering in some ways." In "steering" children into activities they see as appropriate to their gender, adults eventually transform gender norms into their children's personal preferences. Harrison's explanation serves as a corrective to Rick's, which posits that men's desire to dominate others stems from sex-specific evolution. Harrison explained how men are socialized to engage in activities where they can compete against and dominate others.

Gender norms and socialization combine in what sociologists refer to as gender performance.[27] Harrison explained how men, and college-aged men in particular, perform their gender to gain what he alternately referred to as "street cred" or "social capital." In Harrison's fraternity and in the campus's broader Greek culture, fraternity brothers are expected to act a certain way. He thought it was conspicuous when brothers performed those behaviors to fit in:

> To me, it feels so transparent, the extent to which guys will perform this kind of frattiness. They'll drink a ton. They'll smoke a ton. I'm just not convinced they like it that much, but they do it. And I feel like to me, it feels so obviously performed and so I don't see that as very impressive because it's so not authentic. And yet other really, really smart guys are like, "Awesome. You're killing it. You're the man." I had this friend, probably the smartest guy I ever met in my life, and in freshman year he barely smoked or drank. Well not barely—he smoked a little bit. But then he did more and more and more and his cred in our fraternity increased and increased.

Harrison's use of terms like "social capital" and "perform" reflected the context in which he was first exposed to these ideas: the university. He was critical of men in fraternities who exaggerate behaviors that make them "fratty." He saw their performances as inauthentic, transparent, almost pathetic. He implied that men should resist the forces that compel them to perform masculinity.

Yet Harrison admitted that he too performs his gender, at times in an over-the-top way with his fraternity brothers:

> We have this tradition where if someone says something cool or fratty then people bang on the table and then there's a point in which people become aware of how silly it is and how animalistic and hypermasculine it is to be like, "tough guy." And so, then everyone does it as a joke now so it escalates and becomes more intense. And then the whole house is just like, [pretending to scream] "Yeah!" And we're jumping on tables and in that sense, people are very much aware of the absurdity of it.

Harrison described his fraternity's almost farcical enactment of a "tough guy" hypermasculinity. While Harrison believed the ritual to be "absurd," he also saw how a performance like this one can be transformed into something more:

> But there's this funny thing where . . . you're both making fun of it and embodying it. . . . When there's just the people in the frat [present], everyone's kind of in on it, that it's kind of like a joke. But I think it's interesting when you have people [present] who aren't in that group who don't know it's a joke or aren't in on it. Because they think it's just real and maybe it is real [laughs]. It's all very confusing.

Harrison and his fraternity brothers make gender "real" for themselves and others. He recognized how such rituals, even done in jest, reinforce gender norms: "There's so much more to [my brothers], but for this night when we're all playing beer games, we're just going to be this frat star. It's almost done ironically sometimes but still not ironic." In other words, while his fraternity brothers are multifaceted and unique people, their ritual, communal gender performance transforms them for the evening, reducing them to a hypermasculine stereotype in a way that is at once a joke and dead serious.

Harrison acknowledged how he and his fraternity brothers are complicit in gender expectations. Throughout his interview, he described resisting gender norms as a very difficult task. On the one hand, he perceived there to be negative consequences to a man's failure to perform his gender. When I asked him what would happen to a man who didn't conform to gender norms at his university, he said,

> I think they would definitely be less successful. . . . And success being defined as for your career stuff, and your job. And women's stuff—they would be less successful with women. For socializing, they would be less successful in making friends, I think. Which is not to be discounted. Those are serious things to be less successful in, just for not conforming to the norms.

On the other hand, gender performance comes with particular benefits. Above, Harrison described the immense pleasure he and his fraternity brothers gained from performing their hypermasculine, animalistic ritual. Additionally, Harrison performs his gender out of what he called a "rational calculus": "I would be more successful if I do conform to them [gender norms]. There's more to be gained by conforming. I mean, it's hard because I conform to a lot of the main ones already." By this last statement, he meant that he unthinkingly conforms to gender expectations because of his personality traits and interests, like his romantic interest in women, his enjoyment of drinking and smoking, his interest in fitness, and so on. Harrison let himself off the hook for his complicity in some hypermasculine expectations, describing his gender performance as both compulsory and coming naturally.

Unlike Rick, Harrison saw the value in interventions meant to reduce gender inequality. For example, he attributed positive changes in his fraternity's culture—brothers' willingness to talk about masculinity and gender issues—to new leadership: "Basically the leadership was like, 'This is the way it is.' Our president was like, 'Look, if you're in [this fraternity], these are your values.' And I've been stunned by how. . . . They said [that] to us, then [the] new guys [were] like, 'Okay.'" Harrison's deployment of the structural lens in understanding gender shaped his understanding of solutions for gender inequality. Here, he described how changes in leadership in an organization can have big effects on culture and members' beliefs.

But Harrison's approach to social change was similar to Rick's in some ways. In many instances, Harrison portrayed gender inequality as nearly insurmountable, not because it is natural or biological but because individual people can do little to challenge it when it is baked into structure and culture. When discussing how he sometimes unconsciously engages in gendered expectations, he said,

> There's definitely times that I've been feeling insecure for whatever reason and I've emphasized [in conversation with other men], "Oh, I was with this girl," or something. So, you know, I see in myself all these little times when I've struggled or failed and I think that's just a hard thing as a man or anyone who's kind of working against the structure that rewards acting in a certain way.

Harrison's assessment that the social structure rewards individuals for performing their gender is exactly right. But his focus throughout our interview on the ease of complying with gender norms is illustrative of a limitation of his perspective. Namely, Harrison almost exclusively considered small, individual actions as solutions for gender inequality, even while he saw such actions as difficult.

For example, when I asked him what being a feminist entails for him, he replied,

> The first is trying to learn more about this stuff. And that comes through reading stuff. I'm in the [gender studies] zone right now and going to classes with people that know a lot more. Also, talking with female friends, asking them about their experience. I've been just blown away by how open and candid female friends of mine have been in talking about stuff and then just being humble in listening. And then even if things don't make sense at first, asking more questions rather than being just like, "Oh, that just doesn't make sense." So, the first part is learning and the second part is thinking about what I can do to make some small change. I think small things like really em-

bodying completely and exactly consent in my own actions, which I think I didn't always do when I was a freshman.

In practice, Harrison's feminism translates to reading, listening, and adjusting his small, everyday behaviors, like around consent. When I asked Harrison whether he does anything he would consider activism, he responded, "Not really. No. I mean I'll attend marches every now and then, but. . . ." The forms of everyday resistance that Harrison engages in are important, and I do not wish to dismiss them. But his narrow focus on everyday (and individualized) resistance reflects an incomplete internalization of the structural lens, which could otherwise help him understand how coordinated, collective action (rather than individual action) is a powerful tool for structural change. It is difficult for people to deploy the structural lens because the neoliberal hyperfocus on the individual agent permeates every facet of American culture, including feminism, and feminist men like Harrison are not immune to it.[28]

While Harrison discussed how men like himself could challenge gender inequality with small, everyday actions, he thought women were better suited to it. This is an additional and, I argue, more problematic limitation to Harrison's perspective because it meant he placed the burden almost entirely on women to solve gender inequality. Moreover, he thought that women would need to approach change in a particular way to convince men, even feminist men like himself. For instance, Harrison had been dating a woman for a while and she had discussed with him her experiences with inequality on several occasions: "One thing I appreciate is that she's very open about times when she feels like she's been treated a certain way, based on the fact that she's a woman." He explained why he thought their discussions had made an impact on him:

> She's very confident in doing things and I like her a lot, so I'm less likely to dismiss it as weird or stupid. I hate to push it on women but I think some of the women that are the most successful are those that are able to both work within the system to gain a lot of social capital but then also be very vocal about feminism, about patriarchy, because then their words are heard more. I have some friends who are hardcore activists and they are dismissed a lot more. It's [like], "Oh, it's just their agenda." And I've kind of tuned out.

Harrison expects women to perform a sort of respectability politics to appeal to men. He also recognizes that the strength of his and his girlfriend's relationship contributes to his willingness to listen to her. While he "hates" to do so, Harrison does put the onus on women to navigate a tightrope in their individual efforts to tackle inequality. What remains unsaid is how men, in fact, must change: they must overcome their resistance to women's "hardcore" or angry voices, practice listening to women even when they don't like what they say or how, and develop empathy for women with whom they do not have relationships.

This point was underscored at the very end of our interview, when I asked Harrison if there was a question that I should be asking interviewees that I had not asked yet. He proposed I ask men, "If you could say something to women about how men like you could be [changed], what would be effective?" The question implies that women must change men if they wish to be equal to them and thereby positions women as ultimately responsible for ending gender inequality. I asked Harrison how he would answer that question. He told me,

> I think I would say be—and this is a lot to ask—courageous, persistent, and patient. Courageous in bringing this stuff up in the first place. [It] is taking on risk. Persistent in that, a lot of guys aren't going to get it at first. And it might hurt a lot when you get dismissed over and over again, as I have dismissed women when they have processed thoughts like this. And then also to be patient because it's like, keep trying because there's a lot of guys I think, who with time and compassion, unfortunately that the woman has to show, I think will get it.

Harrison expects women to risk their feelings and perhaps more in pointing out to men instances of inequality. He expects women to do so again and again, even when men don't get it. He expects women to practice emotion management—to be patient and compassionate—as they explain to men about their privilege.

Variations and Combinations

Rick and Harrison are exemplars of the individual and structural lenses, respectively, but it was not always the case that men's rights activists used the individual lens and feminist men used the structural lens. Brian, a straight, white, cis men's rights activist in his thirties, consistently used the structural lens to make the case that men are the true victims of gender inequality. He criticized the individual lens and its popularity:

> Most people, I would say, believe men and women are fundamentally different, almost to the extent that they're made out of different material, just completely different things. They each have a different obligation, like men would be obligated to do something, women obligated to do something else. Probably most people believe that women are generally weaker than men. I'm not saying that this is my belief by any means, because I believe the opposite.

Brian explicitly rejected the individual lens. While Brian and Rick count themselves part of the same social movement, Brian dismissed the beliefs of people like Rick that construct men and women as "fundamentally different" and, in particular, describe "women [as] weaker than men."

When I asked him what he thinks it means to be a man, Brian responded,

> I can't really answer that because is a trans man a man, even though their private parts don't match? Well, of course, because you can suffer terrible mutilation and not have those parts and still be a man. Then you can go to chromosomes, but that's kind of silly because people have the XY [sic] chromosome and can still also be men. I'd say it comes down to how society perceives you. You are perceived to be tougher, to be more tolerant towards violence being inflicted on you, to withstand higher degrees of pain, to be more muscular. You're expected to have a set of expectations put on you, but I would say those are not really reasonable expectations.

Despite being a men's rights activist, Brian's understanding of gender is much more similar to Harrison's than to Rick's. He rejected definitions of gender that relied on anatomy and chromosomes. Brian explained that gender is predicated on other people's expectations and thus embedded in relationships with others.

Some feminist men, particularly those in the oldest cohort of men I interviewed, exclusively used the individual lens to explain gender inequality. George, a straight, Black feminist in his sixties, told me,

> Women are different [from men], their different strengths.... One of the things, which is totally not feminist creed, is I believe that . . . a mother or a grandmother, some woman in your family, should raise children. Not that men can't do that, but I think women, however they're wired together, just do a better job.... I just think that women are just wired to be more protective and maternal. And I don't think that's a bad thing. That's just like a genetic thing. But that doesn't mean they should be trapped in that role, you know. That's a choice.

George described women as "wired" in a way that makes them better caregivers than men. He was clear that he believes this gender difference not to be learned but rather to be genetic. While George did not explicitly use evolutionary psychology to justify his view, he and Rick agree that women are fundamentally and biologically different from men. George also recognized that his views are not "feminist creed," as did other feminist men who favored the individual lens.

George's reliance on the individual lens shaped his understanding of how policies can reduce gender inequality. In defining feminism, he said,

> I think feminism is still about equality. You know, being paid the same wage, but it's also about allowing women to be women, you know, in the context that they're in. And until it's not necessary, the creating [of] institutions to protect them from discrimination, protect them from like what used to be in the fifties, the pat on the ass, and the eventual like forcing you to have sex with your boss if you wanted to keep your job stuff. Like really creating an atmosphere where women can be themselves and have like our culture and the world benefit from the difference that women bring to the same job.

In George's view, men and women are intrinsically different, and feminist policies like protection against sexual harassment allow "women to be women" in the workplace. He understands sexual harassment and assault not as creating gender difference but rather as the result of the presence of gender difference in the workplace. Unlike Rick, who saw women's physical weakness as a disqualifier for certain jobs, George believed that "the difference that women bring" to work is a "benefit." The outcome for their theory of change is the same, however. Reminiscent of how Rick believed women must necessarily "sacrifice" to be CEOs, George said that women have "got to understand the differences and make adjustments" if they choose to have children. As a result of his biologically essentialist understanding of gender, he charged women with the responsibility to both raise children *and* navigate a workforce that is not set up for primary caregivers.

Most of the men I interviewed deployed both the individual lens and the structural lens, though not necessarily equally, in their explanations. Russell, a straight, white feminist in his sixties, stitched together the structural and individual lenses to describe his own unhappy childhood: "[I have] an unconventional temperament for a male, I'm not a conventional guy. I've never had an interest in athletics, and part of the male sex role, it's assumed that that's in your genes. It's a cultural expectation, like what women experienced in the fifties where they were all expected to be happy being in the home. It's oppressive and absurd." Russell described himself as "unconventional" and suffering in the face of "cultural expectation[s]" that insist men act in a certain way. Through therapy, he "learned a lot about what was going on in the culture" and how that impacted him psychologically. He said, "My view is men and women are not really that different. The culture is what makes us different. It expects different things." Thus, he used the structural lens.

Yet when I asked Russell why men are expected to enjoy sports, he said,

> Well, back in our history, back in our evolutionary history, men basically were the warriors. They were the ones that fought the battles and did most of the active actions for providing food—the hunting stuff. Women, of course, would do that. They would hunt and they would gather, but they usually use nets rather than the things that required real upper body strength. And so, there's been a long history of the male sex being rated—the hierarchy of self-esteem in groups and cultures—based on those abilities. I think that a natural expression of that is sports.

Despite saying earlier that sports are "*assumed* [to be in men's] genes," here Russell said they are in fact in men's genes as the result of sex-specific evolution and biological differences in strength.

Russell combined both lenses and concluded that while gender norms are based in biology and evolution, they have become a part of culture in a way that does not serve people like him:

> My concern is the absolutism of these sex roles, is that it oppresses certain people that don't comfortably, or at least within a range, fit within them, and so that was the case with me. . . . These things [norms] are dinosaurs, they're on their way out, but there's a lot of people, right now, that are still very invested in them. Many people, in our current climate, want us to go back to them, even though they're absolutely obsolete. They're part of an intellectual, scientific, and technological culture that no longer exists.

While Rick argued that culture has outpaced men and women's biological needs to society's detriment, Russell argued almost the opposite: that culture must leave biologically based gender norms behind to catch up with humans' realities. In using the structural lens, he still supports efforts toward change. "The culture is flawed," he said.

Yet like interviewees who exclusively used the individual lens, he questioned whether gender inequality could ultimately be fixed. Referring to the author of a book he read recently, he said,

> She thought that it may be that we will never get away from the biological basis of men having to play a dominant role [in romantic relationships] with women because of just all our evolutionary history. It's disconcerting to me, not that I need to play a dominant role or anything, but it's disconcerting to me as someone who would like to see more of an egalitarian kind of thing that, maybe, the genetics are going to be dictating things for a long, long time, you know?

It is curious that Russell, who identifies as part of a social movement that aims to end gender inequality, questions whether that goal is even possible because of what he perceives as the biological natures of men and women.

In many cases, feminist men brought up biological explanations as one reason why gender inequality exists in addition to other social and structural reasons. For example, Richard, who is straight, Asian, and in his fifties, told me, "People will say that, . . . 'I try to give my kid dolls and all he wanted was Legos and trucks. I tried to give my daughter this.' Look, I will say that there probably is some genetic encoding at whatever level that puts us on a spectrum between frilly and dolls and nurturing to trucks and sticks and all that. . . . I think that might be internal." Richard believes that gender differences in toy preferences could be the result of genetic differences. Yet he went on to explain that parents' enforcement of early biological differences in their interactions with their children is also influential for gender inequality:

> I think the difference is that what gets enforced are things like not crying. So a parent will say, "My kid wants a firetruck." Okay, fine, but he trips over his firetruck and now he wants to cry because he's in pain. Now what do we say about that? . . . One example I give is that I was at the local amusement park with an eleven-year-old boy. He didn't want to go on a roller coaster. This is early in my career, but I had started to look at these things and I felt a rising in my gut of like, "What do you mean? You're a big eleven-year-old boy. You're scared of roller coasters?" I said to myself, "Would I have done that with a girl of the same age?" Probably not.

Thus, Richard also deployed the structural lens to describe how social processes compound biological differences.

Men's rights activists also combined the structural and individual lenses. Jeremy is straight, white, and in his thirties. He came to the men's rights movement after feeling isolated in a gender studies class. Feeling that his class completely skipped over the role of biology in gender inequality, he sought out more information:

> There's a lot of data on things like the effect of testosterone on human behavior that I found really, really interesting, partially because so much of it is kind of culturally constrained too. I was reading this one paper that found that like when you tell people that they got a shot of testosterone, their behavior is different in this totally different way than if they actually

get a shot of testosterone. It's different than if you give them a placebo, right? It's like culture matters but biology matters, it just gets so mixed up together.

In Jeremy's view, culture and biology both matter.

While Jeremy's recognition of the social origins of gender difference and inequality made him more open to possibilities that people like Rick rejected (e.g., that legislation should intervene in sexual assault), he still struggled with the question of whether gender inequality was solvable: "I don't want to go hard core traditionalist or anything like that, because I'm definitely not, but at the same time I guess I've heard some people say, and I think this is true, that gender equality is probably not really possible because you can't have equality between things that are different." Understanding men and women as fundamentally different made it difficult for Jeremy, like other interviewees who used the individual lens, to envision a world without gender inequality.

The Limitations of Men Gender Activists' Perspectives on Gender

Interviews with men gender activists reveal important limitations in their understandings of gender and gender inequality. First, as is clear from Rick's interview, the individual lens can perpetuate deeply misogynist ideas about women's "natures" and legitimize men's violence against women. While feminist men who used the individual lens did not express themselves in the same hostile terms, their beliefs similarly perpetuated gender stereotypes and reified gender differences.

Additionally, men's rights activists and feminist men alike could imagine only a very narrow range of solutions for gender inequality when they understood gender through the individual lens. These men saw individual people—their biology, personality traits, and decisions—as responsible for gender differences. They largely fit into two camps when it came to solutions to gender inequality. Some saw themselves as lacking any agency to change inherent, natural gender differences and so understood gender inequality to be unsolvable, while others saw exercising individual agency as possible and in fact the only solution to gender inequality.

Men who saw gender differences as unchangeable believed inequality to be insurmountable. Recall Jeremy's belief that equality is impossible between "things that are different," or Russell's claim that "genetics" will slow progress toward gender equality. Rick believed rape was inevitable and that biology would eventually undo much of the progress feminists have made toward gender equality. Pablo, a straight, white, and Latino men's rights activist in his twenties, used the individual lens to justify his view that the state would be unsuccessful should it intervene in women's underrepresentation in leadership positions:

> Because women more often want to take care of children, they don't focus on their careers so much. . . . Even if you could have this idea of the state caring for babies only and women being completely free from that or just men caring for babies equally or even more [than women]. . . . If that happens and women are still not at the top, then we need to look at other reasons. I think that would actually, in fact, happen. And I think that's a problem that cannot be solved very easily, which is that it's not only culture and society shaping these gender roles. It's also thousands and millions of years of gender roles in nature, in shaping genes, shaping a lot of behaviors and that's something you cannot reverse.

Pablo attributed women's underrepresentation in the upper echelons of business and government to their desire to take care of children, which he saw as the outcome of generations of sex-specific evolution. He summarized his view: "I don't think there's a way to fix it." Men like Pablo conceived of individual people as powerless in the fight against gender inequality because they saw gender differences as unchangeable. Understandably, men with such a pessimistic perspective did not engage in any meaningful action to challenge gender inequality, despite identifying as gender activists.

In contrast, some men who used the individual lens were able to imagine solutions to gender inequality. Yet the solutions they devised were narrow and placed the responsibility on individual people to engage in different actions under unchanged structural and cultural conditions. For instance, George explained how individual men must resist their biological natures so they can reduce gender inequality:

Let's say I went out with a bunch of guys. I know there's a different criteria and you got to amp up your assertiveness and your testosterone and, you know, do locker-room talk or some other stuff. And a lot of times I won't participate in that, you know, because I always try to remind myself that, "that could be your daughter they're talking about," or some other stuff. . . . Even though I think it's, on some level, it's a biological thing, too, like objectifying people. But you know, I try to at least be aware that it's going on and if I can, not participate. And sometimes my desire to just be part of the group overrides that too.

Individual solutions are flawed because all people cannot make different choices that would reduce gender inequality absent larger structural changes.[29] In this case, it is unlikely that all men can resist engaging in locker-room talk when objectifying women is still rewarded in masculinized spaces. Thus, individual solutions often end up blaming individual people for what is actually a structural and cultural problem. While George described this individual action as a solution to gender inequality, even within his own incomplete understanding of how gender operates, he recognized it was ineffective. He is sometimes unsuccessful because, in his view, objectifying women is biological and he desires to be part of the group. Still, men like George saw individual people as agentic and, through small, everyday actions, able to undo gender inequality.

Men who relied on the individual lens were thus divided between believing people were powerless to stop inequality and believing individual action alone could solve it. While men who used the structural lens understood gender in different terms, they had similar ideas when it came to solving inequality. On the one hand, some men recognized individual agency could not serve as a practical or effective solution to inequality that was embedded in relationships, institutions, and culture. Gil, the feminist I introduced in chapter 1, said that gender inequality must be solved by "government decisions," like affirmative action.

In his support of structural solutions, however, Gil proved to be rather exceptional. It was more common for men who used the structural lens to have no solutions at all. Amy Johnson and I have written previously about how some individuals, in internalizing the structural lens, feel a sense of hopelessness in the face of structural inequality.[30] I observed this especially among feminist men. Many believed that gender equality could not be achieved in their lifetimes, or in any person's lifetime. They were largely unable to articulate solutions because they believed gender inequality to be too entrenched in social structures to be solved. For instance, speaking specifically on the entrenchment of sexism within religion, Abe, a straight, white feminist in his seventies, told me, "Once it's in place, firmly in place, then nothing you say or do, no evidence is going to change it." Tim, a straight, white men's rights activist in his thirties, said, "Once you see things clearly, you yourself can change, you can impact the people around you, but are you ever going to be able to change society? No. No. It will always be something there."

Likewise, some men did not see how they personally could contribute to structural change. Matthew, the feminist I introduced in chapter 2, had a distinctly structural view of gender inequality and related his identity as a feminist to his identity as a socialist:

> Capitalism [is] just a fundamentally unjust and ecologically unsustainable system that just ruins, commodifies, and is destroying the planet, and creates all kinds of misery and pain through war and through economic deprivation. Then that of course ties in with feminism because of the inequality, both the economic inequality between women and men as well as between classes, but also the patriarchal masculinity that's promoted by imperialist wars.

For Matthew, capitalism and patriarchy are both systemic causes of inequality. He described a new Left coalition—made up of a revitalized labor movement, Black Lives Matter, feminism, and socialism—as the solution to both. Through the structural lens, Matthew saw collective action, not individual action, as a means to solving gender inequality. But he described this ideal leftist coalition as something far removed from him, referring to "the people"—not himself—who would participate in it. When I asked him if he engaged in any feminist activism, he said, "I don't know. I mean, I'm just not . . . I'm fairly introverted, so I don't go out and do a lot of things, just in general." Matthew recognized the power of collective action but did not recognize the power he had as an individual contributor to it.

Most commonly, however, men who used the structural lens still endorsed individual-level solutions akin to "changing hearts and minds." Recall the individual solutions Harrison endorsed: that women should, one by one, teach the men in their lives about inequality. Richard argued that it was up to parents to avoid socializing their children in gendered ways and instead to teach boys "emotional intelligence." He suggested that parents must essentially rise above gender norms when parenting their children. This ignores that children come into contact with other agents of socialization (media, school, extended family) and that children will be rewarded and policed vis-à-vis gender norms in contexts outside the nuclear family and over the life course. Similarly, Noah, a queer, white feminist in his twenties, endorsed "the kind of lived politics where men start ignoring a lot of the restrictions that are placed upon them and on women." Despite seeing the world through the structural lens, Noah did not recognize how such a political stance may be almost impossibly difficult for most men, given that gender structures our society.

It is unlikely that the individual-level actions men like Harrison, Richard, and Noah undertake will effect swift and significant change when it comes to the structural foundations of gender inequality. This is not to say such actions are unimportant; building men's feminist consciousness is a key step to investing them in more radical change efforts, and small changes around consent and socialization can have an impact on feminist men themselves and the people with whom they interact. Still, individual solutions are limited, and it is a problem that feminist men, presumably a best-case scenario, do not consider structural solutions or, worse still, see them as pie in the sky.

Most men who envisioned the world through the structural lens but endorsed individual-level solutions recognized that people would have to purposefully act against structural and cultural forces to change their behaviors. This was evident throughout Harrison's interview, for instance when he described how much easier it is to comply with rather than resist gender norms. When I asked Ian, a straight, white feminist in his thirties, about how men can adjust to a changing culture, he replied, "I think it takes a lot of personal courage to do that, to reflect on your heritage, reflect on your values."

Importantly, feminist men thought women were less susceptible to structural and cultural pressure than men. Because of this, they believed women would necessarily be responsible for both changing men and ending inequality. In advising women to be "patient, courageous, and kind" in broaching gender issues with men, Harrison painted women as responsible for teaching and coddling men in conversations about gender inequality. Recall also how Theo (in chapter 2) relied on his women of color colleagues to explain the gender and racial dynamics of his work meetings. Similarly, Joe, a straight, white feminist in his seventies, rejected structural solutions: "It's not like throwing a switch. It's not like you can enact a law. It's really you have to change how people think, men, mostly." Unspoken here is that, if men need changing, women will need to change them. Tomás, a straight, white feminist in his twenties, told me, "I saw a shirt the other day that said, 'The Future is Female.' And I was like, 'Yeah, I hope so.' I don't know why women still date men by and large. I don't know if that's just me, or like other people are going to realize that too, but like in a big way, men aren't going to be needed anymore as men, as we move forward in the world." The idea that men are irrelevant to a feminist future reflects a contemporary "choice" feminism influenced by neoliberalism, meritocracy, and hyperagency.[31] The feminist men I interviewed were embedded in this popular feminism, and it influenced how they understood men's and women's responsibilities over ending gender inequality. They described women as necessarily leading the charge and men as simply coming along for the ride or else risking being left behind.

* * *

Men's gender beliefs and their limitations are, in part, the outcome of their incomplete internalization of the structural lens. While both lenses are needed for a full picture of gender inequality, sociologists largely agree that gender is structural, not an individual attribute.[32] Both groups of men deployed the individual lens to explain gender and gender inequality, which shifted their focus from structural causes and solutions to individual ones. Even feminist men who primarily used the structural lens were fixated on individual solutions. This dynamic is not necessarily surprising; feminist men too are subject to the same psychological and cultural forces that promote reliance on agentic explanations. Feminist men's contradictory views on gender show that it is not easy for any one individual, no matter their intentions, to transcend beliefs that are baked into our culture, institutions, and interactions. Still, it is a limitation: the men we expect to be interested, invested, and participating in radical, structural change are not.

Men's identity projects present an additional obstacle to their thinking more critically about solutions to gender inequality. If, as I have argued, men are motivated to identify as gender activists to feel like and present themselves as good people, adopting the structural lens (and structural solutions in particular) would make achieving this goal much more difficult and labor-intensive. Focusing narrowly on individual solutions enables men gender activists to construct themselves as agentic and moral simply by reporting their engagement in rather unremarkable, everyday behaviors. It also allows them to absolve themselves of blame when they backslide, since biological, structural, and cultural forces compel them to conform. In other words, their prioritization of individual solutions (or insisting there are no solutions) allows men gender activists to portray themselves as doing all that is within their power to combat gender inequality.

In reality, a majority of the men I interviewed reported doing very little work to advance the goals of their social movement. Interviewees became uncomfortable when I asked them whether they do anything they consider "activism." This revealed that avoiding thinking about how they might contribute to collective action and structural solutions allows men gender activists to avoid guilt—guilt related to their own privilege and to not doing more to challenge inequality. Positioning women as ultimately responsible for changing men and solving inequality serves the same purpose. In essence, men's understandings of gender inequality were in and of themselves privilege renegotiation strategies. They allow men gender activists to forge new, moral identities without fundamentally challenging the gender order. Ultimately, the limitations in their understandings of gender inequality impede their ability to challenge it.

4

The Limitations of Identity-Driven Activism

Nick is a queer, white man in his twenties who began identifying as a feminist sometime in college. He couldn't pinpoint a particular moment that transformed him into a feminist. Instead, he explained that feminism was a more common topic of conversation in college than it had been in high school, and he began to feel more and more that it was time for him to consider the matter: "I don't think it was a conscious choice. I guess, just there was no time before where it felt like you either had to decide if you were a feminist or not. In high school, it was never brought to my attention. I probably didn't even know the term very well. . . . It was just at college, . . . it seemed to make sense to either decide if I would consider myself a feminist or not." While Nick didn't describe his feminism as a "conscious choice," his sense that he "had to decide" indicates the pressure he felt in a new context where more of his peers were discussing gender issues and feminism was becoming more visible online. He said, "Just the idea, that the word 'feminism' was around social media, on the internet. I'd see headlines about it, I would read articles, there'd be articles about it in the school newspaper. It was just a term that was being talked about by other people around me." Nick adopted feminism as his strategy for navigating these new and more frequent discussions around gender on campus and online. To paraphrase Alex's description of identity labels (chapter 2), feminism allowed Nick to declare which side he was on.

Nick defined feminism simply as "the belief that either sex or gender shouldn't be held against someone." He saw his feminism as a natural consequence of the broader lens he applied in his everyday life, which he described as a highly rational way of seeing the social world:

> I think [my worldview] just derived from not believing in God and picking the philosophical view of determinism, which is cause and effect and you're a product of your environment. If you [pick] four vari-

ables and you set them to one, two, three, four, whatever result happens would happen every time you set the variables to one, two, three, four, or if you set them to four, five, six, two, there would be [a] different [result]. That's how things make sense to me.... Then from there, I think about how you define fault and blame and, if we're all products of our environment and things that we had no decision over, why should you be penalized for it? So, that kind of derived from there, a sense of fairness or equality.

Nick saw individuals' outcomes as largely determined by forces outside of their control—that is, by the random variables they were assigned—making the uneven distribution of those outcomes unfair.

He saw gender as one of these arbitrary forces:

> I view feminism as a subset of a more basic worldview. I find it as a kind of derivative viewpoint, really, in the sense that I view all things through—I try to be objective and just pragmatic and deterministic in the sense that if women have.... [You] didn't get to decide whether you're born a man or a woman, so why should you be penalized for it?... Feminism comes from that.

Because Nick saw a person's gender as a matter of random chance, he didn't think it was fair that it should determine income, treatment, rights, and so on. Nick described his approach as obvious and hyperlogical: *if A, then feminism.*

While Nick had reflected carefully on how the world operates, constructing a cohesive and comprehensive philosophical worldview, he had thought less about how his worldview could translate into direct action to fight inequality. He told me,

> I don't think there's been a huge overarching shift in my day-to-day treatment of people or how I act as a result of identifying as a feminist or whatever. It's just made me more aware.... There's some scenarios where if I see something on the street, I'm more willing to step in or say something. But that's just because I'm more aware of it, so I guess that's how it's translated in one sense.... But those are few and far between because the scenarios that I consider egregious enough to say anything happen very

infrequently. It could go for a month where I wouldn't say there's anything that it directly translated [to].

Nick freely admitted that he engages in little feminist activism. He felt he had become more attuned to gender issues as a result of his feminist identity—for example, recognizing sexist advertisements on the subway—but had not changed many of his behaviors.

Nick explained that his self-identification had not catalyzed action toward feminist goals:

> I think once you self-identify as something, you start to think of the concept more. So, since identifying as feminist, I would say my thought and worldview might have changed. But how much that translates into day-to-day life, I guess not that often, because I just go about [my day] and go to my work. I'm not really exposed to scenarios where identifying as a feminist—[where] there would be a fork in the road. Does that make sense? I don't feel like I'm forced to make decisions on if I was going to do something radical.

Nick didn't consider most of the "scenarios" he encounters on a daily basis egregious enough to do something about. Moreover, he didn't feel he identified strongly "enough" as a feminist to do more: "Maybe if I identified as a feminist enough and felt I had to fight for the cause or get a job that maybe is furthering, I don't want to use the word 'agenda,' but 'cause,' I guess. But since I'm not doing that, there's not really a middle ground that I feel. I'm not faced with a lot of decisions where it would translate." As a casual rather than professional feminist, Nick felt that he wasn't often confronted by "forks in the road" that would test his feminism. Feminism was more a personal and philosophical project for Nick, not an activist one.

This is not to say Nick never acted on his feminist worldview. He described, for example, intervening when he saw a man and a woman arguing on the street and traveling to Washington, D.C., for the 2017 Women's March. However, Nick explained why in other contexts he did not intervene despite recognizing problematic gender dynamics. For instance, he took issue with the emails his company sent to announce the births of employees' children: "They always color code it in the sense that they always put a picture at the bottom, like an animated picture or whatever that they pull off clip art, that they pull off the internet. If it's a boy, it'll say, 'It's a boy,' and it'll either be a blue balloon or if it's a girl, they might have a little girl there with a little pink bonnet or hat on or whatever." In addition to what he called "unnecessary" and stereotypical color coding, Nick problematized the emails' conflation of sex and gender: "In a perfect world, you would say, 'We had a child,' and wait until it's at the point to decide whether its gender is a boy or a girl or whatever you want to say." Despite his annoyance with these birth announcements, Nick had not brought up the issue with his higher-ups: "I would never say anything at this point because it just seems like you got to pick your emotional energy and that seems like something not worth [it]. It's more of a symptom than a cause, kind of thing. So why draw a line in the sand there?"

Nick believed that people must pick their battles; at the same time, it didn't seem he had picked many. He summed up his feminism by saying, "I'm more feminist in theory than in practice." When I asked him if it was still important to him to identify as a feminist, he said,

> Yeah, because it impacts my perception of myself and my ego. I don't know. I obviously want everything to be equal and [for] me to treat people fairly and not manipulate them and do my fair share. So, it's important for me to think that I'm a good person. Most people want to think they're a good person. But I think when it comes down to it, I pick the easy, manipulative way more often than what would be the feminist moral obligation.

Nick was candid about what his identification with feminism achieved for him. Despite not fulfilling his feminist "obligation," Nick is able to use his feminist self-identification as a tool to construct his moral self-concept.

Like Nick, many of the feminist men I interviewed did little feminist activism. Indeed, I categorized the level of activism of 45 percent (14 of 31) of the feminist men I interviewed as minimal, meaning they participated in only low-commitment activities like posting opinions on social media, talking with friends and acquaintances about gender issues, and signing online petitions.[1] Yet they volunteered for a study explicitly calling for participants who identify as feminists. This is evidence that men's feminist identities are not built upon distinctions that social movement scholars might use to determine who is a "participant" or who has been "mobilized," like engagement in in-person activism.

Instead, men's feminist identities hinge upon *moral* distinctions. The men I interviewed constructed moral boundaries to define what it means to be a feminist. This is clear in how Nick described his feminism as derived from a larger moral philosophy. He defined feminism as a "belief" and being a feminist essentially as being fair and just. That men's feminist identities are defined through moral boundaries fits with the argument I have made thus far. Feminism allows men to feel like good people and portray themselves as such to others, and they construct their feminist identities toward that end.

This also fits with broader changes in the culture and in feminism specifically. The ascendance of neoliberal feminism has transformed feminism from something to be practiced with others to a personal lifestyle and aesthetic. This means individuals can "be" feminists without engaging in feminist activism at all. For the men I interviewed, feminism is largely a moral framework with which they can align themselves to serve their identity project. This is not to say identifying as a feminist does not shape them, their beliefs, or their actions. We see this in Nick's greater awareness of everyday sexism.

But Nick also didn't see himself as "enough" of a feminist to "draw line[s] in the sand" on many of the instances of sexism he recognized in his day-to-day life. This is a limitation of the feminism of many men I interviewed. The decoupling of men's feminist identification from activism means the promise of men's feminism goes largely unfulfilled.

Still, feminist men told me how they engage in practices of everyday resistance, even when they did not participate in any organized activism. Scholars contend that everyday resistance is not less meaningful than more collective and visible forms.[2] I do not disagree. The concept of everyday resistance has been most often applied to describe the resistance that people without power—peasants or prisoners, for instance—undertake when "public collective resistance would be futile, self-defeating or too dangerous."[3] While they may face social sanctions for engaging in more public activism, the men I interviewed do not live in a state that makes feminist collective organizing dangerous. Even more importantly, the men I interviewed are not powerless. Feminist activists recruit men to the movement precisely because they are powerful. If men were to wield that power through public activism to effect broad-based change, it would have a striking impact. As I argued in chapter 3, men's focus on individualized solutions for gender inequality impedes their ability to imagine more effective, structural ones. While I do not discount the good that men's everyday resistance can do for the women in their lives and themselves, I do argue that it is a problem—and a serious one—when men who identify as feminists do not consider how they can engage in collective and public acts of resistance.

This is not, of course, a limitation exclusive to *men's* feminism. As the most visible strain on the national stage, and one that melds seamlessly with neoliberal rationality, "lifestyle" or "choice" feminism is popular among people of all genders. Neoliberal feminism commits women to their own personal happiness projects geared toward striking the perfect work-family balance, while it commits men to their own personal identity projects aimed at reconstructing themselves as good people.[4] Still, men's focus on developing new moral self-concepts through feminism at the expense of activism presents particular problems to ending gender inequality.

For one, they do not leverage their disproportionate power, status, and resources toward feminist goals through more visible activism. Additionally, as men define their feminist identities through moral boundaries, they construct hybrid masculinities, reifying inequalities between femininity and masculinity, and among masculinities. I find that feminist men's identity work draws on boundary-making strategies that link morality with masculinity and emphasize the primacy of masculine traits, like rationality and agency, to situate themselves as more moral and status-worthy than others and, very often, other types of men. This was true of Nick when he described feminism as hyperlogical, creating an implicit comparison between himself and nonfeminists in terms of a markedly masculine characteristic. Elsewhere in his interview, Nick recalled altercations with nonfeminist men—counterprotestors at the Women's March and catcallers—whom he described as "inappropriate," "cringey," "aggressive," and having an "inferiority complex." In defining their identities as feminists, men constructed themselves as superior through their particular and particularly moral masculinity. Men who are men's rights activists used similar strategies for defining their activist identities, with similar results. In leveraging their identities as gender activists to remake themselves as morally good people, both groups of men subordinate femininity and other masculinities to what they view as their own idealized masculinity.

In this chapter, I provide Tyler, a feminist, and Aaron, a men's rights activist, as examples of how men gender activists use traditionally masculine characteristics—agency and rationality—to bolster their identity projects, inadvertently reifying gender inequality.

Agency

Tyler is white and in his thirties. Like Nick, he began identifying as a feminist in college, after taking a women's literature class. As a gay man, he felt an instant connection to women's struggles as portrayed in the course readings. He recalled, "I had just come out of the closet, and understanding aspects of identity, . . . really understanding that behind all these core issues there is almost a linkage between all of us, that we all feel and experience. . . . Just understanding that the fight that women have to undergo just for basic equality or autonomy from any aspect of life, it's just really troubling to me." Tyler chalked up his feminism to his ability to empathize with women and to see them as human. He called women's need to fight for equality and autonomy "really troubling," hinting at the moral boundaries he would use over the course of our interview to construct his feminist identity.

I quoted Tyler in chapter 1 as he defined manhood as doing "as much as I can to make the world a better place [each] day." He thought manhood meant "showing up" and "being a force for good." In contrast, he thought most people accepted that being a man meant having "a position of privilege and power in today's world." Unlike most people, Tyler questioned men's power and privilege:

> Still today in this world [it's] very basic knowledge, the knowledge and understanding that like, these reactions that we [men] think we can just say stuff, and just raise our hands—that's just still intact. No one challenges that. That's the one thing that a lot of my professors in undergrad, you know, they said, "We're not going to call upon you, Tyler,

because you have to learn your place. You have to learn your position, you have to learn your privilege, and you have to check it. Yeah, we know you know the answer, and we want you to know the answer, but we're not going to call upon you, because you need to understand what it feels like to be this other student that doesn't have that innate ability to feel so inclined to automatically jump into a conversation and give their opinion."

Tyler learned to "check" his privilege in college. He credited his professors with why he understands masculinity differently than others. Through these experiences, Tyler said he unlearned his privilege, which distinguishes him from most people who don't "challenge" the idea that men are entitled to dominate conversation and volunteer their opinions. Moreover, he learned "what it feels like to be this other student." Tyler described himself as particularly humble and empathetic, which he suggested makes him unique among men.

Tyler was often the only man in feminist spaces. While he found this problematic from an organizational and social movement standpoint ("I should not be the token male feminist in one of the most metropolitan areas in the world"), he also seemed to derive great pride from his uniqueness as a feminist man. After taking the women's literature class, Tyler became involved in feminist activism. He recalled, "And then, I started getting heavily involved with women's politics on campus, and I was always the sole male voice for a lot of stuff, but always going and showing up, and doing what needed to be done." Tyler again positioned himself as exceptional: "the sole male voice." While he attributed his feminist consciousness to his empathy and humility—two feminine-typed characteristics—his description of his activism has a particularly masculine quality: he continued to "show up" and "do what needed to be done." He simultaneously portrayed himself as especially committed to feminism despite his gender and as particularly masculine.

Tyler was proud of being "the sole male voice," but he also explained that being a man in feminist spaces was not entirely straightforward. He described how he navigated this during college:

My whole motto that entire time is that, you know, I'm a white, six-four, two-hundred-pound, midwestern boy, so I very much don't look the part in many aspects. So, I always say that you have to show up, but you have to be quiet in the sense that this isn't your space that you can dominate. . . . You always have to be willing, I guess, to sit at the back of the bus, and until you're invited to the front of the bus to take part in that community, you have to be okay [with it].

Tyler pointed to a real problem for feminist men: just like in the classroom, they can feel entitled to dominating feminist spaces. As Tyler explained, feminist men must feel comfortable "being quiet" and being a sort of outsider "at the back of the bus." By his own description, Tyler embodies a very particular masculinity: one that is physically big and strong but emotionally intelligent and humble.

While he implied that navigating feminist spaces might be difficult for some men, he described it as a nonissue for himself:

So, it's really about getting rid of your internalized privilege that society says that you have, either because you're X or Y. And that's always kind of been how I approached a lot of these spaces, because I already know that I am an outsider, and whatever that means, in those spaces, but I had to learn what it meant to be that way, and feel that kind of singularity of being that only person there, and why I'm there, and how I can be worthy of being there at the same time.

In describing how he had to adapt to being a man in feminist spaces, Tyler suggested that "getting rid of [one's] internalized privilege" is a difficult process but one that he ultimately overcame. Above, he implied that many men would not "be okay" with taking a back seat to women, even in feminist spaces. In discussing the very real challenges of being a feminist man, Tyler also juxtaposed himself—dedicated and humble—with the men who are absent from feminist spaces—presumably lacking the same virtues. He suggested he is more agentic than other men, able to rise above his socialization and entitlement to join with women in feminist struggle.

It was common for interviewees to describe themselves as having a remarkable degree of agency, which in turn allowed them to become gender activists. Peter, a straight, white, cis feminist in his thirties, told me he faces some resistance when others find out he identifies as a feminist, but he is not dissuaded. He played it off, saying, "I think it's easy to navigate if you know what you believe. . . . I don't find it challenging, personally." The implication, of course, is that some men do find it challenging. When I asked Sid, a straight, white, cis men's rights activists in his sixties, what he believes it means to be a man, he linked his masculinity with his will and ability to solve gender issues: "Being a male certainly has something to do with having the grandiosity, the ambition, the chutzpah to tackle gender politics and believe that I could come up with a solution. Me, Sid, a nobody. I was gonna do that. I was gonna take that on, by God, I'm gonna do that. And I believe I did." Sid explicitly linked masculinity with agency, confidence, and ambition. He explained that these masculine-typed qualities allow him to pursue his moral calling—men's rights activism.

Unlike many of the feminist men I interviewed, Tyler did engage in feminist activism, both during college and afterward. He had been the "first" or "only" in a variety of feminist organizations on campus:

> Basically, I became the first male director of our [campus women's group]. I was the only man on the [campus gender council], and we worked on issues like getting lactation rooms on campus, because they didn't have such things, to being the public relations director for a women's center, being really the only male voice there, to being the first man to graduate with a women's studies minor.

Tyler was motivated to work toward feminist goals because he thought it was the right thing to do.

But he also used his feminist activism to bolster his identity:

> I'm very proud of myself, to call myself a feminist. I don't like the [term] "male feminist," because I think that, I don't know, it just places some type of difference on me. I mean, if that's how people wish to identify me, that's fine, but I have staunch feminist friends that say, "Tyler's one of the few people I actually feel comfortable calling a feminist, and not putting that misnomer in front of it."

Tyler objects to the term "male feminist" because he feels that it qualifies his feminism, perhaps as not as real or as dedicated as that of women feminists. His "staunch feminist friends," who we are left to assume are women, endorse his identification as a feminist without qualification.

Tyler's insistence in using the term "feminist" to describe himself stands in stark contrast to the debates within men's consciousness-raising groups in the 1960s and 1970s, which questioned whether men should call themselves feminists at all.[5] Lou, a Black, gay, cis man in his sixties who identifies as "profeminist," explained these debates, which were in full swing when he first came to the movement:

> Because to many of the men of my age, my generation—and today I stand very strongly for the use of "profeminist" rather than "feminist"—is that to me, for a man to call himself a feminist is to appropriate women's lived experience. You know, if you were my ally along the lines of race and you are not Black or a person of another culture that's identified as of color, then at what point would you then start referring to yourself as Black? Well, one wouldn't, because you would always recognize that your challenge was to be an ally and that was the best that you could hope to be. But you never had exactly the same experience. And that's exactly how I feel about the issue of gender and use of the terms "feminist" and "profeminist."

Lou explained that the decision of an older generation of men to use the term "profeminist" stemmed from their recognition that they were allies, not members of the oppressed group for whom they fought. They consciously differentiated themselves from women, who had direct experience with oppression and inequality, in an effort to avoid appropriation. Lou continued, "No matter what a man does, he is always going to be a man. He can seek to relinquish himself of the powers and prerogatives of being a man in this patriarchal structure but he can never totally achieve that as long as patriarchy survives and no matter what he achieves, he never lives the experience that a woman has lived."

In contrast, Tyler is uncomfortable with the term "male feminist," which he called a "misnomer," precisely because it "places some type of difference on [him]." He wants to be—and believes he should be—seen as the same as his "staunch" feminist friends who are women. Lou's description of this historical debate within men's consciousness-raising groups sheds light on why Tyler is so adamant that he be called a "feminist" rather than a "male feminist." Tyler's goal is not only to give up his privilege but *to be seen as having given up his privilege.* Terms like "profeminist" and "male feminist" purposefully signal men's power and privilege. In contrast, Tyler prefers the term "feminist," which does not. Moreover, his assertion that he has gotten "rid of [his] internalized privilege" is at odds with Lou's claim that a man cannot truly do that while patriarchy survives. To support his moral self-concept, Tyler represents divesting himself of privilege as a process that he has already completed rather than one that must necessarily be ongoing. He believes his feminism is fully realized, and he wants others to recognize this too by referring to him as a "feminist" rather than as a "male feminist."

While Tyler wanted to be seen as a feminist without qualification, he also clearly enjoyed being the only man in feminist spaces. In other words, he at once hoped to be seen as just another one of the feminists *and* as unique among men. These seemingly competing desires served Tyler's identity project to be and be seen as a good man. Being simply a "feminist" allows him to portray himself as deeply committed to a moral cause and as having already and completely relinquished his privilege. Being the only man in feminist spaces allows him to portray himself as exceptional as compared to other men.

Toward this second goal, Tyler distinguished himself from other men through moral boundaries, often using agency as a measuring stick for morality. In explaining why there are so few men in feminist spaces, he said,

> I think that men often may be afraid to show up, because they might have to understand aspects about themselves that they thought maybe were already realized, and super progressive, and fully in tone with the equality that they really believe in, and understand that those core truths [they believe about themselves] may not be right. Because when you show up to an activist space, you have to be prepared to challenge not only somebody else, but yourself most importantly, and a lot of people can't handle that.

In describing the difficult process of self-reflection that feminist activism requires of men, Tyler called men who do not "show up" "afraid" and unable to "handle" the "challenge." He implied that feminist men like himself have overcome this challenge through sheer will. He thus differentiated himself from other men through agency. In describing agency as underlying his commitment to feminism (a moral cause), he linked agency with morality. What is more, because agency is a masculine-typed characteristic, Tyler also linked *masculinity* with morality. He portrayed himself as more agentic and masculine, and thus more moral, than nonfeminist men.

Likewise, Tyler drew a line between men who have considered their privilege and power in private and those who do so in public:

> We are literally taught, whether through unconscious or conscious actions in the world, that there's a certain order to things. I try to deconstruct that, and I live my life based on a certain way. You can do that in private, but when you go out there in public, and you show up in that way, and you're not prepared to do that, there's a resonance to it, that it's hard for people to understand. And we need more men to show up. So, it's great that they're doing this in their private lives, they're doing whatever they need to do in that way, but at the end of the day, we need you [out] there.

Tyler believes that the work other men ("they") do privately to rid themselves of internalized status hierarchies is less meaningful than what men like himself ("we") do publicly and that public feminism is more difficult and demands more strength and dedication. Again, he used agency—the ability to overcome, to "show up," to choose feminism—as the characteristic that distinguishes the most moral men from the others. Moreover, he reified another gendered binary—private versus public—and reinforced the importance of the masculine domain.

Men's rights activists used agency in a similar fashion to describe themselves and others in their movement. Pablo, a white and Latino, straight, cis man in his twenties, told me, "I never bought into this whole idea that women are more disadvantaged than men, in general. . . . Most people work with social pressure. I feel I work less that way, but a lot of people get socially pressured and they don't even question it much." Pablo, who is a college student, explained to me that his university peers are generally profeminist. He defies the expectation that he should be a feminist. Pablo thus frames himself and his fellow men's rights activists as uniquely agentic, which makes them different from and superior to others. Reminiscent of how Tyler described feminist men, Pablo portrayed men's rights activists as showing up and choosing their movement despite the odds.

Men gender activists, including Tyler, often drew moral boundaries related to appropriate sexuality. This worked in tandem with boundaries interviewees constructed based on agency: men portrayed themselves as being able to rise above their basic sexual desires to pursue their activism in contrast to other men, whom they portrayed as singularly focused on sex. Tyler, for instance, used such boundaries to distinguish himself from then-president Donald Trump and his supporters. This was common among feminist men, as I interviewed many of them in the wake of Trump's election or inauguration. Tyler remarked, "Well, we have a sexist, and Groper in Chief in the White House." He attributed Trump's and other politicians' sexism to their obsession with sex:

> That's why women didn't get the right to vote. They were like, "Oh, what's going to happen to the house?" It's not what's going to happen to the house. These men didn't care [about] what's going to happen to the house. They were worried that these women would be outside the house, so they couldn't have sex with them anymore. I mean, it really comes down to this sexual nature that possesses a lot of people's minds, and almost paralyzes them. And it paralyzes them, sadly, sometimes through their legislation, and that's what we're really seeing a lot lately.

Through his activism, Tyler had worked at the state and local levels to support legislation that would benefit women and girls. Here, he described men politicians as being "paralyzed" by their lasciviousness when it comes to meaningful measures to reduce gender inequality. He drew a moral boundary between himself and other men (viz., Republicans), through both their agency (his action vs. their "paralysis") and the appropriateness of their sexual desire.

Because stereotypes often paint gay men as sexually promiscuous, Tyler may have been especially concerned with representing himself as having appropriate sexual desires, but it was common for feminist men and men's rights activists alike to describe other men as immoral because of their obsession with sex and themselves as able to rise above such base instincts.[6] For example, Lenny, a gay, white, cis men's rights activist in his sixties, believed that feminist men are not actually interested in equality: "We're finding that a lot of them are the abusers, that they're hanging around . . . these women as—I think there's a modern word for this that's really ugly—'allies,' but they're really trying to get in their pants. We're finding a lot of them are assaulting women." Likewise, men's rights activist Travis, a bisexual, white, cis man in his twenties, said feminist men are "trying to appear sensitive and score brownie points for their own perception," especially with women. It was common for men's rights activists to describe feminist men as sexual opportunists. This perception might stem from many men's rights activists' conceptualization of gender as biological. They often framed feminist men as acting on base sexual desire, which they portrayed as relatively natural. On the other hand, men's rights activists described themselves as more moral than feminist men because they were involved in their social movement for the "right" reasons—that is, to end gender inequality. Men's rights activist Arnold, a straight, white, cis man in his fifties, put it succinctly: "We [men's rights activists] are really the true people who are for gender equality." They thereby constructed feminist men as sexual savages and themselves as civilized proponents of equality.

While collective identity formation is a necessary process for social movement mobilization, the way men like Tyler accomplished this task had several unintended consequences. For one, the moral boundaries they construct stratify men on the basis of their agency, willpower, and moral toughness, thereby reinforcing a traditional hierarchy among men where the most masculine are also the most status-worthy. They presume that agency is the most appropriate measure of a person's morality and juxtapose morally strong men against morally weak ones. There is an implied denigration of characteristics seen as feminine—lack of agency, inaction, weakness—within the moral framework Tyler and others construct. In addition to reifying inequalities among men, then, such moral boundaries reinforce the inequality between masculinity and femininity too.

Second, such an understanding of feminism and morality locates men's feminism squarely within neoliberal feminism. The centrality of the individual actor and personal agency is reflected in Tyler's conceptualization of the feminist man: a strong-willed individual who can rise above his own natural instincts and self-interests to act morally. We cannot expect feminist men like Tyler to be exempt from neoliberalism's cultural influence. Still, neoliberal feminism is less radical, less collective, and less effective than other feminisms because it does not critique the economic, political, and cultural system.[7] While not unique to *men's* feminism today, this remains an important limitation of men's gender activism.

Last, men's construction of personal agency as the measure of morality means that they must provide evidence of their own agency to demonstrate that they are good people and fulfill the unconscious motivation underlying their activism. In an effort to portray himself as agentic—as having risen above social norms and perhaps biology to become moral—Tyler insists that relinquishing privilege is a one-time process, which he has already completed. My concern is that conceptualizing privilege as easily shed stops men like Tyler from engaging in deeper, ongoing reflection that might be more likely to translate into sustained change, both in men's behaviors and for gender equality more broadly.

Recall, for example, that Tyler thought that feminist men must be prepared to "sit at the back of the bus"—in essence, to follow the lead of women in feminist spaces. He believed most men would try to dominate feminist spaces, as they are accustomed to doing in other contexts. Similarly, he recognized being chosen for leadership positions as an advantage of his gender: "Leadership positions—people automatically think you [as a man] can step up over somebody else. . . . So yeah, I totally think there has always been an advantage being a man, and I've tried to really understand that, because when someone chooses me for X, is it because of X? And so, there's a lot of second-guessing involved, I guess." What Tyler said throughout his interview indicates that he believes women should lead feminist spaces and action and that men should be critical and careful when offered leadership positions.

But at the time of our interview, Tyler was serving as the president of a women's organization. He described being handpicked for the position:

> My friend had started the chapter that I am currently the president of, and my other friend has been in charge of it as well. I had worked my way up through various circles, and was leading them, and then I said, "Well, I should probably get more involved in this." . . . And so, as a result, I started attending—they appointed me to the board, and then my friend

didn't want to be president anymore, and so she had said, "Would you join me, and if you ran, I would totally support you." And so I did, and it really just became kind of a positive force like that.

As these things often happen, Tyler was tapped as a board member and later president through his network on account of his more informal leadership and previous involvement in the organization.

I do not wish to imply that Tyler is not a qualified leader or wasn't the correct choice for the future of the organization. We did not discuss the other candidates, and I am certain Tyler's work as president has been productive. Instead, I want to point out that Tyler's description of his becoming the president of a women's organization contrasts with what he said men in general must do in relation to feminist spaces and leadership. He described becoming president both as happenstance—it was not something he sought but rather something raised by a friend—and as completely logical—it followed from his increasing involvement in the group. He suggested that the nomination was well deserved while simultaneously denying he had any deliberate leadership ambitions.

Tyler believes that men should relinquish control in feminist spaces, but this is an abstract belief that he does not seem to apply to himself. He did not hesitate when his friend suggested he run for president, nor did he admit to having any misgivings. Instead, he recounted, "I was kind of just showing, 'Of course I'll do it.'" Why such a disconnect? Tyler's word choice provides an answer. He said he was "showing." What he was "showing," I contend, was his agency and thus moral fortitude. The audience of this "showing" may have been his friend, other members of the organization, or a generalized other that judges what kind of man he is. As he emphasized elsewhere, Tyler believes that being involved in feminist activism requires particular willpower and moral strength of men. In answering the call to be president, Tyler portrayed himself as willing, able, committed, and thus morally superior. In becoming the leader of a women's group, he is able to project to others the way he hopes to be perceived. He does so even though it conflicts with an aspiration to check his privilege and make rather than take space as a feminist man.

The decoupling between what Tyler thinks and how he acts stems from his unconscious motivation: to be seen as morally good. In focusing so much on his identity work, Tyler cannot fully internalize and act on his feminist beliefs. That feminist beliefs sometimes conflicted with Tyler's identity project was evident elsewhere in our interview too. For example, when I asked Tyler how feminist organizations might recruit more men, he replied,

> We have to invite more men to be speakers at women's conferences. We have to not be afraid to, at a women's event, have a man on the panel. I see so many people that are like, "Oh, there is an equally qualified woman for this position that a man is now speaking on," and it's like, "Okay, let's have that conversation. Let's have that conversation." . . . I always was suggesting male speakers, because you know, we had to get them in these spaces. And when they came to the event, people latched onto them like no one's business. They were so entranced by having these people here, these men there. They found their voices to be just as critically important as the female ones that were there.

Tyler's suggestion to make men more visible in feminist spaces is incongruent with what he claimed to believe elsewhere in the interview and what he recognizes as what most feminists ("many people") believe: that feminist men must decenter themselves, especially in feminist spaces. He also failed to recognize that the audience's effusive reception to men speakers was likely informed by gender bias, a sort of glass escalator that propels feminist men into celebrity.[8]

For Tyler, constructing men as "critically important" to the public feminist stage validates his leadership and thus his morality, and so some of his feminist beliefs are not put into practice. It would be unreasonable to expect Tyler (or any person, for that matter) to act on his feminist beliefs all of the time. In many instances, the decoupling between belief and action may be largely inconsequential. But in this case, the result is that the gender status hierarchy that constructs men as natural leaders and experts is re-created within the very organizations that aim to dismantle said hierarchy. More broadly, Tyler's desire to be seen as having freed himself from male privilege prevents him from more deliberate and reflexive behaviors that would better align with his feminist beliefs.

Rationality

Aaron is a straight, white, cis man in his twenties. He was just out of college when he realized his mother was controlling and emotionally abusive. He was listening to a radio program discussing domestic violence, and it dawned on him, "This is what I've been going through for the last many years." His personal experience did not immediately catalyze his joining the men's rights movement. The Affordable Care Act did. He explained,

> There was a lot going on in the news with Obamacare, and especially about the contraception mandate and how it was claimed that those [who] were opposing this were engaging in a "war on women," which I thought was pretty ridiculous, especially since I knew I was born with a congenital heart defect, which is just as much an accident of birth as my gender is, and I have certain medical care I need to get for that. . . . The cost of the copays and deductibles on that can easily exceed what the cost of a year's worth of contraception would be without any insurance coverage at all. . . . If it constitutes waging war on someone to expect them to pay a ten-dollar copay, then where's the outrage about the bipartisan war on people with congenital heart defects?

Feminist anger about conservative opposition to universal coverage for birth control raised questions for Aaron. To him, the problem just seemed overblown. While Aaron had personal experience with one of the issues the men's rights movement champions (domestic violence), what originally piqued his interest in issues of gender was something else: feminist outrage.

He researched the proposed legislation and found that some preventative services, including domestic violence screenings, were covered for women but not for men. From Aaron's perspective as a victim of domestic violence, this didn't make sense:

> So, I'm looking at this, and I'm saying, "If this had been in place, and I had gotten this as part of my annual physical back five years earlier, I probably would have been referred to a mental health professional, been able to do that free and confidential, and would have been able to get

the help I needed. I might not have an anxiety disorder now." So, I was pretty frustrated about that situation, so I decided that it was time to do something about it.

Aaron wrote a petition that demanded preventative services be "available to anyone regardless of their gender." He eventually found the men's rights movement in his effort to gain signatures for the petition. Since then, he has continued to do anonymous online activism, like writing petitions, and some in-person activism for the movement.

Aaron's description of his initial interest in gender issues illustrates how his moral self-concept motivates his activism. When he realized that health care services could have helped him and other men who are the victims of domestic violence, he "had to do something about it." He described reading comments on the petition that took him aback:

> I read some of these comments, and it goes beyond—not just the level of the abuse and not just ignoring it, but it goes to things like, "My wife beat me up so bad that I needed to go to the hospital. I called 911. The cops came, and they . . . I was all beaten up. She was completely unscathed. I had never laid a finger on her, and they go and assume that just because I was a man, and she was a woman, that she had done this in self-defense, and instead of taking me to the hospital, they took me to jail."

Aaron recounted a horror story posted in the comments: being physically abused and then arrested for assault by the very people whom you called for help. He described this as a particularly heinous experience that went "beyond" the typical level of abuse and the typical experience for men victims (the abuse being ignored). He described the police as acting callously and immorally.

In contrast, simply reading about this experience motivated Aaron: "There were a number of these, and it was really a wake-up call for me. I mean, I knew that there was a problem here, but I didn't get just how bad it was until that point. . . . At that point I just couldn't go back to living my life the way I had been. I knew I had to do something about this, and I couldn't just stand by idly." The experiences he read about served as a moral call to arms, and he quickly became embedded in the men's rights movement. Like Tyler and the other men I interviewed, Aaron constructed moral boundaries to define himself and his identity as a gender activist. Here, Aaron compared himself to people who "stand by idly" and the police, who made the situation worse. Like Tyler, he used agency—his springing into action—to differentiate himself from others. In his view, Aaron's newfound knowledge of the problem and his immediate action make him more moral than others.

Aligning with the moral framework men's rights activists have co-constructed—that they, not feminists, are the true defenders of equality—allows Aaron to build his self-concept as a morally good person. In explaining the philosophical perspective that guides his activism, he said,

> We're all equally human. We're all equally capable of both good and evil, and we should all treat each other with basic respect and all be held accountable for our own decisions. . . . It's just that I think that should hold across gender lines, within gender lines, whatever. Especially, I think that when you look at just the history of the concept of tolerance, that ultimately what it was based on was the idea of do unto others as you'd have them do unto you, and that's not just people who are like you, that's people who are different as well.

Aaron described the men's rights movement as an extension of the golden rule. He constructed men's rights activism as simple and almost pure in its morality:

> When you look at the history of various movements, and I mean even some that are still very much in progress today, like say the gay rights movement, that has generally been about just gay people deserve to be treated with the same humanity as heterosexual people, and it should be the same with gender and with race. Historically, that was what the civil rights movement and the like was also about. I mean, Martin Luther King, "I have a dream that my children will be judged, not by the color of their skin, but by the content of their character." Do unto a Black person the same as you would want to be done unto you as a white person.

Here, Aaron likened the men's rights movement to gay rights and civil rights, constructing them as based on the same moral principle. He evoked Martin Luther King Jr., who since his death has been transformed into an almost mythical symbol of virtuousness. Aaron's point is clear: in being a men's rights activist, he is supremely moral.

While Tyler primarily relied on agency as a measuring stick for his and others' morality, Aaron more often used rationality, and this too is reflected in the quotes above. He described insurance coverage for birth control as a special dispensation for women that is not provided to other groups. He deployed a seemingly hyperlogical approach and compared what he sees as two equivalent groups: women and people with congenital heart defects. He made a step-by-step argument that feminists claiming there is a "war on women" are overexaggerating and hysterical. In describing the history of progressive social movements, he again used rationality to underpin his claim to moral virtuousness. He constructed his perspective and his activism as logical and based on the most obvious moral principle: do unto others as you would have them do unto you. Aaron implied that the golden rule is self-evident and that his gender activism simply takes it one rational step further ("It's just that I think that should hold across gender lines"). He presented his philosophy and activism as simply *making sense*.

Aaron also linked rationality and morality through his specific contribution to the men's rights movement: disseminating (what he believed to be) factual information about gender issues. In describing his day-to-day activism, he said, "Just in terms of someone points out something that's factually inaccurate, or someone's talking about something and says, 'I don't know.' And if I know the facts, I'll make them aware of it." In addition to these more informal conversations, Aaron attempted to spread what he understood to be the truth through a more deliberate method:

> One of the things I've done as part of my activism has been monitoring Wikipedia and going and trying to correct either inaccurate information that's on there or adding information to something that's incomplete or misleading, and there were a couple of times where I wound up in some flame wars with people over that.... I can make sure that the perspectives of both sides are being represented there as opposed to if I just left it to be written [by others].

Aaron had added several articles about the men's rights movement and on legislation related to gender issues to Wikipedia. Rationality was baked into Aaron's activism; he felt a moral responsibility to spread "the facts."

Aaron also linked rationality with morality when discussing the men's rights movement's primary antagonist: feminism. He constructed feminism as immoral by pointing out what he saw as flaws in feminist logic. Studying computer science at a university he described as having "one of the highest concentrations of radical feminism on the planet" allowed him to see "the gory details"—the irrationality—of feminism:

> One of the first places I started seeing it was in the context of the women in science movement.... Before that, I had always just assumed, "oh, it's just a matter of that there was discrimination in the past, and after that's ended, it takes time for things to equalize, takes time to get rid of some of the more subtle biases," that sort of thing, but at the same time, I started noticing that there were a lot of things that just didn't add up.

Aaron drew on a well-established template in the men's rights movement called the "red pill story."[9] Men's rights activists use red pill stories to construct a narrative arc that recounts the storyteller's transformation from ignorant and passively feminist to enlightened men's rights activist. According to Aaron, as he learned more about interventions around women in science, things just "didn't add up." He started to uncover what he saw as inconsistencies in feminist reasoning.

He continued,

> I don't know how much you do or don't know about the history of computer science, but the first programmer was Ada Lovelace. It was literally never an all-male field, yet it has this huge gender gap. Meanwhile, there were a lot of other fields, like say law and medicine, that had historically been all-male, where historically women weren't allowed to participate in those fields, yet now those fields were basically fifty-fifty or even had more women than men in them. So, that didn't exactly add up. I also noticed that the gender ratio in a class depended a lot on what the subject matter was, and that if you have subject matter that's very pure computer science, then you could wind up with an all-male class or a 90 percent

male class or something like that, whereas if you had something that was more interdisciplinary, you would wind up with something pretty close to fifty-fifty or in certain cases even more women than men. So, that didn't add up with many of the things that were being said about [how] women were afraid to go near a computer science department because of the geek stereotype and whatnot, and things like that.

Aaron explained that feminist explanations for why there are so few women in science (e.g., the historic exclusion of women, the geek stereotype) simply do not make sense in the computer science context. He implied that something else that feminists ignore must be at play. As he repeated again and again, it "didn't add up."

It became evident to Aaron why feminists were wrong when he began "looking at some of the research studies" they use as proof of their claims:

[I] realized, wait a minute, these studies have huge problems with the way that the methodology is being used, like they're just polling what percentage of women say they've experienced X, and they don't even ask what percentage of men have experienced the same thing, and then when you find a study that does, it turns out that, oh yeah, the ratios are not really all that different. But they would do things like that. They would use things that were very imprecise.

Aaron critiqued feminism as unscientific. It is worth noting that feminist theorists and methodologists critique positivism and objectivism as approaches that center men's experiences and perspectives.[10] Aaron's reasoning was both positivist and objectivist as he made the case for his activism and moral virtue. In showing how feminism is illogical and men's rights ideology makes rational sense, he constructed his activism as true and moral.

Aaron concluded his conversion story by explaining how gender is more complex than how feminism portrays it and that, in recognizing the nuances, he felt compelled to act:

There was a lot of stuff that was sort of pushing me in that direction that this was more complicated than what we were taught to believe, and by the time I got to seeing those restrictions, it was like, "wait a minute, this is something where there isn't moral gray area here anymore. There's no way in which it hurts women to allow men to be able to get psychological counseling if they're victims of domestic violence," and it was just at a point where it was the last straw for me, and I just said, "I can't put this aside anymore. It's time to do something."

Throughout his interview, Aaron explained his activism as a natural extension of his rationality, logic, and newfound knowledge. As is clear when he said, "It's time to do something," he also constructed his activism as a moral imperative, thereby linking rationality with morality. Like agency, rationality is masculine typed. In describing rationality as underlying morality, Aaron linked morality with masculinity, just like Tyler did.

As Aaron claimed, it would be inconsistent for feminists to organize to reduce the services available for men victims of domestic violence.[11] As is clear from the previous quotes, Aaron often misrepresented feminism as overly simplistic and lacking nuance. Yet his understanding of feminism was far too black-and-white, as was common among the men's rights activists I interviewed. It's likely that this is, in part, a function of the inaccurate information about feminism that is available in men's rights spaces. Additionally, portraying feminism as an irrational strawman was strategic for Aaron as he constructed himself as particularly rational and morally good. For instance, he said,

> Well, I think that ultimately, the most important thing and what's going to really effect change is when we change how we talk about gender to be able to recognize that, as I said earlier, both genders have and continue to face injustices. It's not about who has it worse and who has it better. I don't think anything good is going to come out of fighting over that, because different people have different experiences and are going to reach different conclusions, but hopefully we should at least be able to agree that both genders have nonnegligible issues that they face, and people of both genders should be able to make a good-faith effort to understand the perspectives of people of the other gender and the issues that they face and try to craft solutions that are going to be fair to everyone.

Here, Aaron implied that feminists are so ideologically driven and irrational that they are incapable of appreciating the perspectives and experiences of men. He painted feminists as too busy competing in what men's rights activist Alex called the "Victim Olympics" to admit that men too face "nonnegligible issues." In Aaron's telling, feminism fails to reach the lowest standard of morality ("we should at least be able to agree") because it is nearly nonsensical. Importantly, in being so nonsensical, feminism ignores the "injustices" to which men are subjected. It is worth noting that Aaron's unnuanced portrayal of feminism does not allow him to recognize how identifying power, privilege, and hierarchy is essential to combatting even the gendered problems men face.

In making his case that feminism is irrational and immoral, Aaron compared feminism to a religion. In recounting an argument he had with another man about the gender wage gap, he likened the "seventy-seven cents on the dollar" statistic to religious dogma: "I said [to him], 'That's such a misleading statistic.' [He said,] 'Why is it misleading?' So, I explained it to him, and he says, 'Oh, come on. You know that women are paid less than men.' And it was like, okay, it's dogma, so God forbid we should check our facts." When I asked him what the biggest obstacles are to solving the issues men face, he responded,

> Closemindedness. I think for a lot of people, certainly for your hardcore, radical feminists, their beliefs on gender issues are almost like a religion, and trying to persuade them to sympathize with the perspectives of men and boys is almost as difficult as trying to persuade a religious fundamentalist that they should be tolerant of people of other faiths. I think it's a very similar mindset.

Aaron compared feminists to religious fundamentalists to describe their total lack of tolerance for men. He implied that religious faith and rationality are incompatible. Through this comparison, he constructed feminists as both irrational and immoral.

Using rationality to draw moral boundaries between oneself and an antagonist was not the sole purview of men's rights activists; it was also common among feminist men. When I told Tyler the basic ideology of the men's rights movement, he said, "Well, I think that they really need to speak to their Lord and Savior, and understand a lot of stuff that is wrong with that sentiment." When I asked Tyler what he thought might draw men to the men's rights movement, he told me,

> Those people are the ones that are constantly online, or on their phones, or reading and absorbing stuff that is not based in any credible source or type of academic or sensible fact. But they're believing it like it's the word of God. When someone tells you something is blue a zillion times, and you know it's yellow, you're going to believe it's blue, because just the repetition of how people are banging that over your head.

Tyler was, like many of the feminist men I interviewed, dismissive of men's rights activists. He described them as brainwashed—as religious fanatics. Tyler explained that *reason* distinguishes himself from men's rights activists.

In keeping with his broader, hyperrational approach, Aaron believed that the solution to feminism was "factual accuracy." He said, "I think another factor that's important is—and I think ultimately, this has to supersede everything else—factual accuracy. That ultimately, as Senator Moynihan said, 'We're all entitled to our own opinions, but we're not entitled to our own facts.'" He used the gender wage gap as an example of feminist propaganda, miscalculated and used to drum up hysteria:

> So, when you have something like say the gender wage gap, for example, where that gap comes from taking the average earnings of all men and all women who work full-time, averaging them together, and not taking into account factors like how many hours a week a person works or the type of job they do, how much experience they have, and that when you normalize for those things, that seventy-seven cents on the dollar goes up at least into the high nineties. And you have someone like President Obama getting up there and saying, "Women are getting paid seventy cents on man's dollar to do the same work." I mean, it's simply not true. And in the case of something like that where there's just an outright lie, the truth needs to come out, and facts need to supersede emotions.

There are merits to calculating the gender wage gap when controlling and not controlling for occupation, hours, and years of experience, and these choices are both statistical and theoretical.[12] They are also political because even when a portion of the gender wage gap can be explained by gender differences in those variables, that portion still contributes to inequality between men and women. In controlling for such variables, researchers can sometimes treat the explained portion of the gender wage gap as justified. Aaron, however, constructed these methodological and political questions as having obvious, right answers ("it's simply not true"; "there's just an outright lie").

At the same time, Aaron denied that his perspective was political: "I should also make it clear in terms of me saying that—in terms of President Obama saying that, I am not someone who is dogmatically opposed to Obama or anything like that. I'm a Democrat. I voted for him twice. This is not about liberal-conservative. This is just about both factual accuracy and basic human decency." Despite identifying as a Democrat, Aaron borrowed from the right-wing playbook, essentially saying "facts don't care about your feelings" to dismiss feminist claims about women's disadvantage.[13] At the same time, he tied rationality and morality together when he declared the issue is "about both factual accuracy and basic human decency." In Aaron's view, you cannot have one without the other.

Aaron's story illustrates that men's use of rationality to undergird their moral self-concepts had similar drawbacks to their use of agency. Aaron associated the men's rights movement with positive and traditionally masculine traits (e.g., rationality, logic) and feminism with negative, femininized traits (e.g., imprecision, hysteria). At the same time, he linked those masculine traits with superior morality. As a result, he discursively reinforced masculinity's supremacy over femininity. He also reinforced a hierarchy of masculinities, for instance, when describing his interactions with other men who bought into feminism (like the seventy-seven-cents-on-the-dollar statistic).

* * *

Feminist men and men who are men's rights activists defined their activist identities through moral boundaries, rather than other distinctions, like engagement in in-person activism. Among feminist men, this reflects the broader decoupling between identity and activism within neoliberal feminism, which reconfigures feminism from praxis to lifestyle or aesthetic.[14] For both groups of men, this also reflects what I have argued is their subconscious motivation. They rely on moral boundaries because their aim is to build their moral self-concepts.

Men's rights activists' unique conceptualization of "gender inequality" means they, like feminists, believe they are fighting to reduce it. They believe men are discriminated against and thus define gender inequality as men's disadvantage relative to women. As they understand it, their agenda would reduce gender inequality. So both feminist men and men who are men's rights activists purport to advocate for equality. While constructing collective identity among activists is a necessary task, men gender activists' identity work also accomplished two other incidental yet consequential things that run counter to their intentions.

First, it reinforced the association among masculinity, morality, and status-worthiness, reifying the inequality between masculinity and femininity. Tyler, Aaron, and other interviewees measured their and others' morality through masculine-typed traits, like agency and rationality. Others described masculinity itself as having and following firm moral principles. Adrian, a straight, Asian, cis feminist in his twenties, told me that he defines manhood though "older metrics" like "having a value system that you believe in and follow." Bradley, a straight, white, cis men's rights activist in his fifties, described how his grandfather served as a "great model of how to be a man," which influences his activism:

> What he would do, and I think what a lot of men aspire to do, is to speak up when there's a need to speak up, . . . if there's some real serious injustice going on, or some real serious problem. But when there is, the manly thing to do—and also the womanly thing to do, but since you asked about men—the manly thing to do is to fight for what's right. And that's also part of the reason why I've done this activism, because it just feels like the right thing to do to me.

Bradley interrupted himself to note that acting upon a moral code can be "womanly" too, but he used masculine language ("*fight* for what's right") to evoke imagery of traditional manhood. Men gender activists described traits like "having a value system" and "speaking up" as masculine. In associating morality with masculinity and constructing moral boundaries to delineate their activist group from less status-worthy outsiders, they reaffirmed the supremacy of masculine traits over feminine ones.

Second, in comparing themselves explicitly to other men, they bestowed primacy on a particular type of masculinity, predicated on "having a value system," "fighting for what's right," leaping into action, transcending sexual instinct, and being hyperrational. They positioned their masculine-typed ingroup as superior to masculine-typed outgroups. For example, Bradley told me "there's many ways to be a man." In asserting that his and his grandfather's fighting for what is right is "the manly thing to do" and morally superior, he implicitly subordinated other masculinities. Very often, interviewees explicitly compared themselves to other men in moral terms. Adrian described a memorable incident during a gender studies course that served as a cautionary tale:

> We talked [in the course] about . . . whether or not gender plays a part in academia or your success in your classes and we had a member of my fraternity, a man, who straight up said, "Of course not. We are in a time now where it's merit-based grades." All the women in the room were not on the same page and so it was a clear example to me of, as the person in the place of privilege, you get to be blind to inequality or lack of power, right? Because you have the power, you don't see other people lacking the power and so that was a great moment where I realized I could easily be that guy.

Adrian contrasted himself against his fraternity brother, who stood in for the type of masculinity—privileged and willfully ignorant—that he himself works to avoid. Comparisons to "that guy" were common. While downward social comparisons to other men allowed interviewees to build a positive and moral self-concept, they also reified status inequalities between themselves and other men. In contrasting themselves with "that guy," interviewees reconstructed a hierarchy of masculinities.

These unintended repercussions constitute important limitations in men's identity-driven activism. Interviewees' identity work was their central task and the re-creation of inequality a consequence. How can feminist men construct a collective identity without drawing on old tropes that re-create the gender hierarchy? The bad news is that feminist organizations cannot, alone, tackle neoliberal rationality, which structures both the narrative resources interviewees use (i.e., their focus on themselves as individual agents) and the decoupling of activism from feminist identity. But Tyler's account suggests another strategy: feminist men must understand that dismantling their privilege is an iterative and ongoing process that, in fact, cannot be achieved until patriarchy is itself dismantled. Such a shift might limit the impetus for men to prove that they are supremely moral and have overcome their privilege, and allow them to more fully consider how their actions and beliefs are shaped by privilege. Feminist organizations can take deliberate action through educational programs, social media campaigns, and other tactics to shape the public discourse about men's privilege. Feminist organizations might also work with men to develop new and liberatory narratives they can use toward their identity work, rather than ones that rely on traditionally masculine characteristics like agency and rationality.

5

Contexts of Mobilization

Adrian is an Asian American, straight, cis man in his twenties. Daniel is white, straight, and cis and around a decade older than Adrian. Both men majored in English in college. When we spoke, Adrian was on the cusp of graduating. He was unsure what he would do postgraduation but was considering both the Peace Corps and graduate school. While Daniel had taken some graduate school courses, he worked in sales at the time of our interview.

Adrian is a feminist, Daniel a men's rights activist. Unlike many of the men I interviewed for this book, both men regularly participate in public organized activism. Adrian works as an intern at his university's women's center, where he helps organize events for men students to learn about feminism and discuss masculinity. Daniel created and manages a men's rights website. In contrast to similar websites, Daniel's is not a blog or forum; rather, it provides resources for boys and men—what he calls "a data-driven platform"—and connects professionals working on men's issues.

Both men described activism as a constant process—as "work." Adrian told me being a feminist means "working towards alleviating some of the disparities in power and status that exist as a result of systems of oppression." Considering what it means to be a men's rights activist, Daniel said, "Advocacy—it's a job that has to be done. I think that's how you have to look at it. It's not just a hobby. It's not just something that you can do when you feel like it. If you're going to do it you have to get into the mentality of it's a job that needs to be done and you need to have good high standards for yourself."

Adrian's and Daniel's journeys into gender activism follow the typical trajectory I have outlined thus far: when confronted with the idea that they are privileged as men, they sought out a strategy to recoup their moral sense of self. Their personal identity projects invested them in gender activism. How, though, did they become invested in such different social movements? The answer, I argue, is the social contexts in which Adrian and Daniel are embedded. In this chapter, I detail Adrian's and Daniel's accounts of how they became interested in feminism and men's rights activism, respectively. Together, their narratives show which dimensions of men's social environments can encourage them to undergo identity change and think and act like feminists.

Adrian: The Picture of Everyday Life

Adrian is disarming in his honesty. A minute into our interview, he told me,

> I'm not super close to my father. I think he represents to me a lot of the Korean masculinity, which is a little bit distant and emotionally unavailable. I definitely feel like I grew up with great examples of how to act my gender and I think coming to college, I've been thinking more recently, more critically about why do I behave in the ways that I do? Who's teaching me and who's teaching young men generally how to behave?

Adrian grew up in a conservative household. His family is Christian, and he attended a religious, all-boys high school. His upbringing did not encourage him to notice gender inequality or interrogate masculinity but did encourage him to perform a traditional masculinity like his father.

While Adrian has experimented with gender during college, his family continues to exert a conservative force on his gender performance:

> I think when I go home, I actually take on more traditional fatherly characteristics which does make me feel like I'm sort of going back to this older model where I don't speak very openly with my siblings about how I'm feeling emotionally or I take a lot of initiative on getting our family to do things together or go somewhere. I do feel a little bit pigeonholed when I go back home to fit the role within the family that I filled growing up. And also because I think my parents are much more conservative and even my siblings are more conservative because that's where they live. I think that there are certain things that I am more wary about, like I removed my nail polish when I went home. I have kissed a guy but I would probably never tell anyone in my family

about that. I did get a piercing and I took it home and it was surprisingly well received.

Adrian said that he falls back into old, gendered patterns when he visits home. As the oldest sibling of five, he takes on a "fatherly" role. He does not share his inner, emotional life with his family members and alters his outward appearance to be more masculine. In sum, Adrian's feminist transformation did not begin at home.

Only when Adrian came to college did he begin to think about gender and masculinity:

> I think I was confronted with some of the privileges that I got because I identified as a man and I think growing up, I hadn't seen those, I had been blind to them. But coming to college I had people that I really care about sort of show me the things that I didn't have to deal with because I didn't identify with a different gender or group, and the things that I benefited from, like assumptions that were made about my capabilities or my leadership abilities, because I was a man. I think that was really important and humbling when I did learn about them because I had been so oblivious to them in the past.

Adrian described himself as undergoing an important transformation. Before college he was "blind" and "oblivious" to his privilege as a man. During college he was "confronted" with the idea that men are privileged. While he described learning about his privilege as a "humbling" experience, suggesting a slight embarrassment, Adrian's story lacks the threat responses—anger, defensiveness, denial—that many men's rights activists displayed. In fact, he described learning about his privilege as "really important."

Adrian described the realization that he is privileged as a social process: "I think it was mostly other people pointing things out to me as opposed to my just suddenly realizing them, because it's comfortable to just go about your day the way you always do." In other words, other people intervened in Adrian's understanding of gender and male privilege. Adrian believed he would not have come to the same understanding without such interventions because maintaining his sense of self (as unprivileged) was "comfortable." According to Adrian, his trajectory into feminism was indelibly shaped by the people who surrounded him in college.

Adrian learned about the benefits he receives as a man from people he "really cares about." In particular, Adrian's former romantic partner exposed him to new ideas about gender and inequality during college:

> I was in a serious relationship for two years with someone who identified as a woman and she was able to explain to me what her life was like around her gender. And that was something that helped because, although I had grown up with my mom and my sister and friends who are women, I don't think I had been that close to someone to the point where they were able to share the daily stresses and the daily social implications of choosing to identify as a woman.

Adrian attributes his new perspective on gender inequality to a woman with whom he had a long-term, romantic relationship. He described their relationship as close—closer than his relationship with his mother or sister. According to Adrian, the intimacy of their relationship facilitated more open communication between them, including about her gendered experiences.

In describing the "daily stresses and daily social implications" of womanhood, Adrian's former partner revealed to him a new "picture" of gender relations:

> When she told me about the underlying fear to any sort of romantic encounter, or getting your own taxicab, or like these really small things, or being catcalled, these microaggressions that build up over time and develop this sense of general fear. I had no idea. Even if I could acknowledge that the act of catcalling was really misogynistic and harassment, I couldn't see it in the picture of everyday life and how that moment could affect a moment with another man who had never displayed any sort of harassment or misogyny, how the other man's behavior does affect the way you see that man.

Adrian's partner provided the context for understanding the claim that women are disadvantaged in their daily interactions, what he called "the picture of everyday life," making concrete what was only abstract to him before. She communicated to him a new understanding of what it means to be a woman and thus what it means to be a man. In this intimate context, Adrian avoided the strong threat responses that accompanied some men's realization about their privilege.

It is worth noting that Adrian constructs two types of men: those who contribute to women's "sense of general fear" and those who are judged because of it despite their good behavior. Adrian sympathized with his former partner and so understands why women are suspicious of men who, for instance, do not catcall, even while he suggested that it is not entirely fair. In differentiating between these two groups of men, Adrian managed some of the negative feelings that might accompany his realization by aligning himself with the "man who had never displayed any sort of harassment or misogyny." This indicates that Adrian may not, in fact, have the full "picture." While he understands that other men's bad behaviors impact him, he does not really identify himself as benefitting from the same systems of oppression that facilitate said behaviors. In one reading, he portrayed himself as unfairly maligned because of these "other" men.

Adrian described his university and social circle as generally profeminist, which he recognized even before he started identifying as a feminist himself. He said his understanding of gender inequality began to crystallize during his junior year: "I started to have a lot of friends who would tell me about their own experiences or my intimate partner would tell me about what it's like to feel that lack of power generally on a daily basis." In other words, Adrian's social network played a large role in steering him toward a feminist perspective. Through interpersonal relationships and personal stories, Adrian began to learn more about gender and inequality.

Even his fraternity contributed to his trajectory into gender activism. When the fraternity president arranged with the gender studies department to host a seminar in the fraternity's house, Adrian enrolled in the course:

> It was a one-unit seminar on just feminism in the news today, but all these news stories time and time again, which show that the systems that were making decisions about like justice or about really bad things that have happened—not only was the event a representation of how men

have a lot more power than women in society, it was that the systemic responses were also decided by mostly men.

The gender studies course revealed to Adrian the more structural and institutional roots of gender inequality that conversations with his friends and romantic partner had only implied. He continued,

> A classic example was, if you think about sexual assault is an issue where the actual act of sexual assault is largely a display of men's dominance over women most of the time, and then on top of that, the governing body, which is like the university or the legal system that decides to enact justice on sexual assault, is also a patriarchal body that can't avoid some of these instances of power. So, in that case, this class was perfect in that it showed me twofold how power plays a huge part in the way we engage with our gender and made me more aware of the ways that I was benefiting from this.

The course helped Adrian recognize how sexual assault and adjudication of sexual assault (or lack thereof) are both manifestations of men's power and dominance.

The gender studies course was influential in Adrian's trajectory in part because the course was concrete; as he noted above, it focused on "feminism in the news today." In particular, Adrian's understanding of sexual assault was facilitated by a specific and deeply emotional example: "I would say the Brock Turner case played a huge part in my thought process around it and the witness's statement was really important." Here, Adrian referred to the highly publicized sexual assault of Chanel Miller in 2015 at Stanford University. Turner, then an undergraduate student, was convicted and sentenced to only three months in jail for raping Miller, sparking outrage. The case is notable for several reasons—it happened on a college campus on the brink of the #MeToo movement and led to a successful effort to recall the presiding judge.[1] As Adrian indicated, the case is also well-known for the victim impact statement Miller read at Turner's sentencing, which detailed the horrifying physical and psychological effects of the assault and court case on her.[2] The statement was released online and read by millions of people.[3] Adrian specifically referred to this statement as "really important" when it came to his understanding of sexual assault. As was the case with his conversations with his former romantic partner, Adrian was moved by Miller's statement because, I argue, it was deeply personal and concrete.

It's also possible that this case was important for Adrian's understanding of sexual assault because of the role men bystanders played in it. Two men graduate students interrupted the assault, restraining Turner until police could arrive. Miller specifically thanked them in her impact statement.[4] Beyond his emotional connection to the case through the impact statement, then, it may have allowed Adrian to see himself as a different kind of man from Turner—one who might intervene in the most heinous manifestations of gender inequality.

Adrian had never taken a gender studies course before and attributed his enrollment to the course's meeting place in the fraternity itself. He was of two minds about hosting a gender studies course in a men-dominated space:

> I think some people would argue that we're spoon feeding men and going out of our way to educate them and—it's essentially like going to their doorstep and telling them like, "Please, just come downstairs and we'll teach you things you need to know." And part of me understands that that's frustrating that we have to go to that length to get men to care about a class like this but I think it's super effective and the impact can be huge and to be honest, had the class been hosted anywhere else, I probably wouldn't have taken it.

Adrian admitted that he enrolled in the course out of convenience. This too speaks to the importance of his social network and social context in informing his views about gender. After all, the fraternity president sought out the opportunity to host the course in the fraternity house, which indicates the fraternity as an organization and its members may be more attuned to issues of gender.

Despite being held in a men-dominated space, the course was largely successful in changing Adrian's understanding of gender because of the women enrolled in it:

> It opened my eyes to things and I really wish that that kind of seminar would be required for men in general because I feel it made evident to all

the men in the room that there are a lot of blind spots of our experience that women knew about and I didn't really feel like there was much going the other way. A lot of the class did feel like the women in the class educating the men so part of me does feel like because we are given a lot of privilege as men, there should also be a lot of responsibility to understand where that comes from and how it happens.

Adrian described a one-way flow of knowledge from the women in the class to the men. While this instilled in him a sense of "responsibility" to understand and grapple with his privilege, it also echoes the theme present throughout Adrian's narrative and that of other feminist men: men's reliance on women and other marginalized people as they attempt to learn about inequality and privilege. Adrian believed that such a course was a good intervention in inequality precisely because learning from women peers was so effective for him personally.

Adrian's connection with women and feminist peers also facilitated his first foray into activism. When I asked him how he first became involved in feminist activism, he told me, "One of my friends asked me to be a part of this conference. It specifically focused on sexual assault, but I think that's what made me see the implications of these power dynamics that I was learning about in the class." Adrian was personally invited to help organize a feminist event that directly reinforced the new knowledge he had obtained in the course. This again illustrates the role of men's social networks in their trajectories into feminism. Additionally, it speaks to the importance of timely and relevant activism opportunities in cementing men's understanding about gender and inequality. Following the conference, Adrian took another gender studies course and began to work at his university's women's center. Most recently, Adrian participated in an initiative meant to prevent sexual violence in the Greek system. He is responsible for training fraternity leaders in "how to be advocates for women in general or against sexual violence."

Adrian's story is one of identity change. With his father as a role model, he was raised to believe being a man meant being the stoic head of the household. Adrian admitted to sometimes defaulting to these more traditional definitions of masculinity, but he also said being a man "means acknowledging and navigating the privileges that have come with traditionally being a man or the way society treats a man." In other words, he thought that men should be obligated to grapple with their privilege. Burgeoning feminist men, who had glimpsed how the world is organized to their advantage, had to reconcile their newfound knowledge with their understandings of themselves and their ingroup. To adopt a feminist perspective, they had to see men as privileged, even if they envisioned themselves as exceptions to that rule. Identity change is complex, but as Adrian's narrative shows, one's social context and network can facilitate it.

While Adrian's interview indicates several reasons why he was ultimately able to adopt new definitions of masculinity, there was another important, structural one. He explained that frustrated entitlement was a major issue for men today:

> I think men are facing a huge problem with entitlement where the kind of realizations that I'm having and the acknowledging of power does conflict with the previously advertised message from society that you as a man are entitled to a lot of things and I think there's disparity between what I thought I should get and what society is now saying is right for me to be entitled to. That is hard. It feels like something is missing or that you're being cheated. I think a lot of men are feeling that.

Why is Adrian able to resist feelings of aggrieved entitlement?

> I think that maybe because I'm not a *white* man, I don't feel it as intensely. I think there were less things that I was being told by society implicitly that I deserved so it has been easier for me, I think. But of course, it is difficult to acknowledge that a lot of the success that I have is tied to the power that I get from being a man, which inherently separates it from my own deservingness or diligence.

In the previous chapter, Tyler claimed that his entrée into feminism was shaped by his sexuality. As a gay man, he felt solidarity with women. Being a member of another marginalized group may facilitate men's sympathy for women and make men more practiced in identifying inequality.[5] Additionally, each man's structural position informs his relationship to male privilege. Adrian's social location as an Asian man tempered his expectations and entitlement, perhaps making identity change easier for him to navigate.

Daniel: Reading, Reading, Reading

Like Adrian, Daniel grew up in a conservative family. His upbringing instilled in him traditional values when it came to gender. When I asked him what he thinks most people believe manhood means, he said,

> If I could put it down to one word, "responsible." . . . I've pretty much always known that. Because my father is a very traditional man, a lot more traditional than I am. He's always been like, "A man's got to do what a man's got to do. No matter what else happens the man is responsible for making sure that there's food on the table." My dad is very old school in that. He's much more an advocate of, I would say, traditional gender roles.

Daniel grew up in a working-class family. He started working summers at his father's construction business at the age of twelve. At work and at home, he learned a particular version of masculinity predicated on "doing what a man's got to do." Indeed, his older brother left school at fourteen to work construction full-time.

Like Adrian, then, Daniel was not encouraged to interrogate gender and masculinity at home. But also like Adrian, Daniel's understanding of masculinity and gender today was different from that of his family:

> I've always been like, "Let the best person for the job get it." For example, if a wife happens to know more about financial management in a household, then she can make most of the decisions, or if the wife has a better job or is a better worker and the dad happens to be a better parent, why not have that? I don't really agree with everything that my dad . . . with my dad's lifestyle. . . . I just look at a lot of stuff from the previous generation of my father's and I say, "That may have worked for them, but that's not really the life for me."

Daniel believed his mother was happy in her marriage to his father, as she also subscribed to traditional ideas about gender. But Daniel didn't believe such strict ideas about gender would suit him. In fact, Daniel hesitated to define manhood at all: "I would not place any kind of limitation on that definition. Because, once you define something you sort of give power to . . . it, but you also limit it, and I just don't think that there should be any definition of a man or what is a real man."

While Daniel's stance here may appear profeminist, his quarrel with traditional gender roles was largely that they unfairly pigeonhole men, not that they disadvantage women. His angle, then, was entirely in keeping with the early origins of the men's rights movement, which focused on the constraints men face because of their gender, and still-influential men's rights texts like *The Myth of Male Power*.[6] Providing dating as an example, Daniel continued,

> The man is responsible for approaching the woman if he wants a date. The man is responsible for paying for dinner, for possibly driving the woman. That's a social norm that still exists in a lot of society. And there's definitely an obstacle in women's initiation or level of responsibility. For my wife, herself, she was the first one to reach out to me whenever we were dating. But I think that it's still usually the case, that the man is expected to be the one to be responsible for initiation, for dating, even for money.

In men's rights discourse, women are simultaneously positioned as immensely powerful (e.g., they control the state) and as shirking responsibility (e.g., they expect men to provide for them).[7] Daniel juxtaposed his own wife, whom he describes as exceptional in her initiative, with the majority of women to make the case that men are unfairly put upon because of their gender.

If Daniel was not encouraged to think critically about gender at home, how did he first begin to consider it? He described his graduate school experience as central to his development of a gender consciousness:

> So, in humanities in particular you're often exposed to a lot of theories which have a foundation in identity politics and I was taking a look at just a lot of the conversation. A lot of the conversation of identity politics, most when you look at a lot of scholarly literature, and as well as just when you talk to people in that community, just seems very one-sided. There seem to be a lot of assumptions in the conversation that were kind of taken for granted and were not open to examination. And so, at first it seems kind of unacademic for me. I mean, I didn't really have a concept of gender. To me I was . . . I mean, I guess I was seeing

myself as gender-neutral for the most part. But for me, what struck me at first was just the unacademic nature of a lot of the conversation that I encountered. And when I discovered that there are some other problems, particularly with survey research, particularly on sexual violence on college campuses and that research was being used to spearhead sort of like a national movement to basically lock down on things, I became a little concerned.

Daniel described "identity politics" as foundational in the humanities; later in our conversation, he clarified that he was referring to feminism. He criticized identity politics and feminism as "unacademic" on two counts: (1) it has underlying "assumptions" that are "taken for granted" and (2) its methodology (survey research, in this case) is flawed. I discussed in chapter 4 how men's rights activists construct feminism as irrational to further their own identity project. Additionally, it is worth noting here that all schools of thought have underlying assumptions. Importantly, it is clear that Daniel's exposure to feminism in graduate school was especially jarring to him because he was "seeing [himself] as gender-neutral" then. As was the case for other men gender activists, Daniel's first encounter with the idea that men (including himself) are privileged evoked negative feelings.

Daniel explained that the feminism he was exposed to in graduate school unfairly stereotyped men:

> My very first introduction into gender politics and academia was a colloquium course, which was basically a required course of my department in advanced rhetoric and argumentation. . . . Unfortunately, I think we spent too much of the class on really ideological interpretations of rhetoric. For example, . . . I was basically given a feminist lesson in rhetoric for about two weeks. And the rhetoric tended to be highly stereotypical, I think. It tended to stereotype traditional rhetoric as masculine rhetoric that was focused on dominating people and it tended to characterize persuasion as domination, sort of something that subverted the will and consent of the person that you were trying to convince. A lot of it had this constant tone of negativity and stereotyping of men. And so, I thought that you could have removed a lot of that, a lot of the gender aspect from it and had a much more academic piece. I just thought that was unnecessary. The only

thing that tagging it with the feminist perspective seemed to do was just to negatively stereotype men.

Daniel characterized feminism as having a "constant tone of negativity and stereotyping of men." He said, "It also tried to stereotype a good type of rhetoric as a feminist type of rhetoric, which they described as invitational rhetoric, where you invite other people to share your perspective." In keeping with the processes I described in chapter 1, Daniel's exposure to feminism evoked negative feelings for him because of what he interprets to be feminism's implication for men's (and his own) morality. He understands feminism to be condemning men as dominating, perhaps manipulative. In contrast, he sees feminism as elevating itself (and perhaps women) as morally superior.

In interpreting feminist perspectives on rhetoric as a threat to men and his moral sense of self, Daniel could not grasp what purpose such perspectives serve:

> But it seemed like a lot of politics was simply shoehorned in, so to speak. You can tell when politics is—when people try to make something political that doesn't need to be political. A lot of people can feel that. I was a nonactivist at the time and I try to keep this in perspective that people who are nonactivists tend to generally resent, or at least become distrustful of situations where things become unnecessarily politicized. That is definitely something that happened that I felt.

Interestingly, Daniel recognized a dynamic that shaped his negative response to feminist viewpoints: his understanding of himself, at that time, as apolitical—a "nonactivist." Still, he accused his professors of forcing politics into their courses "unnecessarily."

While Daniel continued to complete his assignments and do the readings with "a grain of salt," he decided to do additional research on his own. He entered what he referred to as "the research phase" of his gender consciousness development, which lasted "a solid eight months." He said, "From then, I learned that there were women's issues and then learned there were men's issues. And so, I just started reading, reading, reading as much as I could." He read, for instance, *Against Our Will: Men, Women and Rape*, in which Susan Brownmiller argues that rape is "nothing more or less than a conscious process of intimidation by which *all men* keep *all women* in a state of fear."[8] These readings reaffirmed Daniel's belief that feminists think men are immoral. Reacting to what he perceived to be unacademic and prejudicial interpretations, he sought alternative understandings of gender, masculinity, and inequality. He read popular men's rights texts, including *The Myth of Male Power* and *Who Stole Feminism?*[9] At one point, he read about the 2006 Duke lacrosse case, a high-profile incident in which a Black woman accused three white university lacrosse players of rape.[10] He said, "That was particularly alarming because in that case there were eighty-eight professors basically speaking for five academic departments and ten academic programs, who openly took a side against their own students. I thought that was incredibly alarming, especially for an institution of that level of prestige." In his private reading, Daniel was exposed again and again to the feminist claim that men victimize women. As a response, he sought examples like the Duke lacrosse case that show *men* are the victims. At that point, Daniel "decided [he] wanted to advocate for men in some form."

Notably absent from Daniel's explanation of his trajectory into the men's rights movement—particularly in light of Adrian's narrative—are other people. Despite presumably interacting with professors and classmates during this time, his description centered largely on himself and solitary activities like reading. One of the only times he mentioned other people in describing this early phase of his mobilization—discovering feminism and experiencing identity threat—was when he explained,

> I continued to read. Of course, I did the lessons to the best of my ability. I didn't face any kind of discrimination in the classroom by any of my teachers, I think. I wouldn't say that any teacher was really mean to me or anything like that. Some of the students, I think, were a little swayed by the language in it and I think tended to go along with some of the stereotyping of language that was presented in the academic piece, so that was a little disconcerting.

By his own account, Daniel did not experience mistreatment at the hands of his professors. While he was "disconcerted" that some of his classmates seemed to agree with feminist perspectives, he did not describe getting into disagreements with them or feeling unfairly maligned by them. Beyond this moment, Daniel did not mention how other people shaped his mobilization.

This is not to say that Daniel did not have meaningful relationships. In fact, he visits his parents at least twice a week and "prides" himself on being "a family man." He had also just gotten married. In describing his hobbies, Daniel said, "I like to learn foreign languages, so right now I am about waist deep, I want to say, into learning Spanish. . . . I like to spend a lot of time with family. I was recently married, so I do like to spend as much time as I can with my wife, who I love very much. And really just basic friends and family kind of thing." Daniel's wife is an immigrant from a Spanish-speaking country, and we can assume that his desire to learn Spanish was motivated by his relationship with her and her family. While Daniel says that he "love[s his wife] very much"—something I do not dispute—it is interesting to note how different his description of their relationship is from Adrian's description of his previous romantic relationship that played such an influential role in his feminism. Adrian's description was effusive in its conveyance of intimacy, mutual respect, and empathy; Daniel's was not. I think it is possible that Daniel was less comfortable sharing more personal details of his life with me than Adrian was. Nevertheless, the difference in how central relationships—particularly relationships with women—were to each man's trajectory into gender activism is evident.

As was the case for Adrian, Daniel's first opportunity for activism came from a friend from college. She was working on establishing an organization to support Latino men in higher education. She told Daniel about the project, and he offered to help with grant proposals. Later, he was invited to participate in their conferences. What Daniel learned during those conferences made him more passionate about the organization:

> A lot of what was said there really resonated with me, because it matched with my background a lot. Even though I'm not Latino myself, the reality is that when I was younger, I started working in my father's construction business when I was basically twelve years old. I was doing that during the summer and then, I did it full-time. And whenever you're working in a construction job in the summer and in [U.S. state], then you're going

to be around a lot of young Latino males. Some of these males are people who actually work year-round. They should be in school at some point, but they feel like they have to be the providers for their family and they have this idea of "a man's got to do what a man's got to do." And so, they just work and they chase the money and a lot of the time their education suffers because of that.

The conference also discussed how machismo might stand in the way of young men's education. He recognized in his own upbringing the cultural belief that men should be tough and strong and avoid asking for help.[11] In other words, Daniel felt a social and cultural proximity to Latino men, for whom the organization advocated: "So, having that kind of background, being with those people, it really helped me to understand what a lot of young Latino males are going through and their barriers to education."

Daniel said the organization taught him "what professional advocacy looks like." He returned to his more antifeminist roots when he began blogging on men's rights issues. While previous iterations of his website have been more obviously associated with the men's rights movement, the current version is not. Instead, it misrepresents feminist goals and legislation, frames men as victims of feminism, and connects men with resources that will help them avoid accountability.

Interwoven Dimensions of Men's Social Contexts

Adrian and Daniel's early gender socialization was similar. Neither had felt encouraged to question norms around masculinity, let alone the privilege they receive as men. Instead, both men felt they had taken their first steps toward gender activism in postsecondary education—Adrian in college and Daniel in graduate school.

Through a college girlfriend, friends, and classmates, Adrian began to get the "picture of everyday life" for women. He started to understand, for instance, how threatening seemingly mundane activities, like taking a taxi, can be for women. This more anecdotal knowledge was reinforced in a gender studies course hosted in his fraternity. A friend's invitation to co-organize a feminist conference led Adrian to seek more opportunities to engage in feminist activism.

Daniel's first exposure to feminism was in the classroom. Feminist ideas evoked in him immediate, negative feelings. He did research—"reading, reading, reading"—on his own to find out more about feminism and to seek out other information that could assuage his feelings. Like Adrian, Daniel's first experience with activism came from a friend. His work supporting Latino men in higher education was only somewhat related to men's rights activism; he later began blogging on men's rights issues and expanded his activism from there.

The similarities and differences in Adrian's and Daniel's narratives indicate what shapes the privilege renegotiation strategies men choose to use to reconstruct their high-status group identities. In particular, two interwoven dimensions of men's social contexts appear to play an important role in men's trajectories into feminism and men's rights activism: (1) relationships with women and (2) interactions with feminism. These two dimensions often coalesced during men's formal education.

Relationships with Women

It is not a coincidence that Adrian and Daniel both became interested in gender activism as students. I find that education, particularly postsecondary education, played a key role in shaping men's mobilization into the feminist and men's rights movements.[12] One primary way education shaped men's understandings of gender inequality and their trajectories into gender activism was by providing the setting in which they formed relationships with women. School—particularly college—was where many of the men I interviewed for this book formed close relationships with women outside of their families for the first time. For instance, Adrian attended an all-boys high school and so didn't have an opportunity to form many relationships with women he was not related to until college. At a young age, boys and girls are likely to have gender-segregated friend groups.[13] Over the course of adolescence, boys become more likely to form friendships with girls.[14] Later, marriage and parenthood reduce the gender diversity of men's friendship networks.[15] College, then, marks a very particular time in many men's lives when they are most likely to form friendships with women.

The friendships men formed with women in college were instrumental in many men's journeys into feminism. This is because women exposed men to new information about gender inequality and male privilege. As I have described throughout this book, such information provided a shock to men's moral sense of self. But when the threat came from a trusted source, like a close woman friend or romantic partner, men were sometimes able to avoid immediate threat responses and absorb new information about the gender order. We can see this clearly in Adrian's story, when he described how his former romantic partner put gender inequality into context for him.

Sam is a straight, white, cis feminist in his thirties. He told me about one moment when the idea of male privilege became crystal clear to him:

> I had a very good friend—an ex-girlfriend, actually, we then became friends later on—was beaten up and raped by some asshole. And I visited her the day after, probably about twenty-four hours after it happened in the hospital, and that was the last time I saw her. She moved back to her home state. She moved away, and we never saw each other again. Yeah, I was certainly aware of male violence when I saw the bruises on her face.

Sam had formed a relationship with this "very good friend" during college. He witnessed the brutal, physical effects of gendered violence on her body and a huge disruption to (and possibly the end of) her college career. Over ten years later, he still found it difficult to talk about. While Sam's experience was particularly extreme, it is also representative of a process evident in nearly all feminist men's accounts: despite the discomfort and negative feelings it caused them, feminist men could not maintain an understanding of men as unprivileged, blameless, and virtuous when confronted with the experiences of the women in their lives.

Recall too Harrison (chapter 3) describing how his women friends were "candid" with him about their gendered experiences. He attributed much of his knowledge about gender inequality to these friendships forged during college. Importantly, he believed their experiences had been so impactful on his way of thinking because of the importance he placed on these relationships: "The kind of women that I wanted to be friends with, that I thought were cool and that I admired, were the kind of women who were like, 'You know, this [sexual assault] is really wrong,' and would stand up and talk about it. And so, I kind of realized that like, 'Oh shit, if I'm going to be friends with these girls, I kind of have to evolve my own thinking.'"

While less common, feminist men also forged influential relationships with women in high school. Patrick, a queer, white, cis man in his twenties, had a revelation toward the end of high school when a friend disclosed her sexual assault to him:

> A friend of mine who I was very, very close with confided in me that she was sexually assaulted a couple of times actually by the same person, and it seemed so unjust that someone as wonderful as this person had suffered something so awful. It opened the door for me into a world of subordination that I had been privileged enough not to see. . . . This friend sharing that was kind of a trigger for me realizing there's a lot of gender violence and gender subordination in the world that people who are able to do something ought to do something [about].

After his friend disclosed her sexual assault to him, Patrick began identifying as a feminist. His college experience reinforced what he had learned from his close friend: "I began to study feminist critical theory, feminist sociology, a lot of academic feminist literature." Patrick's college courses helped him connect his friend's experience to broader social problems, and he soon began working as a rape crisis counselor.

These data point to the importance of nonfamilial women peers in men's feminist identity formation. Women friends and romantic interests are cited much less often in the literature as influential in men's engagement with feminism, but they proved to be a powerful force in men's narratives.

As previous research has found though, mothers were important for feminist attitudes among the men I interviewed too.[16] For instance, Jacob, a gay, white, cis feminist in his twenties, told me how his mother educated him about the disadvantages women face by describing some of her own experiences as an engineer. He recalled one particular story from her time working at a large company: "She would be on a business trip and they would go to a strip club, and she would have to go to a strip club. And I remember she told me this story when I was in my early teens or something. And it's funny 'cause I now hear that story so much, and it was like, that actually happened to my mother." Jacob described his mother's experience as an "archetype" of how women were historically excluded from the workplace. Despite him thinking the story was rather cliché, it was impactful—Jacob "remembers" it—because it happened to a woman about whom he cared ("that actually happened to my mother"). When Jacob later heard about men's privilege, the claim did not clash with his previous experience; it fit with what his mother had described. In other words, his mother shaped his understanding of gender in a way that might align with feminist perspectives in the future. Feminist men also described grandmothers, sisters, daughters, and other women relatives as central to their feminist identity formation.

It is worth noting an important difference in feminist men's relationships with women relatives and with women to whom they were not related. While men's relationships with women family members did provide them with information about gender inequality, I find that such relationships did not precipitate as radical a transformation in their thinking. This is evident in the fact that feminist men sometimes described their concern for women family members in a paternalistic way. When I asked Ari, a straight, white, cis feminist in his seventies, where his view that "all people are equal and entitled to the same civil rights" came from, he said, "I guess from watching what goes on in the world, and also having a wife and daughters." Joe, a straight, white, cis feminist in his seventies, told me, "I just don't understand why a father who has daughters or is married to a woman . . . would have disdain for women and think that they should have less opportunity or not be paid as well as the man." Men like Ari and Joe wanted their women relatives to be treated well. Their feminist consciousness originated from a sense of paternalism—of protecting *their* women—rather than a recognition that women are human beings deserving of the same rights, privileges, and status. That some men couch their interest in feminist issues through women's actual or potential relationships to men (e.g., "what if that was your mother" or "she's someone's daughter") is self-centered and reflects male supremacist dehumanization of women.[17] Men who described relationships with women family members as influential in their trajectories into feminism did not seem to have developed the same deep reflection and empathy as men who had built relationships with women to whom they were not related. Ari, for instance, reified gender stereotypes (e.g., that women are more nurturing than men) and professed some benevolent sexist attitudes (e.g., that men should "care" for women) throughout his interview.

Why were nonfamilial relationships more transformative? I argue it's because nonfamilial relationships, unlike relationships with relatives, were fairly egalitarian. They were often formed in the college setting between two students of the same age. As a result, men saw these women as peers and interacted with them as such. They listened to and learned from their experiences. It is clear in the previous quotes from Patrick and Harrison that they had developed a great deal of empathy for their women friends, which catalyzed a broader process of reflection about women's inherent worth that they could extend to women beyond their social network. Men's relationships with women family members may encourage them to form relationships with women to whom they are not related and are thus an important part of this story.[18] But familial relationships are typically unequal, whether due to generation (e.g., parent-child), age (e.g., siblings), or strong gender norms (e.g., those pertaining to the husband-wife relationship). They may more immediately evoke a sense of paternalism rather than true empathy.[19]

While the depth and intimacy of feminist men's relationships with women varied, men's rights activists were far less likely to talk about their relationships with women as influential to their trajectories into activism, or at all. More often, men's rights activists learned about male privilege outside of their relationships with women and therefore outside of the context of women's lived experiences. Daniel, for instance, described a seemingly solitary path into the men's rights movement. While a class piqued his interest in feminism and gender issues, he did not seem to have meaningful relationships with any of his classmates or professors. He discovered the men's rights movement through solitary research and reading. Sid, a straight, white, cis men's rights activist in his sixties, had a similar experience reading feminist theory in a college course. He described feminist writings "going on [about] how men should feel very guilty, having dominated and oppressed women throughout the millennia." When he told me about this experience, he did not describe relationships or interactions with women in the class. As compared to feminist men's experiences, the threat Sid experienced was not contextualized by the women in his life.

That future men's rights activists were less likely than future feminists to learn about gender inequality from women suggests that these two groups of men had social network ties to different types of women. It also suggests that men's rights activists' relationships with women were qualitatively different from feminist men's. Both are reasonable assumptions, considering men's rights activists often expressed explicitly misogynist views and subscribe to a male supremacist ideology. Consider, for example, how Phil, a straight, white, cis men's rights activist in his sixties, described his divorce. He only briefly outlined his and his wife's relationship, before telling me, "Unfortunately after she had a child, she went completely psycho.... Believe me, she changed from the nicest girl ever to violent. She did not want to kill me, she just didn't want to talk to me. She didn't care how I felt and what I thought, it was practically all over." He then chronicled a lengthy divorce and custody process, in which he framed his wife and her woman attorney as perpetrators of crimes against men. Relationships with men's rights activists may be emotionally taxing for women; at worst, they may be physically harmful. We can assume that men's rights activists' beliefs about women make it difficult for them to form and maintain relationships with women, especially egalitarian relationships.

Certainly, when men's rights activists talked about women, they did so differently than feminist men. They did not describe the quality of their relationships. Rather, they almost exclusively talked about women as having done something to them—that is, as perpetrators. Sid, for instance, described the end of his relationship with a woman friend: "We would go in the shoe store and she's bringing over the women's shoes and she's showing me, 'Look, see how much more I pay for my shoes than you pay for yours? And while you have these comfortable shoes to wear, I'm stuck wearing these high heel shoes, one size too small just to make my feet look smaller, raise up my behind for men to look at.' I just got this whole diatribe. Over time I got tired of it." Sid's account differs markedly from those of feminist men. While he stated that they spent considerable time together and were "very close," he did not describe the quality of their relationship or how he felt about her, unlike feminists Harrison ("admired") and Patrick ("wonderful") did of their women friends. Instead, the focus of Sid's story is what this woman had done to him—that is, her subjecting him to a "diatribe."

It is not that feminist men did not have deteriorating relationships with women; for instance, six of the feminist men I interviewed were divorced from women, and one was separated from his wife (compared to five men's rights activists who were divorced and three who were separated).[20] Abe, a straight, white, cis feminist in his seventies, had a lengthy divorce process similar to men's rights activist Phil, during which he lost custody of his daughter. Despite being their daughter's primary caretaker before the divorce and having evidence that his ex-wife neglected their daughter while she was under her care, he did not frame his ex-wife as a perpetrator. Instead, he described the family court system as at fault. Of the court's decision to award his ex-wife custody, he said, "And that's so prejudicial against a man because if you remove gender or sex from that whole issue and you just simply looked at two people who could be parenting, it was asymmetric totally." Having lost custody of his daughter, Abe did not make his ex-wife out to be the villain. This indicates that Abe's relationship with his ex-wife before and during the divorce was different from Phil's.

Interactions with Feminism

In addition to enabling or constraining men's relationships with women, college campuses were also important to men's trajectories into feminism because they were very often where men were first exposed to feminism in a meaningful way. Nick, the feminist I introduced in chapter 4, told me, "In college, you start thinking about a lot of things. . . . We had an LGBT club in high school. We didn't have a feminist club, so it just wasn't there." Men were exposed to feminism in gender studies or related courses (as was the case for both Adrian and Daniel), through feminist programming, and through more informal conversations with feminists on campus.

Of course, men form opinions about gender, gender inequality, and feminism before they arrive at college. Feminism has been portrayed negatively in the larger culture for centuries, and negative stereotypes about feminism and feminists are still common.[21] But as I have described, feminism has become more mainstream, particularly as new technologies have enabled its proliferation and celebrities and social movement campaigns, like #MeToo, have amplified it.[22] The men I interviewed have been exposed to numerous and conflicting narratives about feminism, gender, and gender inequality as a result of their generation, geographic location, family background, political ideology, and so on.

For some men's rights activists, their disagreement with college feminists boiled down to feminists' structural understanding of gender. As I described in chapter 3, men's rights activists were less likely to use the structural lens compared to feminists. Recall how Jeremy, a straight, white, cis men's rights activist in his thirties, majored in gender studies as an undergraduate student but ultimately found feminism's failure to recognize the importance of biology unsatisfactory. He turned to conducting his own "research" online. Likewise, Frank, a straight, white, cis men's rights activist in his sixties, described being "ticked off" throughout his doctoral program because academic studies do not acknowledge "the male sex drive." He believed that, as a result, feminists and society do not understand men "biologically, what makes them male, what makes them different from females," and so do not "honor and respect and have equal consideration for those differences." Because these men did not agree with academic feminists on a fundamental level about the nature of gender, they were not interested in learning more.

As I pointed out in chapter 3, however, there was considerable overlap in feminist men's and men's rights activists' use of the individual and structural lenses, so the way men make sense of gender and gender inequality does not neatly predict alignment with a movement. The lenses men use to understand gender before they first step foot on campus are influenced by myriad social, cultural, and personal factors. They are not what I chose to focus on as a site for intervention.

Instead, I want to point out how feminist frames on campus both enable and constrain alignment with men's diverse, preformed opinions about gender and gender inequality. Frames are the interpretive orientations social movements use to identify the problem, solutions, and justifications for participation.[23] Researchers working within this perspective stress the importance of frame alignment, or "the linkage of individual and [social movement organization] interpretive orientations," for mobilizing individuals toward social movement aims.[24] Campus organizations' choices—for instance, to emphasize that gender differences are socially constructed or that men and other high-status groups, like whites, are privileged—shape which men will be interested. In keeping with this body of literature, men began to identify with feminism if the way they understood gender and gender inequality aligned with the particular brand of feminism on their college campus. Feminist framing was thus one source of variation in whether men were attracted to feminism.

Doug, a queer, white, trans man in his twenties, told me he had never considered identifying as a feminist before talking to an older student (and feminist) during his first year of college: "I think she was the first person to ever expose me to this idea that feminism could be about people of 'all' genders instead of 'both' genders. I thought that was really important because I felt like I had a place in that, and I had a stake in there because I didn't have a stake in 'both' genders." Doug once thought he didn't have a "stake" in feminism because of what he then perceived to be the movement's narrow conceptualization of gender. When Doug was exposed to the idea that feminism can incorporate a nonbinary understanding of gender, he began to "feel like this is something I want to be having conversations about." The older student's use of an expansive understanding of gender in conversation with Doug made him feel included in the movement, like he could invest in learning and discussing more about it.

In contrast, college feminists failed to convince soon-to-be men's rights activists that they had a "stake" in feminism. Oliver, a bisexual, white, cis men's rights activist in his thirties, described his experience as a graduate student in a discipline where some scholars use feminist theory. He said, "Feminism is almost like a quasi-official religion, and it's taken very seriously. . . . I guess I eventually realized that feminism never has nothing [sic] to offer to men." Oliver had previously read *The Myth of Male Power*, which he found "whimsical" but educational.[25] He compared the gravity of statistics about wartime deaths of men referenced in the book with the issues he heard feminists in his program discussing—namely, that the air conditioning in most workplaces is set to a temperature that is comfortable for men but too cold for women. He said, "If that's a grievance that feminists are seriously discussing and if that's an issue in mainstream media, how [do you] compare that to the fact that millions of people are dying just 'cause they are men? It's such a disproportionate violation of human rights." The way feminists described feminist issues did not match Oliver's understanding of the world. When campus feminist frames and men's frames did not align, men developed new frames or doubled down on preexisting antifeminist beliefs, as Oliver's narrative illustrates.

In my interviews, feminist men were keenly aware of how different movement framings restricted their access to certain populations of men on campus. For example, many feminists described avoiding buzzwords in conversation with men they hoped to recruit. Theo told me he organized an on-campus event about "locker-room talk" so he didn't "have to say, 'Come interrogate hegemonic masculinity and destroy the patriarchy with us,'" because "no one would have come to that." Again and again, feminist men described avoiding words like "privilege" and "patriarchy" when they were trying to recruit other men to feminism. Beyond meeting men where they are metaphorically (e.g., avoiding jargon), Theo also recommended coming to them physically (e.g., doing events in the engineering school).

In addition to their alignment with campus-specific feminist frames, universities also shaped men's interactions with and ties to feminists. Adrian enrolled in a gender studies course because his social network—his fraternity—made it convenient to do so. In the broader sample, interactions with feminists were important in shaping men's mobilization into feminism and the men's rights movement. Feminist men described these interactions as preceding their feminist identification and being central to it. They described positive interactions with feminists that facilitated their alignment with feminist frames. This is evident, for example, in Doug's story earlier.

Social network ties with feminists provided men with more opportunities to engage with the movement. Recall that Adrian first became involved in feminist activism because of an invitation from a friend. Men who would later identify as feminists described forming these important ties with feminists primarily during college. George, a straight, Black, cis feminist in his sixties, contrasted his high school, where few people were "pushing for equal rights for women," with his college: "When I went to college there were way more people [talking about feminism], which I think [is] what college is about, is people ... pick causes or stake out moral ground." George described making friends with women in a feminist co-op, where feminism "rubbed off" on him. As another example, Diego, a straight, white, cis feminist in his twenties, was involved in organizing around labor issues in another country before moving to the United States for graduate school. He found that feminism was a more prominent social movement among students at his new university: "What attracted me to the feminist movement was that it existed, and that it was happening, and that I could feel like it's happening. People are talking about [it], there's emails, there's events, there's stuff, there's discussions." In other words, there were people Diego could connect with and easy ways for him to become involved in feminism on his campus.

Men who were men's rights activists, on the other hand, very rarely described having close relationships or positive interactions with feminists. While they expressed very strong antifeminist sentiments and condemned feminists writ large, actual, specific interactions with individual feminists were largely absent from their narratives. Men's rights activists evoked the specter of the "evil feminist," but presumably had not interacted with many in real life.

Evan, who identified as white, heteroflexible, and genderqueer and was in his twenties, was one of the few men's rights activists I interviewed who had cordial relationships with multiple feminists. He described discussing his belief that men are demonized with a feminist friend. The conversation ended when she said, "Well, that's all well and good, but when I walk down the street, I do have to fear men because of all these experiences." Evan described the effect of this statement on his sense of self: "Like when I'm walking through a world where I can feel that half the population is afraid of me, not for anything I've done, not just for who I am, that really eats away at . . . a sense of just being okay. It's a constant reminder of, 'You are bad, you are violent, you are dangerous,' and [I] have to get over that in every interaction." Unlike in Doug's experience, Evan's interactions with his feminist friends make him feel excluded from feminism. He is not drawn into feminism; he feels villainized by it. These interactions serve as a repeated threat, a "reminder" of how others see him because of his gender. He also felt like he could not address his concerns with his feminist friends: "No one from that side, from that contingent—and I hate using that language but I have no other way of describing it—is willing to hear it." Thus, those few men's rights activists who did have relationships with feminists often described them as strained.

In contrast to feminist men's experiences, men's rights activists' interactions with feminists largely took place outside the university context and outside established or burgeoning relationships. Instead, they took place online with anonymous strangers or with people they only assumed to be feminists. Phil's trajectory illustrates both. Phil referred to the woman attorney his ex-wife employed during their divorce as a "feminazi" throughout our interview, despite not having any evidence that she identified as a feminist. He repeated several times that she worked to secure his ex-wife with a favorable alimony arrangement and sole custody of their children for "fun." He saw her as targeting him because of her (presumed) feminist ideology. But when I asked Phil whether this was his first experience with a "feminazi," he said,

> No. This is something that I learned from my observations of reading countless blog things. . . . After a while you start to understand this small minority of people, who they are and what they want to do, and you start to see them and you start to identify [them]. There are all kinds of men and women with all kinds of ideas about all the subjects, every aspect of the subject. . . . Then there're just the haters, there're the destroyers. The people who don't care who dies, and they do want you dead. They want you to commit suicide is what they want. They want me to die. . . . They have a commitment to this. It's true in their heart. They're pure of heart. Their hatred is really what compels them to live. They're just that kind of animal, they're like bacteria. They're just there to eat.

Phil was particularly extreme in his language, but other men's rights activists told me about similarly negative interactions with people (nearly always women) they assumed to be feminists. As was true in Phil's case, they based this assumption on the individual's mistreatment of them. In other words, they assumed anyone who was mean to them was a feminist. Phil's antifeminism was merely reinforced by his negative perception of his ex-wife's attorney; he acknowledged that his antifeminist beliefs started long before his divorce, online ("countless blog things").

If we assume that the villains at the center of men's rights activists' stories are actually feminists, it would be unsurprising if their attitudes toward men's rights activists were negative. As is made crystal clear in the quotes from Phil above, men's rights activists are virulently antifeminist and misogynist. Indeed, the fact that many of the men's rights activists I spoke to assumed that any woman who is assertive, insists on what she is due, or is competent at her job is a "feminazi" is evidence of their misogyny. (It perhaps goes without saying that, for instance, working to make sure one's client gets a favorable alimony and custody arrangement does not make one a feminist.) Men's rights activists' misogyny makes them an obvious and deserved target of feminists' complaints. Feminists are unlikely to get along with men's rights activists or indeed to permit them to express such misogynist views in their presence, whether in person or online. As Evan described above, experiences feeling censored by feminists were common, but in light of men's rights activists' misogyny, they are—I would say—warranted.

* * *

Men's feminist identity formation is, in essence, a process of *identity change*. Feminist men came to understand men as privileged and (at least partially) responsible for gender inequality. In the case of Sam, whose experience visiting his friend in the hospital served as a visceral realization of violence against women, he became exposed to an alternative definition of manhood: being a perpetrator. In that moment, Sam began to adopt this as his own definition of being a man—that is, as his identity standard. Sam's new identity standard was not comforting. In fact, he told me traditionally masculine behaviors do not make him feel good: "It's not like, 'well, that makes me feel masculine.' It doesn't. It makes me feel crappy that I know people I love and care about are being treated poorly." Identifying one's ingroup as responsible for harm runs counter to the psychological need to see it as moral.[26] Why are some men, like Sam, able to adopt a new identity standard that recognizes men's privilege? Why do some men turn to feminism to navigate the process of identity change?

Social contexts enable and constrain identity change. The two factors I have described—relationships with women and interactions with feminism—and the setting in which those factors often exert influence on men—college—interact with one another. Together, they shape men's understanding of gender, feminism, and themselves. Having strong, egalitarian relationships with women and learning about women's lived experience exposed men to alternative understandings of what it means to be men. In some cases, these women identified as feminists and exposed men to positive narratives about feminism and connected them with opportunities for activism.

These findings support the large body of research on how social networks and social movement frames encourage participation in social movements. Social networks can influence micromobilization because they serve as conduits through which actors can receive information about activism opportunities, offer assurance that others will cooperate in costly forms of activism, encourage the formation of collective identity and feelings of solidarity, increase the rewards of participation and the costs of nonparticipation, and shape actors' values related to political issues.[27] In feminist men's narratives, relational ties with women and feminists served all of these functions. Through social network ties, men were also exposed to feminist frames. Close relationships with women seemed to facilitate frame alignment especially through frame transformation, or the reconstitution or redefining of men's frames around gender and gender inequality.[28] In their particular social contexts, feminist men's understanding of their gender ingroup and themselves shifted to accommodate knowledge about men's privilege and women's oppression.

One question is whether selection explains the link between men's relationships with women and their gender activism. I have shown evidence that certain men's greater and stronger ties to women facilitate their identification with the feminist movement. Do feminist-leaning men seek out relationships with women that further reinforce their profeminist tendencies? I agree that this is a likely scenario, but I do not see such selection effects as at odds with the argument I advance. First, men's profeminist tendencies and relationships with women are likely shaped by their mothers, and feminist men do not select into their families.[29] I described in this chapter how mothers are influential in men's profeminism, and previous research has found the same. Research with children also has shown that family structure—namely, having a different-sex sibling and living in a one-parent (probably mother-headed) home— encourages the formation of cross-sex friendships.[30] This research provides additional evidence that family relationships with women facilitate relationships with women to whom men are not related, which in turn facilitate men's feminist identity formation. Second, research shows that social contexts shape opportunities for cross-sex friendships.[31] Thus, even if feminist-leaning men are more likely to seek relationships with women, the social environment also influences the likelihood of such friendships.

Additionally, while I argue that social context is influential in men's attraction to and engagement with their particular social movement, I agree that individual factors I do not examine here are likely important. In other words, I do not argue that social context alone can cause mobilization. The data I have presented here and my other research indicate that men's antifeminism and misogyny are key for mobilization into the men's rights movement.[32] These beliefs begin to coalesce before men enter the environment on which I have focused in this chapter (college), but these data also show such beliefs are flexible even throughout adulthood. Recall, for instance, that Craig joined the National Organization for Women shortly after graduating from college but later denounced feminism and became a men's rights activist. As another example, Jacob initially believed that feminists "hate men" but later began identifying as a feminist in college. Both Adrian and Daniel described growing to disagree with the traditional gender socialization they were exposed to as children. I have chosen to focus, therefore, on how such attitudes can shift in adulthood as a result of one's social context, particularly college, not how they are established in childhood.

The temporal order of these events, as I have presented them, should be questioned. Is it truly the case that strong relationships with women and positive interactions with feminists *precede* men's feminism? The opposite order is probably true: that identifying as a feminist causes one to have stronger relationships with women and better interactions with feminists. These data are *accounts*, meaning they are socially constructed and may not reflect "true" causes, but they are men's own understandings of their activist identity formation and at the very least reflect a shared schema for what it means to become a gender activist.[33] It is worth noting, then, that men describe these factors as *preceding* and *shaping* their activist identities, and not the other way around. Of course, relationships with women and experiences with feminists change over time, and identifying as either a feminist or a men's rights activist is likely to affect both moving forward. For instance, many men's rights activists described restricting their social circles once they became involved in the movement by seeking women romantic partners who were at least sympathetic to the movement or forgoing intimate relationships with women altogether. While educational experiences, relationships with women, interactions with feminists, and engagement with gender activism certainly influence each other in multiple ways, I have focused in this chapter on how engagement with gender activism is shaped by the others.

As I have shown, education did not have a singular role to play in men's mobilization. It is not that universities are liberal bastions and convert all men to feminism. Instead, men's social networks and the particular feminist frames to which they were exposed on campus shaped whether they adopted feminism as a privilege renegotiation strategy. Importantly, this means the university can be transformed into a site for intervention where men can be mobilized more meaningfully for feminism.

Conclusion

Where We Go from Here

In May 2022, *Politico* published a draft opinion indicating that the highest court in the land would strike down federal protection of abortion rights, and the outcry was immediate. Thousands protested and marched across the country, yelling, "We will not go back."[1] Some were holding out hope that the court's majority might be swayed. But little more than a month later, the final, nearly identical decision in *Dobbs v. Jackson Women's Health Organization* was published, and abortion rights were immediately rolled back in nearly half of all states.[2] "We hold that *Roe* and *Casey* must be overruled."[3] Thus ended nearly fifty years of precedent protecting a woman's right to choose in the United States.

Dobbs is just one in a series of recent events that have caught some Americans off guard. "This is crazy," one protestor said.[4] "It's so hard to put into words how insane it is that you have to explain it's my body, it's my choice. . . . There is no way this can happen." From Donald Trump's 2016 victory to the fierce opposition to the Black Lives Matter movement, the surge in anti-trans legislation, and pandemic-fueled anti-Asian hate, we have seen time and time again that progress toward social equality is fragile. It can be shattered in what seems like a moment. We have gone back, no matter how much we insist that we won't or can't.

Organized backlash movements like the men's rights movement play an essential role on one side of this tug-of-war. Indeed, anti-abortion activists fought aggressively and strategically to devise the end of *Roe*.[5] A number of factors cause the other side's hands on the rope to slip, so to speak. As I have argued, the failure of allies to commit to collective projects for liberation rather than personal identity projects limits the degree to which they can effectively challenge inequality.

A day after the final *Dobbs* decision was released, the *New York Times* published an article sharing men's experiences with abortion.[6] Some stories reflected anti-abortion talking points, but others reflected a deep respect for the complexity of the decision and appreciation of abortion itself. "This feeling washed over me—I don't know if it was shame or humility—and I remember thinking to myself: 'Why did I think I had a right to have an opinion on this subject?,'" said one man. "Do I wish there had been a way to have kept my children? Yes. Do I regret my decision at the time? Not at all," said another. One in five American men have been involved in an abortion.[7] We need them to do more than tweet, or speak to the *Times*, or march. We need them to *work*. As *Dobbs* proves, the gender revolution is not just stalled; it is being dismantled, brick by brick. Effective allyship will be crucial moving forward.

The findings of this book—that, as it stands, men's allyship is largely ineffectual—may appear bleak, but in one sense they are encouraging. Commentators are often eager to proclaim that feminism is dead, but my research shows that it is still incredibly relevant, even to those with the most privilege.[8] Feminism and other movements for social justice have fundamentally challenged the way straight, white, cis men think about their identities. High-status group members have had to radically reorient their identity work toward being and being perceived as morally good people because of these movements. The men I interviewed benefit from associating with feminism's moral framework precisely because doing so is easily interpreted by others—a testament to feminism's broad cultural impact. Feminism's relevance in the contemporary United States is evidenced by the not-yet-resolved struggle over the meanings of masculinity, whiteness, and straightness, and by straight, white, cis men's use of feminism in their identity work.

Furthermore, men's identification with feminism, however it is motivated, is symbolically, culturally, and materially significant for feminist goals. While many of the feminist men I interviewed did not engage in activism per se, their feminist identification likely influences their attitudes and behaviors in more subtle but still important ways. In chapter 4 I quoted Nick, who said that while he doesn't engage in anything he would call "activism," feminism has made him better at recognizing sexism and gender inequality. Men who identify as feminists as a privilege renegotiation strategy may be more likely to support feminist policies and programs, even if they are not "in the trenches" as activists, because doing so will bolster their personal identity projects. So even though feminist men's motivations and contributions to public activism are less than ideal, their identification with feminism is still a meaningful step in the right direction.

But this book shows that men's profeminism *is* less than ideal. What are the implications for change? In this conclusion I discuss how I believe men can be engaged more effectively in feminist struggle. Before I do that, however, I want to state clearly what I do *not* recommend.

First, I think it is natural when considering the mobilization trajectories of men's rights activists to conclude that feminists and other activists for social justice should avoid calling attention to the privilege of high-status group members. After all, this book illustrates that straight, white, cis men can become invested in a highly misogynist and virulently antifeminist movement to mollify the negative feelings they get when their privilege is named. While we must recognize that naming privilege can lead to backlash, such a recommendation ignores that it can also invest high-status group members in feminism and other progressive social movements, which is a good thing whatever the limitations of their allyship. Men and other high-status group members will not consider how they are privileged and what they might do about it absent confrontation and discomfort. As Adrian said in chapter 5, it is all too comfortable for them to continue living without knowledge about their place in the social order. Equality requires the dissolution of privilege. Liberation is not served when privilege goes unnamed; only the status quo is.

Second, I realize that some readers may interpret this book (particularly the findings in chapter 5) as implying that women, trans men, and nonbinary people must shoulder the responsibility of forming and maintaining relationships with cis men and teaching them that they are privileged. This is not my intention, and moreover I believe such a solution would be ineffective and even harmful absent structural and cultural changes that would transform the nature of relationships between cis men and others. The findings show not that any relationship can be a conduit through which men can learn about gender inequality and privilege but rather that only close and egalitarian relationships enable deeper transformations in men's thinking. What's more, it is unfair to put the onus of solving men's privilege on anyone other than men. Ultimately, I think it is inevitable that some of the labor of teaching men about privilege will happen in the context of their interpersonal relationships, particularly with women. The number of interviewees who relied on women colleagues (e.g., Theo), friends (e.g., Harrison), or significant others (e.g., Adrian) to help them recognize or understand inequality speaks to this. But I have chosen in this chapter to highlight ways that this labor can be replaced or made more mutually beneficial.

I now turn to what I *do* recommend. In the rest of this conclusion I describe what gender studies programs, feminist organizations, universities and workplaces, and the rest of us can do to ensure that men are more deeply engaged in feminism and, hopefully, jumpstart the gender revolution once again.

Gender Studies Programs: Teaching Men about Privilege

Adrian's narrative, detailed in chapter 5, alludes to the possibility of women's, gender, and feminist studies programs playing a bigger role in engaging men in feminism. While Adrian was first exposed to the idea that he is privileged by virtue of his gender through conversations with a girlfriend, the gender studies course he took helped him better understand gendered power and structures. More than conversations with his romantic partner, the course piqued his interest in learning about gender inequality. Adrian continued to take gender studies courses and even wished he had time to double major in the subject: "I came into studies of gender and sociology a little later but it has been one of the most interesting things I've found and want to learn more about." The role of gender studies and similar programs in facilitating men's feminist identification was not unique to Adrian's story. Peter said he "started to get some perspective" on gender inequality when he read *The Feminine Mystique* for a first-year seminar; Patrick remembered thinking "everything makes sense" when he was exposed to Judith Butler's writing in a class; and Richard said his "career started" through programming put on by the LGBT center at his college.

College courses are a logical site for intervention. Classrooms can be leveraged as spaces for personal identity exploration, as they are environments where students are expected to grow and learn. College courses also have the time—repeated interactions over several weeks—to meet students where they are and expose them to important feminist concepts and theories. I recommend that programs offer courses and programming that (1) are concrete, (2) are relevant to students' lives, and (3) replace the labor—often done by women—of teaching men about privilege.

Adrian's story illustrates how a course that achieves these recommendations can be especially effective. As he described it, the course was on "feminism in the news today" and focused largely on examples of gender inequality covered in the media. In other words, it highlighted concrete manifestations of gender inequality. The example from the course that Adrian said was most influential for his thinking was Brock Turner's rape of Chanel Miller. This assault took place on a college campus, and Turner and Miller had been at the same fraternity party beforehand.[9] As a college student and fraternity brother, the case was particularly relevant to Adrian. It revealed to him the gendered structures that govern his and his peers' lives as students and as participants in Greek life. It was deeply personal, so made him "more aware of the ways that [he] was benefiting" from sexual assault and the failures of the legal system.

Broad survey courses, like "The Sociology of Gender," often (understandably) focus on topics, like work-family conflict and the division of household labor, with which many students have little personal experience. When time is limited, course readings and lectures may also ignore how gender intersects with other systems of oppression to structure, for example, the experiences of women of color, poor women, or queer women, instead focusing largely on white, middle-class, heterosexual men and women. This can mean that the information students are exposed to is hard to place in the context of their own lives. Research shows that when young people recognize inequality in their own lives, they are more likely to adopt the structural understandings of inequality that instructors hope they will internalize.[10] Concrete and more narrowly defined courses, designed specifically to speak to a diverse group of college students, would make class content more engaging and legible and potentially make a bigger impact in students' understanding of and interest in challenging gender inequality.

Course topics should be chosen deliberately and should vary based on the student body the university serves. They might include gender in sports, sexual violence on campus, gender and Greek life, gender and mass incarceration, or—like in Adrian's case—feminism in the news. This is not to say gender studies programs and similar departments should offer courses only on narrow topics to appeal to the particular students at their universities. Broad survey courses and courses on feminist theory are undoubtedly important for the curriculum as a whole. Instead, I am suggesting programs offer a handful of courses that fit these criteria that would serve as entrées into learning about gender and feminism. They would be designed to begin to build students' ability to recognize inequality and entice students into the field and into feminist praxis.

As readers who routinely teach courses on gender know, men are less likely to enroll in them. Active recruitment will be essential for attracting men students. Courses could be held in unconventional places, like fraternities or sports fields, where men are likely to frequent. They could be designed in collaboration with instructors in traditionally masculine fields, like science, technology, engineering, and mathematics (STEM). They could be advertised (e.g., by flier, by email, by a visit from the instructor) in traditionally masculine spaces. Buy-in and support among leaders in those spaces (e.g., coaches, STEM instructors, fraternity presidents) will be helpful. As entry-level courses, and to lower the stakes to encourage greater enrollment, programs might consider offering these for fewer credits or as pass-fail.

In addition to offering concrete, relevant courses and attracting men students to them, gender studies programs and similar departments can replace some of the labor women do within their interpersonal relationships to encourage men's feminist identity formation. I have no doubt that the intimate nature of these relationships is important to men's feminist journeys, but I also believe that well-designed coursework can accomplish some of what women's personal stories did in these data. Instructors could assign personal accounts of inequality, like those found in ethnographies, as readings. Indeed, the impression Chanel Miller's victim statement made on Adrian speaks to how personal accounts from women whom men do not know personally can be effective in putting male privilege into context for them. Academic readings may be even more effective than stories recounted in simple conversation since their analysis can illustrate trends across the broader population to link personal experience with social structure. Instructors might also specifically design role-taking activities that would encourage cis men to build empathy for women, trans men, and nonbinary people.[11] Journaling on their own experiences and comparing them with the experiences analyzed in course readings might be particularly effective.

Finally, instead of relying on women to point it out to them when they fail as feminists, feminist men can learn about common limitations in men's gender activism through coursework. I recommend that courses geared toward engaging men in feminism explicitly teach about the dynamics I have analyzed in this book. Doing so can help men think more critically about their deeper motivations. Understanding how identity work can get in the way of challenging gender inequality may help men avoid some of those pitfalls. Reading this book may also help men think of feminism in a new way—as an ongoing and ever-evolving practice, not a strategy to be employed for their own benefit.

Women's, gender, and feminist studies programs are essential for engaging men in feminism. But these and other critical programs are threatened globally by lack of university buy-in and right-wing attacks.[12] University leaders must protect these programs and the courses they offer and support them with essential resources (e.g., tenure-track lines).

Feminists Organizations: Investing Men in the Work

Just under half of the feminist men I interviewed did not do anything they considered "activism" despite identifying as feminists. When I asked these men how their feminism translates to their daily lives, they had a difficult time articulating a concrete answer. They sometimes described the effort they made to treat everyone fairly, regardless of their gender, or recounted instances of gender inequality they were able to recognize through a feminist lens. But generalities like "I try to treat everyone fairly" are unhelpful in dismantling unequal power relations because they can obscure them in ways similar to colorblind racism.[13] Men's descriptions of how they actually achieve this were noticeably vague, suggesting to me that they were exaggerating their effort. Additionally, recognizing inequality is necessary, but only a first step. Men must challenge inequality when they see it, whether that means through feminist organizing or through more everyday resistance.

What lessons can be gleaned from these data for feminist organizations wanting to engage men in deeper feminist practice? Most often, men who were more meaningfully engaged in feminism had been invited to participate in low-stakes activism by a friend. This is not surprising; a large body of literature shows that social networks are an important way the individuals who make up a movement's mobilization potential learn about opportunities for activism.[14] This book shows why this mechanism may be particularly important for engaging men in feminism and, more broadly, high-status group members as allies for progressive social movements. While feminism can offer men a strategy for constructing their identities as good people, men may also feel like their moral self-concepts are at risk when they enter feminist spaces because their privilege is especially visible there. Being explicitly invited into feminist organizing by a network tie may make men more comfortable and less immediately concerned with their own identity project.

Importantly, invitations into feminist activism need to be well-timed and should support men's burgeoning feminist consciousness. Adrian was invited to help organize a conference on sexual assault right after taking a gender studies course that focused on that very topic. His positive experience with the conference reinforced his interest and knowledge, and so he continued to pursue more opportunities for activism. A year later he was working on a new university initiative to engage fraternity leaders against sexual violence. Adrian's social network and on-campus courses and feminist organizations shaped his trajectory in such a way that engaged him seriously and deeply in a specific feminist issue.

Adrian's narrative illustrates how feminist organizations can recruit men who are just embarking on their feminist journeys into relevant activism. Organizations might partner with instructors to connect men in gender studies courses with activism opportunities related to the course subject. Initial activism opportunities should be low-stakes, like attending a consciousness-raising group, tabling at an event, or supporting protests by handing out water and food. As men's feminist identities concretize, organizations should provide higher-stakes, higher-commitment opportunities, like facilitating a consciousness-raising group, fundraising, or organizing a protest. Effective on-ramping is especially important. Feminist men who engaged only minimally in activism reported attending the Women's March, for example, but were unsure what they should do afterward. By defining clear pathways into more involved activism, feminist organizations can capitalize on events like the Women's March that attract more men.

Of course, receiving a personal invitation to an opportunity for activism does not mean a person will say yes, and I think it unlikely that a simple invitation could have persuaded the 45 percent of feminist men I interviewed who did not do any activism to get more involved. Still, it is clear that those men who thought of feminism as an identity rather than a practice had trouble imagining how feminism could translate to their daily lives. Put simply, it was difficult for men to associate feminism with activism if they had not learned to do so early on in their journey into the movement. If feminist organizations are able to recruit men into activism just as they begin to develop their feminist consciousness, men may think of being a feminist as more than just an identity but rather something to be practiced, from the outset. Moreover, engaging men in feminist activism will embed them more firmly in feminist networks, which will reinforce their activism.

Purposeful outreach and on-ramping into activism must be accompanied by education. When designed to recruit men, feminist programming should deliberately teach the meaning of feminist terms, like "patriarchy," "oppression," and "privilege." The men I interviewed understood being the recipient of male privilege as equivalent to being immoral. This association is made in the broader culture, and its focus on individual responsibility fits within neoliberal rationality, making it instantly legible and nearly automatic.[15] But it impeded men's more genuine engagement with feminism because it made them hyperconcerned with proving themselves to be morally good people. Men should instead understand that such terms refer to the ways social structure and culture sustain men's dominance and that men can be complicit in these systems, work to protect them, and/or work to dismantle them. They should not conceive of privilege as a personal moral failure. At the same time, they should understand that privilege conveys power, status, and resources that can be put to use toward feminist ends if they so choose.

I disagree with the recommendation made by some of the feminist men I interviewed that feminists should avoid any jargon when recruiting men. Terms like "patriarchy" and "privilege" describe important ideas that men must comprehend if they are to earnestly engage with feminism. The sooner men understand these terms, the better, but they (like everyone else) require purposeful education to understand them in the way I have described. Suggesting that men will be immediately threatened by such language gives them too little credit and ignores that identity threat seems to be necessary for the sort of identity change men undergo when they become feminists. When feminists give up such terms, they also give up control over them to people like men's rights activists, who provide men with inaccurate definitions that fuel antifeminist attitudes and conspiracism. As bell hooks writes, "We have those definitions. Let's reclaim them. Let's share them. Let's start over."[16]

Feminist organizations (and women's, gender, and feminist studies programs and departments) could host frequent workshops designed to demystify common feminist terms. Teaching men about what feminist jargon means and does not mean might suppress the kind of negative emotions that get in the way of more serious consideration of the ideas such terms represent. Importantly, the definitions used in these introductory workshops should be used by organizers consistently, including in other contexts and at other events, so that men who interact with the organization receive a coherent message about what feminist terms mean.

In these workshops and elsewhere, organizers should stress that privilege is a mechanism and outcome of patriarchy and so cannot be simply cast aside. Dismantling it is an ongoing, iterative process done in collaboration with others, rather than something achieved once through individual moral fortitude. In other words, men new to feminism must learn that gender inequality is structural and can be undone only through collective effort. This requires organizers to consistently challenge neoliberal feminism and rationality and the commonly held myth that individuals can overcome (what are in reality) structural barriers through personal agency.[17] Feminist theorists and activists have been calling for politics to be reinfused into feminism for decades;[18] the limitations of men's feminist activism underscore this need.

To answer this call, organizers could draw on the politics of care, a political theory that conceives of care as an "inherently interdependent survival strategy, a foundation for political organizing, and a prefigurative politics for building a world in which all people can live and thrive."[19] A perspective based in the politics of care requires recognition of the interlinkages between cisheteropatriarchy, white supremacism, capitalism, colonialism, and more, providing an opportunity for solidarity with men who are marginalized through other axes of oppression. The politics of care, which emphasizes the communal and interdependent nature of organizing, also challenges men to look past their egocentric identity concerns to consider how they can work with others toward feminist goals. Then, perhaps, men can practice a feminism based in joy rather than guilt.

What is very clear from these data is that feminist programming (whether from social movement organizations or from the academy) is less effective at seriously recruiting men to feminism when it is gender segregated. I learned from interviewees that programming where only men were present tended to turn to navel-gazing. Organizers who facilitated men-only programming, like Theo, intended to give men space to safely explore the personal costs of masculinity. But such discussions could become almost self-indulgent, ignoring how masculinity also confers power, resources, and status to cis men and harms women, trans men, and nonbinary people materially, emotionally, and physically. In contrast, mixed-gender spaces (often classrooms) provided men with the bigger picture: that gender relations are hierarchical and that, despite the costs of masculinity, cis men are the recipients of immense privilege. Because men's own subjectivities are limited in elucidating unequal power relations, diverse perspectives are required, either through readings and other materials and/or through other participants.[20] Mixed-gender spaces avoid the narrow focus on the costs of masculinity that I sometimes observed in men's contemporary feminism—the same narrow focus that facilitated the emergence of the men's rights movement in the 1970s.[21]

Universities and Workplaces: Creating the Conditions for Egalitarian Relationships

Importantly, this book shows that *egalitarian* mixed-gender spaces and relationships are most influential for men's views on feminism. Universities and workplaces are two common places where cis men form relationships with women, trans men, and nonbinary people. Through structural change, universities and workplaces can ensure that such relationships are not only more egalitarian but also more mutually beneficial.

One way to do this is for universities and workplaces to put in place strong protections against sexual violence. When individuals report instances of sexual violence to their universities or workplaces, they too often experience institutional betrayal, or "institutional action and inaction that exacerbate the impact of traumatic events."[22] Institutional policies and procedures around sexual violence were developed to respond to the legal environment and so are largely symbolic. Rather than create substantive protections for survivors, they protect high-status group members and the institution's own reputation, liability, and legitimacy.[23] For instance, complex university policies around sexual misconduct can cause survivors to rely on university actors (e.g., Title IX coordinators) as they navigate the complaint process. As a result, most complaints are resolved through options that require little university action.[24] Cultures of silence, symbolic compliance with the law, complicated response structures, and an overreliance on ineffective sexual harassment training programs hinder the kind of respectful, trusting, and accountable relationships that are required for feminist change.

Likewise, when cis men enact less severe forms of violence, they cannot form mutually beneficial relationships with women, trans men, and nonbinary people. Microaggressions are "brief and commonplace daily verbal, behavioral, or environmental indignities, whether intentional or unintentional, that communicate hostile, derogatory, or negative racial slights and insults toward people of color."[25] The concept has been used to describe other forms of oppression, including sexism. Microaggressions are pervasive in workplaces and universities, and their cumulative effect on marginalized people is well-documented.[26] Very little research has examined how they can be effectively prevented and challenged, and too often it is up to the target of the microaggression to come up with a response.[27] Structural interventions—policies and procedures—for microaggressions and other commonplace forms of bias are needed to ensure the kind of large-scale change that would enable respectful and egalitarian relationships between high-status and low-status group members.

When universities and workplaces make structural changes that facilitate more egalitarian relationships across gender, through those relationships cis men will adopt more feminist attitudes and behaviors that will, in turn, help efforts toward gender equality. I recognize this is a somewhat circular argument: to make the world more equitable, we must first make the world more equitable. To such a critique, I respond that we have to start somewhere. Far too often organizational change is stymied out of fear that stakeholders—usually straight, white, cis men—will object and that the resulting backlash will move the needle in the wrong direction. My analysis shows that backlash is inevitable under current conditions. Only by changing those conditions—that is, by setting the stage for more egalitarian cross-gender relationships—can we prevent backlash or, more likely, make it so insubstantial as to become unimportant. These structural changes are also likely to contribute to an organizational culture that encourages feminist perspectives and discourages exclusionary ones. Importantly, most organizational change does not require buy-in from all stakeholders. If university and workplace leaders are really invested in equality, they should consider structural changes regardless of whether a minority of stakeholders will oppose them.

In addition to changing the structural conditions in which cis men interact with women, trans men, and nonbinary people, workplaces can incentivize feminist activism. Research has documented how feminist activism has become more professionalized over time and how institutional forms of activism have shaped men's allyship.[28] In my sample too it was relatively common for feminist men to become involved in activism through work. Some men were empowered to pursue feminist activism as a part of their official work duties. Richard, for example, designed workshops on healthy relationships, into which he infused a feminist perspective. Theo worked on his project on men and masculinity during work hours. Even when men practiced feminism as volunteers, they often described being rewarded informally at work for their feminism. One promising mechanism for engaging men in feminist organizing, then, is to reward doing so at work. Feminist activism could be recognized as pro bono work or community engagement and could be considered in employee evaluations. For certain roles, organizing might even be required. Richard and Theo, who work in student wellness and residential life, are good examples.

All of Us: Contesting and Creating Cultural Narratives

Finally, the findings of this book reveal that while feminist cultural narratives have become more visible and have undoubtedly shaped the way men think about themselves today, meaningful cultural change is still needed to achieve gender equality. Namely, folks working toward gender liberation must (1) contest cultural narratives that excuse, obscure, or perpetuate male supremacism and (2) create new cultural resources for men's identity work.

As I have shown, men's rights activists are attracted to the movement because it serves as a privilege renegotiation strategy. Their strategy involves denying men's privilege altogether and instead asserting that men are the true victims of gender inequality and thus have the moral high ground. But the men's rights movement is viable as a privilege renegotiation strategy only if others recognize it as bestowing morality upon men's rights activists. While the men's rights movement is obviously misogynist to some people, it is not so to others. In fact, when stripped of some of the more offensive and outlandish language men's rights activists typically use, Americans tend to agree with men's rights ideas.[29] Talking points long used by the men's rights movement—like that Title IX has wreaked havoc on men's sports and sexuality on college campuses, that men are discriminated against in the family court system, and that affirmative action makes it harder for qualified white men to find jobs—are common in mainstream cultural discourse.[30] This is a testament to the fact that the men's rights movement and its ideology are reflections of the misogyny embedded in the broader culture, rather than something distinct or isolated.

This cultural overlap means that the men's rights movement often has plausible deniability. It shields itself from accusations of misogyny through its use of ideas that appear to be common sense. It leverages these same ideas to make claims to victimhood, which constructs men's rights activists (and men more generally) as morally blameless. Privilege (as I have defined it) in and of itself is not a personal moral failure, but men's rights activists actively contribute to male supremacist ideology and pursue a deeply misogynist agenda. The process through which men's rights activists deny the male supremacism of their movement allows them to attract men looking for solutions to questions of identity. As long as the men's rights movement can sustain itself as a legitimate movement organizing for social justice—even among a small minority of people—it can serve as a privilege renegotiation strategy.

It is therefore essential to name the deep-rooted male supremacism of the men's rights movement. Anyone who writes or talks about the groups often referred to as "the manosphere"—the men's rights movement, incels, pickup artists, men going their own way, and so on—has an opportunity to contest the narratives that obscure the harm these groups do. Unfortunately, it is common for commentators—state actors, journalists, and researchers—to adopt the perspectives of male supremacist groups themselves.

State agencies and actors often operate using a flawed understanding of male supremacism. It is common for authorities to adopt the perspectives of male supremacist actors and groups. For example, after a white male shooter killed eight people, six of them Asian women, at three massage parlors in and around Atlanta in March 2021, police repeated the shooter's own account, saying he had a sex addiction and targeted the spas to eliminate a "temptation."[31] A police spokesperson said the day of the killings "was a really bad day for [the shooter] and this is what he did."[32] Besides the inappropriate sympathy the spokesperson displayed for the shooter, the police statement relies on racist and hypersexualized stereotypes of Asian women to position the victims as blameworthy. As another example, instead of putting grant funds toward tackling male supremacism itself, state agencies have provided money to programs to provide social support and mental health services to incels.[33] Such programs fail to recognize that other populations—particularly ones targeted by male supremacist groups—also experience lack of social support and mental health problems. They are likely to be ineffective because they ignore what actually differentiates incels from others who do not commit violence—male supremacism—when they buy into male supremacists' claims that they are uniquely victimized today.

Journalists can prop up male supremacist narratives when they do not explicitly point out their inherent misogyny and danger. Very often, journalists interview leaders from the Right in an effort to represent "both sides." Journalists describe these "experts" using language seemingly meant to appease them—for example, describing Stefan Molyneux as "unabashed in his views against feminism" or Jordan Peterson as "a critic of 'political correctness.'"[34] This leaves out the fact that they make their living hawking extreme and hateful ideas, with serious repercussions for marginalized people. Newspapers and magazines that provide space in their opinion sections for sympathetic portrayals of male supremacist actors or defenses of male supremacist talking points likewise contribute to the normalization of male supremacism.[35] And when journalists represent male supremacism as a gateway to "real" hate, like white supremacism and antisemitism, rather than hateful in its own right, they underplay its severity.[36]

Researchers can make these same mistakes when they fail to address their own positionality or consider how their perspectives are shaped by the broader (male supremacist) culture. It is relatively common for researchers to identify mental health disorders or autism spectrum disorder as the cause of male supremacist violence rather than male supremacist ideology.[37] When researchers use these flawed and individualized approaches to understanding male supremacism, they often end up suggesting ineffective and even dangerous interventions. For instance, one report suggests that practitioners help incels form intimate relationships with women to curb their "desire for dominance," without considering how such relationships might harm women.[38] As another example, researchers have encouraged participation in misogynist online forums, claiming that it may prevent violence through venting.[39] This solution ignores how the violent speech produced on these forums can encourage misogynists to act violently.

The failure of state actors, journalists, and researchers to name the male supremacism within movements like the men's rights movement has far-reaching consequences. When commentators provide the means for the men's rights movement to deny accusations of misogyny, men looking for ways to construct themselves as moral can use the movement as a privilege renegotiation strategy. The movement can be ruled out as a privilege renegotiation strategy only when it is seen for what it is: dangerous and hateful.

All parties interested in achieving gender inequality must also help create new cultural narratives with which men can define their identities. People are deeply invested in their identities because they define the self and guide behavior.[40] Yet, as I have shown, ways of defining the self and others generate inequality. Adopting a truly liberatory identity that still defines the self is thus incredibly difficult because inequality is written into not only our identities but also the very processes through which we define those identities.

I attribute the problems in men's boundary-making strategies to both men's failure to seriously consider how masculinity operates in their daily lives and the limitations of the narrative resources available to them.[41] I have already spoken to the former in this conclusion. On the latter, ontological narratives—or narratives of who we are—build from and are based in public narratives—or narratives produced and reproduced in the culture and institutions.[42] New public narratives are needed so that men can define the self in ways that avoid reifying the primacy of masculinity. This is an essential task for all people interested in dismantling the link between identity and inequality. It is an especially difficult one though, as new narratives around masculinity can easily be used to create new gendered, racialized, and classed hierarchies.[43] Setbacks and wrong turns are likely, but feminist men must devise and try on new ways of defining the self that can facilitate true liberation.

ACKNOWLEDGMENTS

Thank you to the men who agreed to be interviewed for this research. Your time and trust made my work possible. I hope that this book resonates with your experience.

I am deeply grateful to the mentors and advisors who contributed to this book's development and my training as a researcher. I was lucky to have exceptional mentors in Shelley Correll, Cecilia Ridgeway, Corey Fields, and David Pedulla, who provided insightful feedback on this research. Their enthusiasm and ideas for future directions encouraged me to continue developing the project and shape it into this book. I am also thankful for having a longtime mentor in Denise Anthony, who gave me my first opportunity to do sociological research.

Many colleagues have provided feedback to me through all stages of this research, from when it was just a spark of an idea to its final form. I thank the participants of the Qualitative Methods Workshop, Social Psychology and Gender Workshop, and Family Workshop in the Department of Sociology, and the Feminist, Gender, and Sexuality Studies Graduate Workshop, at Stanford University. When it came time to develop a book proposal, I had generous help from Laura Portwood-Stacer, Shelley Correll, Corey Fields, Megan Carroll, Aliya Rao, Alison Dahl Crossley, and Paloma Villegas. I am incredibly grateful to my editor, Ilene Kalish, and the rest of the team at NYU Press, and to the reviewers who provided excellent feedback on earlier versions of this book.

This research was supported by Stanford University's Graduate Research Opportunity Grant, Diversity Dissertation Research Opportunity Grant, and Sociology Research Opportunity Grant. I am especially thankful to have received the Graduate Dissertation Fellowship from the Clayman Institute for Gender Research, which provided me with time to push this research forward.

I am thankful for my community, which has supported me through the challenges of conducting this research and writing a book. The Clayman Institute for Gender Research, the VMWare Women's Leadership Innovation Lab, and the Institute for Research on Male Supremacism have been my intellectual homes. In each of these spaces, I gained invaluable knowledge and felt seen. I am thankful for my collaborators, who have taught me new ways of thinking and doing: Jurgita Abromaviciute, Jasmine Hill, Amy Johnson, Tagart Sobotka, and Alison Wynn. I am thankful for my friends, who have sustained me while I worked on this book. In addition to those above, I thank Laura Blomgren, Beka Guluma, Priscilla Gutierrez, Amanda Mireles, Colin Peterson, and Jessica Spolarich. I am also grateful for my students, from whom I am constantly learning.

I owe much to the love and support of my parents, Blaine and Susan, and sister, Sara. This book is your accomplishment too. I thank my dog, Lily, for her patience while I took an extended break from petting her to write this book. Finally, to Mark, thank you for your unwavering love and encouragement. You show me every day what it means to be a good man.

APPENDIX

Methods

In this appendix, I provide greater detail on how this project came to fruition, my choice of method, and the strategies I employed to gain access to, recruit, and interview participants and analyze interview data. I also discuss some of the challenges of this project.

THE PROJECT

I cannot remember when I first came across the men's rights movement—it was either during or just after college—but I remember it was online and that I was fascinated. I had identified as a feminist at least since college and had been involved in a campus feminist club. I had come into contact with antifeminism before that moment. I can still vividly recall a disagreement I had with a close friend of mine during my first year in college. We're in my dorm room. He is sitting on my extralong twin bed. I am sitting cross-legged on the ground, my back against my standard-issue dresser. At the time, I was a chemistry major and planned to go to medical school. I was excited about a university program that matched women in STEM with internships at the medical school and a local hospital. My friend angrily told me the program was unfair and that men in STEM like him also deserved such opportunities. I remember being surprised by my usually good-natured friend's reaction. I couldn't understand why he thought the program, which I understood as a proactive intervention into a deeply unequal field, was wrong. I tried my best to explain to him why I believed in such programs, but I lacked the language and frameworks that my sociology courses would teach me over the next four years. Our other friends watched on in silence as we argued.

When I happened upon the men's rights movement online, then, I was already curious about why some people—and specifically some men—hold antifeminist beliefs. The movement did not, at the time, anger me so much as it intrigued me. How did men's rights activists come to believe so wholeheartedly that men were the victims of feminism? Initially, I saw the movement, as many would until Trump's election in 2016, as a curiosity. But as I read more, I discovered both its virulent misogyny and its deployment of more mundane antifeminist talking points that I had already encountered, like those used by my college friend. It became apparent to me how the movement simultaneously leveraged existing, commonly accepted beliefs to recruit men and gain some legitimacy and pushed the broader cultural discourse further toward the extreme. I began to see challenging this growing antifeminist movement as an imperative.

I first thought about the men's rights movement as an object of study during 2013 in my first year of graduate school. From the start, I was most interested in interviewing men's rights activists about their trajectories into the movement. Because of concerns about access, I did not undertake an interview study immediately and instead studied the movement using content analysis and surveys.[1] For a qualitative methods course, I observed a fathers' rights group and made a contact that would be instrumental in accessing men's rights activists later on. I succeeded in interviewing two self-identified men's rights activists for the class and learned several lessons that I describe later in this appendix. By this time, the men's rights movement had gained some notoriety, in part because of the Isla Vista shootings in 2013, the expansion of the so-called manosphere and creation of new groups like the Red Pill, and several articles in outlets like the *New York Times*, *Mother Jones*, and *Vox*.[2]

While I was studying the men's rights movement, feminism was experiencing something of a resurgence. On campus and off, in person and online, feminism seemed to be everywhere. As a graduate student at Stanford University, I witnessed the cultural phenomenon that was *Lean In* and its resonance with people (including men) across Silicon Valley. Celebrities were proudly identifying with the movement; there was a sense that it was about time a woman was president and, after Hillary Clinton's loss in 2016, a tide of women running for public office;[3] and there were new corporate commitments to cracking down on sexual violence and increasing gender diversity, catalyzed by the #MeToo movement. Amid this groundswell, more men began calling themselves feminists. At Stanford, students of all genders stuck "of course I'm a feminist" stickers to their laptops.

At the same time, and as I have discussed throughout this book, the feminism that was so popular in the Bay Area and in the broader culture was a particular kind. It was a neoliberal, choice feminism that focused on individual agency and strategy rather than structural and cultural change. My other research interviewing young people about their beliefs about gender inequality and their ideas for solving it illustrated to me just how limiting this feminism would be, potentially for generations to come.[4] I suspected that men's feminism, while of course a positive development, might not be as productive as one would hope.

When it came time to embark on the interview study, then, feminist men seemed an obvious group for comparison. If I wanted to understand how men are mobilized for the men's rights movement, examining men's pathways into feminism provided a juxtaposition that could illuminate how feminist organizers and others interested in achieving gender liberation could move the needle. These two groups are extreme cases of men's possible orientations toward gender inequality, and extreme cases are useful in shedding light on processes and mechanisms precisely because they "sample on the dependent variable."[5] As I began this project, I didn't know that what would be most surprising to me, and what would become the focus of this book, was the similarities across these two groups, rather than their differences.

CHOICE OF METHOD AND SAMPLE

At the start of this project, I was interested in the process through which men come to identify as gender activists, how they make sense of their gender activism, and what their identification with their movement achieves for them. Interviewing is particularly suited to questions of process and meaning, and so I chose this method.[6] Of course, all methods are limited. Interview methods have been criticized for accessing post hoc interpretations rather than "true" motivations.[7] However, even post hoc interpretations provide useful data in examining how interviewees make sense of their experiences.[8] In the context of social movements, post hoc interpretations are useful in identifying activists' agreed upon accounts of mobilization.[9] Moreover, interview data can reveal a deep story by accessing levels of meaning beyond what interviewees say.[10]

Particularly relevant to this project, the explanations interviewees produce can shed light on what they see as honorable or moral in a way that other methods cannot.[11]

To qualify for the study, individuals had to (1) identify as men or trans men or similar, (2) identify as participants in either the men's rights or feminist movement, and (3) live in the United States. I chose these criteria for several reasons. First, and as I describe in the introduction of this book, men control disproportionate power and resources, making their orientations toward feminism particularly relevant to its success. Second, I relied on potential participants' self-identification with their social movement because I wanted to capture variation in level of participation. I wanted to know what identification (rather than, for example, activism) achieved for them, so I refrained from using a definition that limited my sample to serious organizers. I was especially curious about this when it came to feminist men, whose ranks have grown in recent years and who, by virtue of neoliberal rationality, are encouraged to think of feminism as an individual pastime. In my sample, participants used a variety of labels to describe their involvement in their respective movements, including "men's rights activist," "men's rights advocate," "feminist," and "profeminist." I refer to the two groups as "men's rights activists" or "feminists" for ease of use. Finally, multiple feminisms and men's rights movements exist within the United States alone, and there are important cross-national differences across each movement. To focus the study, I limited participants to residents of the United States.

GAINING ACCESS

Gaining access to participants, particularly to men's rights activists, was my primary concern at the outset of this project. Men's rights activists are typically suspicious of researchers. They are keenly aware that their perspective on gender inequality clashes with academic consensus, and they believe that academics reject any findings that do not support a feminist worldview. Additionally, they are hesitant to publicly identify as men's rights activists, as the movement is typically seen as misogynist even by nonacademics. My previous experience attempting to recruit interview participants for the aforementioned qualitative methods course reinforced these concerns. For the course, I posted my solicitation on one men's rights forum, and the responses were discouraging.

Several posters accused me of wanting to "dox" my participants (i.e., publicly out them and share their personal information on the internet); others believed I would present men's rights groups as "scary nazi [sic] misogynist clubs." I spent hours crafting messages to respond to these comments and communicate to potential participants that interviews were strictly confidential and my intentions were academic. While I was able to complete the requirements of the course (i.e., interview two people), I was concerned that attempting a larger interview study would prove difficult indeed.

But from this experience, I learned several important lessons from forum participants who responded to my first (ill-conceived) solicitation. I put these lessons into practice when I began this project, and I share them here with the hope that they will be useful for other researchers studying extreme groups. First, and perhaps obviously, I needed to provide proof of who I purported to be. One poster recommended that I provide links to my LinkedIn and department profiles. I did this in my interview solicitations for this project. While students of qualitative methods are often told to use their university as a credential to gain access, this had mixed results in recruiting men's rights activists: my department signaled that I was part of an institution that (they believed) subscribed to a feminist interpretation of the world, but also that there was some institutional oversight of my project (i.e., Stanford's Institutional Review Board, or IRB). While some participants were suspicious of me because I identified myself as a graduate student in sociology, others were quite reverential toward the Stanford name.

Second, I learned that my offer to interview using Skype—intended to allow me to access individuals outside of the Bay Area and still be able to use some of the visual cues that are so important in interview research—was perceived by potential participants as a confidentiality risk. One poster noted that I might be able to identify a person's IP address using Skype; another said that I could use a screenshot from Skype to identify them via Facebook. For the current project, I offered to interview nonlocal participants over the phone and provided my phone number to those who wished to keep theirs private. While interviewing over the phone presented some challenges (which I describe below), doing so allowed me to access many individuals whom I would not have been able to otherwise. Out of similar concerns, when I undertook this project, I obtained a waiver of documentation for informed consent from IRB so that no paper documentation could link my interview participants with the project.

Third, I learned that having a forum account without any significant history of posting, commenting, or otherwise engaging with the community made me more suspicious. This presented a more difficult problem since I did not participate in men's rights forums or even the broader sites that hosted them; I had created accounts only to post my interview solicitation. While I frequented these sites to stay updated on important discussions within the men's rights community, participating in them felt ethically murky to me. I did not want to inadvertently mislead participants who might look up my account history and interpret my virtual actions in ways I had not intended. For instance, if I "upvoted" an article about a men's rights issue to show my engagement with the community, did that mean I approved of the sentiment expressed by the poster? Instead of working to improve my account's credit, I sought help from key gatekeepers who could recruit participants on my behalf.

RECRUITMENT

TABLE A.1. Method of recruitment for sample of interview participants

Method	Men's rights activists	Feminists
Email	1 (3%)	4 (13%)
Flier	3 (10%)	0 (0%)
Event	4 (13%)	—
Social media / online forum	17 (55%)	1 (3%)
Organization	2 (6%)	16 (52%)
Snowball	4 (13%)	10 (32%)

Note: n = 31 for each group. The table shows frequencies, with percentages in parentheses.

I used a variety of methods to recruit participants, some of which were more successful for one or the other group, as shown in table A.1. First, I cold-emailed potential participants. With one exception, these were not people with whom I had preexisting relationships but men who I knew to be involved in either the men's rights movement or feminism.

Second, I put up fliers on the Stanford University campus. One version advertised that I was doing a study of men who are men's rights activists and the other advertised that I was doing a study of feminist men.

Third, I attended two Bay Area screenings of the documentary *The Red Pill*, which is sympathetic to the men's rights movement and was highly anticipated by the men's rights community.[12] I hung fliers near the theaters before each screening. I also approached individuals after the screenings, told them about my project, and gave interested and qualified men my business card. The reception my solicitation received varied tremendously. While I found my earliest men's rights participants through these screenings, I also observed some men laugh at one of my fliers and rip it down as they waited for one of the screenings to begin.

Fourth, I posted my solicitation online and asked others to post it on social media sites on my behalf. I had kept in contact with a woman who identified as a men's rights activist and organized a father's rights group I observed years before. She introduced me to several other men's rights activists, one of whom posted my solicitation to six Facebook pages and thirteen Facebook groups, all of which were associated with the men's or fathers' rights movements. I personally posted solicitations to two men's rights forums, but this proved to be far less successful as compared to when the insider posted it for me. A picture of one of my posters advertising my study of men who are men's rights activists was posted on Twitter and retweeted several times, which provided another means of recruitment on social media.

I also contacted two Facebook groups geared toward feminist men and requested they post my solicitation. One group forwarded my solicitation to the group's email listserv, but the other did not respond. As I worked to find online spaces where I could access feminist men, I realized that recruiting them would be more difficult than I had imagined. While men who are men's rights activists were not easy to recruit, they were easy to find: since the majority of men's rights activists are men, I could simply recruit from men's rights spaces and groups. The majority of individuals in feminist spaces and groups do not identify as men. I therefore had to cast a wider net to access this population. One way I did this was by contacting organizations that feminist men were likely to be a part of. I asked such organizations to send my solicitation to their members. I contacted organizations that specifically identified as feminist as well as those only tangentially related to feminism and those composed largely of men, including political party organizations and unions. I did the same for organizations whose members might be interested in men's rights.

As shown in table A.1, organizations proved to be a more fruitful recruitment site for feminist men than for men who are men's rights activists. For the most part, feminist and progressive organizations seemed happy to forward my solicitation to their members and affiliates, but I rarely heard back from men's rights and conservative organizations. I believe this speaks to the relative differences in the in-person organizing power of these two movements, as well as the acceptance of feminist issues within progressive politics. While conservative politics certainly align with some of the men's rights agenda, they do not fully overlap, and many men's rights activists see conservative politicians simply as paying lip service to men's issues to gain votes. This is evident in my sample: men's rights activists reported "no" or "other" political ideology far more than feminist men (see table A.3). Since the conclusion of my study, male supremacist groups have been incorporated more fully into conservative politics in the United States, but this was not the case while I was recruiting interviewees.[13]

Finally, I asked participants to send my contact information to men they thought would qualify and be interested. So-called snowball sampling uses the networks of previous participants to access new participants, at the expense of obtaining any sort of representative sample. None of my methods, in fact, would obtain such a sample, and it was not the goal of this research to do so.

The solicitation I used was nearly identical whether I was cold-emailing, posting to forums or social media sites, or requesting that organizations forward my information to their members. It opened by introducing myself, my credentials, and my interest in interviewing "men living in the United States who are interested in men's issues." It said the study's purpose was "to understand participants' experiences as men and their understandings of how men and women interact in today's world. My goal is to learn about personal experiences relating to the internet, work, family, dating, and marriage." Depending on the target population, I included a line stating why their involvement in men's rights or feminism would make them good candidates for the study. I then described the interview process, including that their identities would be confidential and that they would be reimbursed for their time with a twenty-five-dollar gift card for Amazon.com. The solicitation did not state that I was interviewing both men's rights activists and feminists, although I often disclosed this toward the end of interviews to ask participants what they thought of men involved in the other movement.

It was my priority to equalize the samples, not in terms of the way they were recruited but by a select number of participant characteristics. I sought to match the two samples' age, geographic region, and level of movement involvement to answer several theoretical questions about the factors that influence an individual's mobilization and activism. I recognize that an individual's structural position likely contributes to their mobilization into a social movement, but because the populations themselves are fairly different from one another, it would be artificial and incredibly difficult to construct a sample of men's rights activists and a sample of feminists that are identical in terms of demographic characteristics like race, class, and education. I therefore decided to match the samples in terms of age and region to determine if and how men's rights activists and feminists in similar life stages and places respond differently to similar pressures and contexts. I also attempted to match respondents based on level of movement involvement since involvement was an outcome of interest to this project.

I characterized each participant's level of movement involvement based on the activities he reported as part of his activism. I define "minimal involvement" as participating in sporadic movement activities or those not typically considered traditional activism. These generally included posting on social media, confronting friends or acquaintances about related issues, signing petitions, or interacting with other movement participants online. I define "recreational involvement" as participating in routine and prolonged movement activities as a hobby, which generally included attending rallies and conferences, participating in fundraising, and contacting political representatives. I define "organizational/occupational involvement" as either holding an elected or appointed position in a movement organization or participating in activism as part of one's occupation.

Recruitment was iterative: as I interviewed more participants and the characteristics of my samples changed, I employed purposeful recruitment techniques to make the samples similar in terms of these three characteristics. For instance, early in my data collection process, I had interviewed many men's rights activists who were involved in activism at a recreational or organizational/occupational level, whereas my feminist participants were more likely to be involved at a minimal level. As a result, I sent more solicitations to feminist organizations, which I hoped would reach individuals more involved in activism than, for instance, posts on social media sites. Likewise, the men's rights activists I interviewed early on in the project were much older than the feminist men I had interviewed. Thus, I posted on online men's rights forums, hoping to access a younger population. I also declined to interview older men's rights activists. This process of iterative and deliberate sampling is called theoretical sampling. As shown in table A.2, the process was generally successful in matching the samples.

While I attempted to match the samples only by age, region, and level of involvement, table A.3 shows that the samples are, by and large, similar to one another in terms of other demographic characteristics.

Table A.2. Results of theoretical sampling method

	Men's rights activists	Feminists
Age		
Mean	44.4 years	45.4 years
18–29	8 (26%)	9 (29%)
30–54	12 (38%)	10 (32%)
55+	11 (35%)	12 (39%)
Location		
San Francisco Bay Area	8 (26%)	10 (32%)
West (including SF Bay Area)	16 (52%)	13 (42%)
Midwest	8 (26%)	10 (32%)
South	4 (13%)	5 (16%)
Northeast	3 (10%)	3 (10%)
Level of involvement		
Minimal	13 (42%)	14 (45%)
Recreational	10 (32%)	10 (32%)
Organizational / occupational	8 (26%)	7 (23%)

Note: n = 31 for each group. With the exception of the mean for age, the table shows frequencies, with percentages in parentheses.

TABLE A.3. Other demographic characteristics of interview respondents

	Men's rights activists	Feminists
Race†		
Asian	1 (3%)	2 (6%)
Black	0 (0%)	3 (10%)
Latino	3 (10%)	1 (3%)
White	29 (94%)	26 (84%)
Other	0 (0%)	1 (3%)
Education		
Less than high school	1 (3%)	0 (0%)
High school / GED	2 (6%)	0 (0%)
Some college / associate's degree	8 (26%)	7 (23%)
Bachelor's degree	11 (35%)	13 (42%)
Advanced degree	9 (29%)	11 (35%)
Sexual orientation		
Straight	26 (84%)	24 (77%)
Gay	1 (3%)	3 (10%)
Other	4 (13%)	4 (13%)
Marital status		
Single, never married	15 (48%)	8 (26%)
Married	8 (26%)	14 (45%)
Separated	3 (10%)	1 (3%)
Divorced	5 (16%)	6 (19%)
Widowed	0 (0%)	2 (6%)
Ever divorced†	8 (26%)	8 (26%)
Parent		
	15 (48%)	15 (48%)
Religion		
Christian	5 (16%)	3 (10%)
Jewish	3 (10%)	3 (10%)
Other	3 (10%)	4 (13%)
None	20 (65%)	21 (68%)
Political ideology‡		
Liberal	6 (19%)	26 (84%)
Moderate	3 (10%)	1 (3%)
Conservative	7 (23%)	0 (0%)
Other	7 (23%)	2 (6%)
None	5 (16%)	0 (0%)

Note: n = 31 for each group. The table shows frequencies, with percentages in parentheses.
†Race categories are not mutually exclusive. "Ever divorced" is not exclusive to other marital status categories, except "single, never married."
‡Political ideology is unknown for five interviewees.

DATA COLLECTION

I began conducting interviews in November 2016 and completed interviews in December 2017. In total, I conducted thirty-one interviews with men whom I refer to as "men's rights activists," thirty-one interviews with men whom I refer to as "feminists," and one interview with a man who identifies as a member of both groups (who was excluded from analyses for the purpose of this book).

Interviews lasted just under two hours on average. Interviews with men's rights activists tended to be slightly longer (114 minutes on average) compared to those with feminists (103 minutes). Interviews were semistructured, meaning I conducted each interview using a protocol of interview questions but often excluded certain questions to follow up on a participant's line of thought. I did attempt to ask a handful of questions that were central to the project (e.g., "When did you first start calling yourself a [men's rights activist / feminist]?") to every interview participant, but generally prioritized asking follow-up questions over sticking to the protocol.

The protocol evolved as I interviewed more subjects and analyzed the data over fourteen months of data collection. Generally, I asked background and introductory questions at the beginning of the interview. Then I asked questions related to the respondent's participation in his social movement, including why he first became involved, how he defined his movement, and what types of activism he did. Next, I asked questions to determine how the respondent defined manhood and how he believed larger society defined manhood. I then transitioned to a set of questions probing whether the respondent believed there to be gendered expectations of men in different settings (like work and home). I then asked the respondent questions about his perception of gender inequality and men's issues. Finally, I asked the respondent whom he talked to about his activism, before ending the interview with a set of demographic questions. Interviews were audio recorded.

I conducted interviews with participants who lived in the greater San Francisco Bay Area in person, with two exceptions.[14] In light of men's rights activists' privacy concerns, I conducted all other interviews over the phone rather than a video platform like Skype or Zoom. This meant that I lacked the visual cues that are often helpful throughout the course of an interview. It was sometimes difficult, for instance, to determine when a participant was pausing to think and when a participant was done answering a question. Likewise, it was more difficult to show participants I was listening over the phone; I used subtle verbal cues (e.g., "mmhmm") to do this. While phone interviews presented distinct challenges, the quality and richness of participants' answers did not seem to suffer. Moreover, using the phone proved to be helpful in interviewing (especially) men's rights activists, as I could spend less energy managing my facial expressions when interviewees professed explicitly misogynist views.

In addition to interviews, I had a few opportunities to observe men's rights activists in person. As previously mentioned, I attended two Bay Area screenings of *The Red Pill*, a documentary about the men's rights movement made by a "former feminist."[15] The film was eagerly awaited by men's rights activists, many of whom had financially backed it and hoped it would present their perspective to a wider audience. The men's rights activist I met observing a fathers' rights group two years earlier invited me to join her at one of the screenings and eat dinner with a small group of her friends beforehand. I attended another screening by myself. I took field notes after each of these observations. These screenings helped me understand the broader context of the movement, observe interactions between men's rights activists, and make connections with potential interview participants.

DATA ANALYSIS

I used conventional qualitative content analysis to analyze the wealth of data I collected.[16] Data analysis was iterative and comprised three stages: (1) preliminary code generation, (2) a first round of transcript-by-transcript, line-by-line coding and memoing, and (3) detailed within-code analysis and comparison.

I used notes from my interviews to generate a preliminary list of codes. After each interview, I immediately took extensive notes on its content and what I perceived to be its major themes. As a result, these notes were a combination of summary and analytic memo. My postinterview notes totaled more than thirty thousand words. From November 2016 to February 2017, I conducted ten interviews each with men's rights activists and feminists. I then analyzed my notes from these twenty interviews using Microsoft Word to develop a preliminary list of codes.

At the end of data collection, audio recordings of my interviews were transcribed verbatim by a professional transcription service. I coded transcripts using Dedoose, a qualitative analysis software that allows the user to attach codes to text and analyze themes across transcripts. I applied the preliminary list of codes I had developed using my interview notes and also created new codes and returned to previous transcripts to recode them. During this first round of coding, I wrote and rewrote twenty-five memos in which I explored similarities and differences within and across each group. I revisited these memos to determine which themes I would explore in further coding.

Next, I reexamined excerpts that had been coded with common themes. I exported excerpts tagged with particular codes of interest and reanalyzed them to draw out themes. I used Microsoft Word to add marginal notes to these excerpts. I did this targeted analysis and memoing instead of a second round of transcript-by-transcript coding because it allowed me to better compare across interviews and explore nuances within themes I had already identified.

CHALLENGES

Whenever I present work from this project, I am asked the same question: how did my identity as a woman affect the study? As with all kinds of sociological research, many of my identities—yes, as a woman, but also as a biracial person and as an academic—affected this project.

My being a woman had both expected and unexpected consequences for my research. Perhaps most obviously, my identity as a woman affected my recruitment of men's rights activists. In this and my previous research on men's rights activists, it is clear that they often assume most women are feminists. In my particular case, this assumption is correct. I can only assume that the men's rights activists who decided to speak with me are more trusting than the general population, and potentially less radical too. There is also the issue of social desirability bias. Men's rights activists are well aware that their views are perceived as misogynist. It's possible that my being a woman dissuaded men's rights activists from expressing some viewpoints. However, I think their candor is well evidenced by the quotes in this book.

Even the men's rights activists who agreed to participate in this research were likely less trustful of me than the feminists I interviewed. In taking a critical approach to the men's rights movement, I know I will inevitably encounter accusations of bias, and I was cognizant of this while conducting this study. For instance, during interviews, I tried to give men's rights activists (and feminists) every opportunity to explain their viewpoint by asking probing and follow-up questions. In data analysis, my goal was to apply a critical yet fair eye to *both* men's rights activists' and feminists' accounts. In writing this book, I aimed to truthfully represent men's rights activists' opinions and perspectives.

More surprisingly, I believe my gender identity influenced feminist men to be more careful about their responses too, but for different reasons. My sense during interviews with feminist men was that they believed I was far more knowledgeable about feminism and gender issues than they were because I am a woman and a gender researcher. Some seemed to worry about whether what they were saying was "correct." For instance, when I asked Theo how he defined feminism, he said, "Yeah, I was afraid you were going to ask me that." Russell prefaced his answer with, "I don't know what the current models are." Patrick said, "This probably isn't textbook" before providing his answer. Nick asked me, "How did I do?" once the recorder was off. While perhaps counterintuitive, my sense is that feminist men were more guarded and careful with their answers than men's rights activists, as these examples show. Men's rights activists, after all, are already aware that their beliefs are different from many people's. In other words, the men's rights activists I interviewed are likely used to their views on gender being scrutinized; feminist men sometimes seemed to think I was sizing up their views. They seemed to be worried that their feminist self-identification (and thus their moral self-concept) wouldn't hold up to my scrutiny.

After the question about my gender identity and how it influenced this research, the second most common question I get is, "Was interviewing men's rights activists difficult?" The answer is a resounding yes. My gender identity certainly made these interviews emotionally taxing. Being a member of the group often discussed by men's rights activists and feminists made some interviews personal in a way they would not have been had I not been a woman. In one of the most difficult interviews, Rick, a men's rights activist, told me that men are biologically driven to reproduce and resort to raping women to do so. He recalled an ongoing debate he has with a friend, who predicted that men would form gangs to rape women if women did not start willingly having sex with them. He often spoke in the second person (e.g., "If you got pregnant . . ."), a rhetorical choice that made his comments even more personal. The notes I took after illustrate my state of mind during my interview with Rick:

> This was a particularly uncomfortable interview for me, as both my first in-person interview and as the most explicitly sexist one I have done. Despite this, I think I did a good job controlling my tone of voice, my facial and body expressions, etc. as he did seem to trust me by the end. . . . By the end of the interview, I was exhausted from putting so much effort into listening attentively, controlling my facial expressions, and maintaining my kind demeanor. When I stood to leave, my legs felt like jelly.

As these notes demonstrate, I had to pay special attention to my self-presentation during interviews, particularly to the tone of my voice and my facial expressions. These challenges occurred for my interviews with men's rights activists *and* feminists. For both groups, I tried to be an attentive listener and conceal my personal reactions from interviewees. The long process of data analysis was also difficult, as I had to read and reread transcript after transcript.

My gender also undoubtedly shaped my concerns about safety. Researchers studying male supremacist groups are often targeted online, and those conducting in-person research must further consider their physical safety. As I geared up to conduct this research, I locked down my social media accounts and, when possible, made them unsearchable. I gave out a Google Voice number or my office number rather than my cell number for phone interviews. With the exception of Rick, whom I interviewed in his office, I offered to interview men's rights activists in my office at Stanford or at a public place of their choosing. In hindsight, I wish I had interviewed all men's rights activists in public places. While public places like cafés don't offer the kind of privacy that helps facilitate honest responses during interviews, I felt uncomfortable being alone with men's rights activists in my rather secluded office in the basement and wondered later whether it was wise to essentially tell them where they could find me in the future. When I interviewed men's rights activists in person, I texted my sister beforehand with my location and the estimated time I would be done and texted her again as soon as the interview was finished.[17] My sister also bought me a taser, which I kept in my desk drawer during interviews in my office and carried with me in my bag to interviews in public places.

Throughout this research, my tendency whenever I felt a pang of concern for my safety was to minimize it—to immediately think of it as silly. In the end, my physical safety was never compromised, but I include this discussion in case it is useful to other researchers. To those planning on studying male supremacist groups, particularly those who are women, trans men, or nonbinary: your concerns about safety are valid. This research is dangerous because these groups are dangerous. Before embarking on your research, make a plan to ensure your safety.

Race emerged as an important identity in my interviews with both men's rights activists and feminists. I am biracial, but my first and last names reflect my white racial background, and my appearance can be racially ambiguous. Because I conducted most of my interviews over the phone, I imagine many participants assumed I am white or at least partly white. I am unsure how much my racial identity affected the recruitment and data collection processes since many participants were rather forthcoming in expressing racist sentiments. There was one case in which I was especially worried about the impact of my racial background. Ken, a men's rights activist and white nationalist, asked about my race at the close of our interview, I assumed because my middle name (Kiyoko) sometimes shows with my email address:

KEN: By the way, is the family Japanese? Half Japanese?
EMILY: Yes. My mother is Japanese. I have that telltale middle name.
KEN: Yeah, yeah, it showed. Obviously, there's no accent, but yeah.

By this time, Ken had spent nearly an hour telling me about the beauty of racial homogeneity and segregation. He had even used Japan as an example. At that moment, I wondered what he thought of me as a biracial person and what he would have disclosed to someone he did not suspect of being biracial. More generally, my racial identity posed similar emotional and self-presentational challenges as my gender identity. It was difficult for me, as someone who identifies as a person of color, to retain my role as a researcher when individuals made racist comments.

While my gender and race made this research challenging for me, they also gave me special insight. For one, participants assumed I knew little about the experience of being a man, so they provided rich explanations of their own and others' definitions of manhood and the expectations men experience in different contexts. Had I been a man, I imagine some participants may have assumed the experience was common knowledge and provided less detailed answers. My racial ambiguity allows me to pass as white and enter into conversations with white folks where they feel safe to express racist views. Both my gender and my race provide me with a particular subjectivity with which I could approach this project. My standpoint facilitates my distinctive and critical analysis;[18] if fish don't know they're swimming in water, I am able to see the water because I am not a fish. Indeed, I doubt that I would have embarked on this project if I were not a woman of color.

I have already described how I believe my being part of a sociology department affected my ability to recruit men's rights activists to the study. My prior research posed an additional complication. When I posted my interview solicitation to a men's rights forum in December 2017, a forum participant responded by posting a conference abstract from another of my papers on the men's rights movement and the title of a second paper. Both papers were critical of the men's rights movement. I spent many hours carefully responding to questions about these papers and other concerns, but the forum ultimately did not prove to be a successful means of recruitment. There was additional fallout: a men's rights activist whom I had interviewed nearly a year before emailed me after reading the comments on my post and accused me of already knowing the conclusion of my research (that men's rights activists are sexist) before conducting it. And this was early in my career. Today, I am a founding member of the Institute for Research on Male Supremacism, have published several articles on the men's rights movement, and have co-edited a volume on male supremacism. I conducted this research and wrote this book knowing it is likely to be the first and last time I have interview access to this population.

There is one ongoing challenge of this research: the tension between my commitment to represent the views of all of my participants fairly and my academic duty to critically assess them. I felt this tension particularly during interviews. It is typical to listen attentively during interviews and to avoid arguing with the respondent or sharing one's own opinion. I worry that many of my respondents understood my demeanor to indicate agreement with their statements. Indeed, several men's rights activists implied at the close of our interview that I must agree with the movement's views. Rick, for instance, predicted I would have a hard time finding feminist men who would agree to talk to me. I think this illustrates that men's rights activists are not used to encountering an active and polite listener when expressing their views about gender.

I imagine some of my respondents will read this book. In fact, many requested I send the results of my study to them. While I think I have accurately represented what feminists and men's rights activists told me during their interviews, I have no doubt that many will feel unfairly judged. How do I make my participants feel like they were heard while still accomplishing the academic aims of this project? Doing anything less would be a disservice to the individuals who trusted me with their reputations, their private information, and the opinions they rarely share with others. I tried to navigate this tension by always rereading the context in which a statement was made, providing that context in my writing, and presenting alternative interpretations of statements whenever I thought one was plausible. While I did not try to satisfy every one of my participants, I hope that this book resonates with their experiences even if it upsets them.

NOTES

INTRODUCTION
1. Mantilla, "Gendertrolling."
2. Vaisey, "Motivation and Justification."
3. I am more comfortable questioning men's rights activists' intentions. As I describe below, the men's rights movement deploys extreme misogyny, and its agenda serves to further men's group position despite activists' claims that they are advocates for equality.
4. Hochschild, *Strangers in Their Own Land*.
5. hooks, *Feminism Is for Everybody*, viii.
6. Freedman, *No Turning Back*.
7. Banet-Weiser, *Empowered*.
8. Crossley, *Finding Feminism*.
9. Rottenberg, "Rise of Neoliberal Feminism."
10. Banet-Weiser, *Empowered*.
11. Banet-Weiser and Portwood-Stacer, "Traffic in Feminism."
12. Rottenberg, "Rise of Neoliberal Feminism," 422.
13. Barroso, "61% of U.S. Women."
14. hooks, *Feminist Theory*, 81.
15. Banet-Weiser, *Empowered*.
16. Ging, "Bros v. Hos."
17. Boyd and Sheehy, "Men's Groups."
18. Messner, *Politics of Masculinities*; Faludi, *Backlash*.
19. Hodapp, *Men's Rights*.
20. I do not debunk men's rights claims in this book, as others have done this effectively. See Hodapp, *Men's Rights*; Coston and Kimmel, "White Men as the New Victims"; Chowdhury, "Conditions of Emergence."
21. Menzies, "Virtual Backlash"; Rafail and Freitas, "Grievance Articulation."
22. Dragiewicz, *Equality with a Vengeance*.
23. Hong, Zaveri, and Rashbaum, "Inside the Violent and Misogynistic World."
24. Kimmel and Mosmiller, *Against the Tide*.
25. Messner, Greenberg, and Peretz, *Some Men*.
26. Dragiewicz, *Equality with a Vengeance*; Coston and Kimmel, "White Men as the New Victims."
27. As an example of more critical work, see Sumerau et al., "Constructing Allyship."

28 This has been documented across multiple realms. As one example, see Coltrane, "Household Labor."
29 Linder and Johnson, "Exploring the Complexities of Men"; Bridges, "Men Just Weren't Made to Do This."
30 Kimmel, *Angry White Men*. I recognize the allegations of misconduct against Michael Kimmel. While I draw on his work to develop my argument, I in no way condone sexual misconduct. See Mangan, "'I Want to Hear Those Charges'"; Ratcliffe, "US Women's Rights Campaigner."
31 See the Appendix: Methods for more information on the challenges of recruiting men's rights activists.
32 Polletta and Jasper, "Collective Identity," 284.
33 McIntosh, "White Privilege and Male Privilege."
34 Acker, "Hierarchies, Jobs, Bodies"; Ray, "Theory of Racialized Organizations."
35 Davis and Robinson, "Men's and Women's Consciousness of Gender Inequality."
36 Wetts and Willer, "Privilege on the Precipice"; Bjorklund, Davis, and Pfaffendorf, "Urine or You're Out"; Major, Blodorn, and Major Blascovich, "Threat of Increasing Diversity"; Mutz, "Status Threat"; Carian and Sobotka, "Playing the Trump Card"; Abascal, "Contraction as a Response to Group Threat."
37 Polletta and Jasper, "Collective Identity."
38 Johansson and Vinthagen, *Conceptualizing "Everyday Resistance."*
39 Hollander and Einwohner, "Conceptualizing Resistance."
40 Masquelier, *Critique and Resistance*.
41 Rottenberg, "Rise of Neoliberal Feminism."
42 England, "Gender Revolution."
43 Fry and Stepler, "Women May Never Make Up Half of U.S. Workforce."
44 England and Li, "Desegregation Stalled."
45 Burstein, "Attacking Sex Discrimination in the Labor Market."
46 Cherlin, *Marriage, Divorce, Remarriage*; Hasday, "Contest and Consent."
47 Cotter, Hermsen, and Vanneman, "End of the Gender Revolution?"
48 Jackson, *Destined for Equality*, 241.
49 Cotter, Hermsen, and Vanneman, "End of the Gender Revolution?"
50 England and Li, "Desegregation Stalled."
51 Weeden, Newhart, and Gelbgiser, "State of the Union 2018."
52 Cohn, Livingston, and Wang, "Stay-at-Home Mothers."
53 Collins et al., "Gendered Consequences."
54 Totenberg and McCammon, "Supreme Court Overturns Roe v. Wade."
55 Cotter, Hermsen, and Vanneman, "End of the Gender Revolution?," 259.
56 Juhn and Potter, "Changes in Labor Force Participation"; Goldin and Katz, "Power of the Pill."
57 Levanon, England, and Allison, "Occupational Feminization and Pay."
58 Arons, "Lifetime Losses."
59 Hess et al., "Employment and Earnings."
60 Acker, "Hierarchies, Jobs, Bodies."

61 Sayer, "Gender, Time and Inequality"; Zamarro and Prados, "Gender Differences."
62 Fry and Stepler, "Women May Never Make Up Half of U.S. Workforce."
63 Carian and Johnson, "Agency Myth"; Williams, "Happy Marriage"; Rudman et al., "Status Incongruity and Backlash Effects."
64 Cotter et al., "Glass Ceiling Effect."
65 Black et al., "National Intimate Partner and Sexual Violence Survey"; Fisher, Cullen, and Turner, "Sexual Victimization of College Women."
66 Ridgeway, *Framed by Gender*.
67 Cotter, Hermsen, and Vanneman, *Gender Inequality at Work*.
68 Bianchi, Robinson, and Milke, *Changing Rhythms*.
69 England, "Gender Revolution."
70 Ridgeway, *Framed by Gender*.
71 Faludi, *Stiffed*.
72 Kimmel and Ferber, "'White Men Are This Nation'"; Ralph-Morrow, "Right Men."
73 Faludi, *Stiffed*; Sherman, *Those Who Work*.
74 Williams, *Reshaping the Work-Family Debate*.
75 Roberts, "Introduction," 3.
76 Connell, *Masculinities*.
77 Pascoe, "'Dude, You're a Fag'"; Levanon, England, and Allison, "Occupational Feminization and Pay."
78 Anderson, *Inclusive Masculinity*.
79 Morris and Anderson, "'Charlie Is So Cool Like'"; McCormack, "Hierarchy without Hegemony"; Baker and Hotek, "Grappling with Gender."
80 Bridges and Pascoe, "Hybrid Masculinities."
81 Bridges, "Very 'Gay' Straight?"
82 Connell, *Masculinities*; Connell and Messerschmidt, "Hegemonic Masculinity"; Messerschmidt, *Hegemonic Masculinity*.
83 Connell, *Masculinities*, 77.
84 Flyvbjerg, "Five Misunderstandings."
85 Washington Post and the Kaiser Family Foundation, "Washington Post–Kaiser Family Foundation Poll"; Carian, "Inversive Sexism Scale."
86 Lamont, *Money, Morals, and Manners*; Lamont and Swidler, "Methodological Pluralism."
87 Hochschild, *Strangers in Their Own Land*.
88 One of the feminist men I interviewed identified as a transgender man and another identified as genderqueer. All other interviewees are cisgender men. Given this, these data speak to how men with substantial privilege—including cisgender privilege—are motivated to engage in gender activism. Future research should examine transgender men's and nonbinary people's pathways into gender activism.
89 See the Appendix: Methods for more information on how participants were recruited.
90 Demographic information for each group of interviewees can be found in the Appendix: Methods.
91 See the Appendix: Methods for more information about how data were analyzed.

92 Carian and Johnson, "Agency Myth"; Pedulla and Thébaud, "Can We Finish the Revolution?"

1. PLAYING THE HERO

1 West and Zimmerman, "Doing Gender."
2 McIntosh, "White Privilege and Male Privilege."
3 Hartsock, "Feminist Standpoint."
4 Banet-Weiser, *Empowered*.
5 Bondi, "Locating Identity Politics."
6 Ridgeway, *Framed by Gender*.
7 Hartsock, "Feminist Standpoint."
8 Friedan, *Feminine Mystique*.
9 Ridgeway, *Framed by Gender*.
10 Burke, "Identity Control Theory."
11 Burke, "Identity Control Theory."
12 Messner, "Limits of 'the Male Sex Role.'"
13 Messner, "Limits of 'the Male Sex Role.'"
14 Tajfel and Turner, "Social Identity Theory"; Leach, Ellemers, and Barreto, "Group Virtue."
15 Farrell, *Myth of Male Power*.
16 Johansson and Vinthagen, *Conceptualizing "Everyday Resistance,"* 81.
17 Hollander and Einwohner, "Conceptualizing Resistance."
18 Burke, "Identity Control Theory."
19 Bridges and Pascoe, "Hybrid Masculinities."
20 Burke, "Identity Control Theory."
21 Banet-Weiser, *Empowered*.
22 Goodwin, Jasper, and Polletta, "Emotional Dimensions."
23 Taylor and Whittier, "Collective Identity."
24 Hunt and Benford, "Collective Identity."
25 A large literature on moral licensing theory shows that when people behave morally they are more likely to behave immorally later. See Blanken, van de Ven, and Zeelenberg, "Meta-analytic Review."

2. STRAIGHT, WHITE, CIS MEN AT THE INTERSECTION OF PRIVILEGE

1 Matthew is drawing on a metaphor used by feminists to contradict the claim that "not all men" are dangerous or threatening. The idea is that even if only a few candies in a bowl of Skittles are poisonous, one would be wary of eating from the bowl. Just a few months before our interview, Donald Trump Jr. used the metaphor in a tweet as a dog-whistle argument against granting refugee status to Syrians fleeing war. See Nelson, "Strange History."
2 Coston and Kimmel, "White Men as the New Victims."
3 Ridgeway, *Framed by Gender*.

4   McCall, "Complexity of Intersectionality."
5   Collins, "Learning from the Outsider Within."
6   Crenshaw, "Demarginalizing the Intersection"; Crenshaw, "Mapping the Margins."
7   See table A.3 in the Appendix: Methods for complete demographic information.
8   Ridgeway and Kricheli-Katz, "Intersecting Cultural Beliefs."
9   McIntosh, "White Privilege and Male Privilege," 377.
10 McIntosh, "White Privilege and Male Privilege," 378.
11 Rachlinski and Wistrich, "Benevolent Sexism in Judges."
12 Hate crimes did increase during election time in 2016. See Levin and Grisham, "Final US Status Report."
13 For example, see Uwujaren, "Why Our Feminism Must Be Intersectional."
14 Fahrenthold, "Trump Recorded."
15 De Boise, "I'm Not Homophobic"; Eisen and Yamashita, "Borrowing from Femininity."
16 François, "Pass the Mic."
17 Levchak, *Microaggressions and Modern Racism*; Jones, "Conflicted."
18 See Hartsock, "Feminist Standpoint"; Hartsock, *Money, Sex, and Power*.
19 See African American Policy Forum, "Say Her Name"; Samuels, Mehta, and Wiederkehr, "Why Black Women Are Often Missing."
20 Berbrier, "Victim Ideology"; Carian, "'No Seat at the Party.'"
21 Parker, Horowitz, and Stepler, "On Gender Differences."
22 Carian, "Men's Rights Activism."

3. MAKING INEQUALITY UNSOLVABLE

1   Risman, *Gender Vertigo*; Martin, "Gender as Social Institution"; Carian and Johnson, "Agency Myth"; West and Zimmerman, "Doing Gender."
2   Ridgeway, "Framed Before We Know It"; Rudman, "Self-Promotion as a Risk Factor"; Prentice and Carranza, "What Women and Men Should Be."
3   West and Zimmerman, "Doing Gender"; Cotter, Hermsen, and Vanneman, *Gender Inequality at Work*; Sayer, "Gender, Time and Inequality."
4   Carian and Johnson, "Agency Myth"; Turner, "Sponsored and Contest Mobility."
5   Carian and Johnson, "Agency Myth."
6   Charles and Grusky, *Occupational Ghettos*.
7   Pedulla and Thébaud, "Can We Finish the Revolution?"; Haas, "Parental Leave and Gender Equality."
8   Carian and Johnson, "Agency Myth."
9   Cotter, Hermsen, and Vanneman, "End of the Gender Revolution?"
10 Carian and Johnson, "Agency Myth."
11 Parker, Horowitz, and Stepler, "On Gender Differences."
12 Carian and Johnson, "Agency Myth."
13 Ross, "Intuitive Psychologist"; Gilbert and Malone, "Correspondence Bias."
14 Meyer and Rowan, "Institutionalized Organizations"; Meyer and Jepperson, "'Actors' of Modern Society."

15 Carian and Johnson, "Agency Myth."
16 Phillips, "'They're Rapists.'"
17 Mason, "Gendered Embodiment"; Bielby and Baron, "Men and Women at Work."
18 Van Valkenburgh, "Digesting the Red Pill"; Jackson and Rees, "Appalling Appeal of Nature," 918.
19 Ruti, *Age of Scientific Sexism*, 15.
20 Ruti, *Age of Scientific Sexism*.
21 Brownmiller, *Against Our Will*.
22 Jackson and Rees, "Appalling Appeal of Nature."
23 Gökarıksel, Neubert, and Smith, "Demographic Fever Dreams."
24 Guzzo and Hayford, "Pathways to Parenthood."
25 Rothermel, Kelly, and Jasser, "Of Victims, Mass Murder, and 'Real Men.'"
26 Ispa-Landa and Risman, "Gender Revolution on Greek Row."
27 West and Zimmerman, "Doing Gender."
28 Carian and Johnson, "Agency Myth."
29 Carian and Johnson, "Agency Myth"; Pedulla and Thébaud, "Can We Finish the Revolution?"
30 Carian and Johnson, "Agency Myth."
31 Banet-Weiser, *Empowered*.
32 Carian and Johnson, "Agency Myth."

4. THE LIMITATIONS OF IDENTITY-DRIVEN ACTIVISM

1 See the Appendix: Methods.
2 Johansson and Vinthagen, *Conceptualizing "Everyday Resistance."*
3 Scott, *Weapons of the Weak*; Scott, *Domination and the Arts of Resistance*; Johansson and Vinthagen, *Conceptualizing "Everyday Resistance,"* 26.
4 Rottenberg, "Rise of Neoliberal Feminism."
5 Clatterbaugh, "Literature of the U.S. Men's Movements."
6 Pinsof and Haselton, "Effect of the Promiscuity Stereotype."
7 Rottenberg, "Rise of Neoliberal Feminism."
8 Williams, "Glass Escalator."
9 Carian, "'We're All in This Together.'"
10 E.g., Harding, *Whose Science? Whose Knowledge?*
11 Men's rights activists have worked to defund services for women victims of domestic violence. See Dragiewicz, *Equality with a Vengeance*.
12 Goldin, "Grand Gender Convergence."
13 This quote is often attributed to right-wing commentator Ben Shapiro.
14 Banet-Weiser and Portwood-Stacer, "Traffic in Feminism."

5. CONTEXTS OF MOBILIZATION

1 Gonzales and Domonoske, "Voters Recall Aaron Persky."
2 Baker, "Here's the Powerful Letter."
3 Brockes, "Chanel Miller."

4. Baker, "Here's the Powerful Letter."
5. Carian and Johnson, "Agency Myth."
6. Messner, *Politics of Masculinities*; Farrell, *Myth of Male Power*.
7. For a discussion of this contradiction and how men's rights activists use "responsibility" toward male supremacist ends, see de Coning and Ebin, "Men's Rights Activists."
8. Brownmiller, *Against Our Will*, 33, emphasis original.
9. Farrell, *Myth of Male Power*; Sommers, *Who Stole Feminism?*
10. The case continues to play an important role in the far right's imagination. See Wiedeman, "Duke Lacrosse Scandal."
11. It is important to recognize that Daniel uses a purely cultural explanation here that ignores the structural reasons (e.g., poverty, immigration status, discrimination) why Latino boys and men might "choose" to work rather than continue their education.
12. All (31) of the feminist men and nearly all of the men's rights activists (28 of 31) I interviewed enrolled in college at some point in their lives (see table A.3 in the Appendix: Methods for the educational attainment of respondents).
13. Crosnoe, "Friendships in Childhood and Adolescence."
14. Crosnoe, "Friendships in Childhood and Adolescence."
15. Kalmijn, "Sex Segregation of Friendship Networks."
16. Bolzendahl and Myers, "Feminist Attitudes."
17. This has been critiqued in popular media. See Mei, "21 Reminders"; Hains, "Pride in Being a '#GirlDad'"; Peters, "It Shouldn't Take Having a Daughter."
18. Kovacs, Parker, and Hoffman, "Behavioral, Affective, and Social Correlates."
19. Handgraaf et al. find that individuals feel what the authors call "social responsibility"—and what I would call "paternalism"—when the person with whom they are interacting has no power. Handgraaf et al., "Less Power or Powerless?"
20. See table A.3 in the Appendix: Methods for complete demographic information.
21. Faludi, *Backlash*; Banet-Weiser, *Empowered*.
22. Crossley, *Finding Feminism*; Crossley, "Facebook Feminism"; Sheinin et al., "Betty Friedan to Beyoncé"; Banet-Weiser, *Empowered*.
23. Benford and Snow, "Framing Processes."
24. Snow et al., "Frame Alignment Processes," 464.
25. Farrell, *Myth of Male Power*.
26. Leach, Ellemers, and Barreto, "Group Virtue."
27. Kitts, "Mobilizing in Black Boxes"; Passy, "Social Networks Matter."
28. Snow et al., "Frame Alignment Processes."
29. Bolzendahl and Myers, "Feminist Attitudes."
30. Kovacs, Parker, and Hoffman, "Behavioral, Affective, and Social Correlates."
31. Booth and Hess, "Cross-Sex Friendship"; Markiewicz, Devine, and Kausilas, "Friendships of Women and Men at Work."
32. Carian, "'We're All in This Together.'"
33. Jerolmack and Khan, "Talk Is Cheap"; Orbuch, "People's Accounts Count."

CONCLUSION

1 Gerstein and Ward, "Exclusive"; Madden, Oliver, and Yang, "Pro-choice Demonstrators Rally."
2 Totenberg and McCammon, "Supreme Court Overturns Roe v. Wade."
3 *Dobbs v. Jackson Women's Health Organization*, no. 19-1392, 597 U.S. ___ (2022).
4 Madden, Oliver, and Yang, "Pro-choice Demonstrators Rally."
5 Ziegler, *Dollars for Life*.
6 Gupta, "Voices of Men."
7 Li, Heyrana, and Nguyen, "Discrepant Abortion Reporting."
8 Reger, *Everywhere and Nowhere*.
9 Brockes, "Chanel Miller."
10 Carian and Johnson, "Agency Myth."
11 Grauerholz and Scuteri, "Learning to Role-Take."
12 López et al., "Understanding the Attacks on Critical Race Theory"; Kerr, "For Scholars of Women's Studies"; Redden, "Gender Studies Scholars."
13 Bonilla-Silva, *Racism without Racists*.
14 Kitts, "Mobilizing in Black Boxes"; Passy, "Social Networks Matter."
15 Bondi, "Locating Identity Politics"; Rottenberg, "Rise of Neoliberal Feminism."
16 hooks, *Feminism Is for Everybody*, 6.
17 Rottenberg, "Rise of Neoliberal Feminism"; Carian and Johnson, "Agency Myth."
18 hooks, *Feminism Is for Everybody*.
19 Woodly et al., "Politics of Care," 891.
20 Collins, "Learning from the Outsider Within."
21 Messner, *Politics of Masculinities*.
22 Smith and Freyd, "Institutional Betrayal," 577.
23 Edelman and Cabrera, "Sex-Based Harassment and Symbolic Compliance."
24 Bedera, "Illusion of Choice."
25 Sue et al., "Racial Microaggressions," 271.
26 Young-Jin Kim, Nguyen, and Block, "360-Degree Experience of Workplace Microaggressions"; Nadal et al., "Sexual Orientation Microaggressions."
27 Metinyurt, Haynes-Baratz, and Bond, "Systematic Review of Interventions to Address Workplace Bias"; Jones, "Conflicted."
28 Messner, Greenberg, and Peretz, *Some Men*.
29 Carian, "Inversive Sexism Scale."
30 Sommers, "Title IX"; Bowles, "Push for Gender Equality." See any number of family law firms using the claim that men are discriminated against in the family court system to attract men clients.
31 Brumback, "Watch."
32 Kornfield and Knowles, "Captain Who Said Spa Shootings Suspect."
33 See, for example, Moonshot, "Violent Misogyny"; Moonshot, "Understanding and Preventing Incel Violence."
34 Schmidt, "'I'm Not a Sexist.'"

35 E.g., Weiss, "Meet the Renegades of the Intellectual Dark Web"; Ferguson, "White Men Are Bad?"; Sommers, "Title IX."
36 E.g., Taub, "On Social Media's Fringes."
37 Moskalenko et al., "Incel Ideology"; Speckhard et al., "Involuntary Celibates' Experiences."
38 Hastings, Jones, and Stolte, "Involuntary Celibates."
39 Morton et al., "Asking Incels."
40 Burke, "Identity Control Theory."
41 Sparkes and Smith, "Sport, Spinal Cord Injury."
42 Somers, "Narrative Constitution of Identity."
43 Prattes, "Caring Masculinities and Race."

APPENDIX

1 Carian, "'We're All in This Together'"; Carian, "Inversive Sexism Scale."
2 Blake, "Mad Men"; Bowles, "Push for Gender Equality"; Rensin, "Internet Is Full."
3 Kurtzleben, "More Than Twice."
4 Carian and Johnson, "Agency Myth."
5 Flyvbjerg, "Five Misunderstandings."
6 Lamont, *Money, Morals, and Manners*.
7 Jerolmack and Khan, "Talk Is Cheap"; Vaisey, "Motivation and Justification."
8 Lamont and Swidler, "Methodological Pluralism."
9 Orbuch, "People's Accounts Count."
10 Hochschild, *Strangers in Their Own Land*.
11 Pugh, "What Good Are Interviews."
12 Jaye, *Red Pill*.
13 Take, for example, President Trump telling the Proud Boys to "stand back and stand by" during a 2020 presidential debate. See Frenkel and Karni, "Proud Boys Celebrate."
14 Though we had originally planned to meet in person, one men's rights activist requested a phone interview instead for an added level of anonymity. I interviewed one feminist over the phone because his schedule did not allow for an in-person meeting.
15 Jaye, *Red Pill*.
16 Hsieh and Shannon, "Three Approaches."
17 It was not lost on me that these techniques are often used by women when dating. See RAINN, "Online Dating."
18 Collins, "Learning from the Outsider Within."

BIBLIOGRAPHY

Abascal, Maria. "Contraction as a Response to Group Threat: Demographic Decline and Whites' Classification of People Who Are Ambiguously White." *American Sociological Review* 85, no. 2 (2020): 298–322.
Acker, Joan. "Hierarchies, Jobs, Bodies: A Theory of Gendered Organizations." *Gender & Society* 4, no. 2 (June 1, 1990): 139–58.
African American Policy Forum. "Say Her Name: Resisting Police Brutality Against Black Women." July 2015. www.aapf.org.
Anderson, Eric. *Inclusive Masculinity: The Changing Nature of Masculinities*. New York: Routledge, 2009.
Arons, Jessica. "Lifetime Losses: The Career Wage Gap." Center for American Progress Action Fund, December 2008.
Baker, Katie J. M. "Here's the Powerful Letter the Stanford Victim Read to Her Attacker." *BuzzFeed News*, June 3, 2016. www.buzzfeednews.com.
Baker, Phyllis L., and Douglas R. Hotek. "Grappling with Gender: Exploring Masculinity and Gender in the Bodies, Performances, and Emotions of Scholastic Wrestlers." *Journal of Feminist Scholarship* 1, no. 1 (2011): 49–64.
Banet-Weiser, Sarah. *Empowered: Popular Feminism and Popular Misogyny*. Durham, NC: Duke University Press, 2018.
Banet-Weiser, Sarah, and Laura Portwood-Stacer. "The Traffic in Feminism: An Introduction to the Commentary and Criticism on Popular Feminism." *Feminist Media Studies* 17, no. 5 (2017): 884–88.
Barroso, Amanda. "61% of U.S. Women Say 'Feminist' Describes Them Well; Many See Feminism as Empowering, Polarizing." Pew Research Center, July 7, 2020. www.pewresearch.org.
Bedera, Nicole. "The Illusion of Choice: Organizational Dependency and the Neutralization of University Sexual Assault Complaints." *Law & Policy* 44, no. 3 (2022): 208–29.
Benford, Robert D., and David A. Snow. "Framing Processes and Social Movements: An Overview and Assessment." *Annual Review of Sociology* 26 (2000): 611–39.
Berbrier, Mitch. "The Victim Ideology of White Supremacists and White Separatists in the United States." *Sociological Focus* 33, no. 2 (2000): 175–91.
Bianchi, Suzanne M., John P. Robinson, and Melissa A. Milke. *The Changing Rhythms of American Family Life*. New York: Russell Sage Foundation, 2006.

Bielby, William T., and James N. Baron. "Men and Women at Work: Sex Segregation and Statistical Discrimination." *American Journal of Sociology* 91, no. 4 (January 1, 1986): 759–99.

Bjorklund, Eric, Andrew P. Davis, and Jessica Pfaffendorf. "Urine or You're Out: Racialized Economic Threat and the Determinants of Welfare Drug Testing Policy in the United States, 2009–2015." *Sociological Quarterly* 59, no. 3 (July 3, 2018): 407–23.

Black, Michele C., Kathleen C. Basile, Matthew J. Breiding, Sharon G. Smith, Mikel L. Walters, Melissa T. Merrick, Jieru Chen, and Mark R. Stevens. "The National Intimate Partner and Sexual Violence Survey: 2010 Summary Report." National Center for Injury Prevention and Control, 2011.

Blake, Mariah. "Mad Men: Inside the Men's Rights Movement—and the Army of Misogynists and Trolls It Spawned." *Mother Jones*, January/February 2015. www.motherjones.com.

Blanken, Irene, Niels van de Ven, and Marcel Zeelenberg. "A Meta-analytic Review of Moral Licensing." *Personality and Social Psychology Bulletin* 41, no. 4 (2015): 540–58.

Bolzendahl, Catherine I., and Daniel J. Myers. "Feminist Attitudes and Support for Gender Equality: Opinion Change in Women and Men, 1974–1998." *Social Forces* 83, no. 2 (December 1, 2004): 759–89.

Bondi, Liz. "Locating Identity Politics." In *Place and the Politics of Identity*, edited by Michael Keith and Steve Pile, 89–106. New York: Routledge, 1993.

Bonilla-Silva, Eduardo. *Racism without Racists: Color-Blind Racism and the Persistence of Racial Inequality in the United States*. Lanham, MD: Rowman & Littlefield, 2006.

Booth, Alan, and Elaine Hess. "Cross-Sex Friendship." *Journal of Marriage and Family* 36, no. 1 (1974): 38–47.

Bowles, Nellie. "Push for Gender Equality in Tech? Some Men Say It's Gone Too Far." *New York Times*, September 23, 2017. www.nytimes.com.

Boyd, Susan B., and Elizabeth Sheehy. "Men's Groups: Challenging Feminism." *Canadian Journal of Women and the Law* 28, no. 1 (2016): 5–10.

Bridges, Tristan S. "Men Just Weren't Made to Do This: Performances of Drag at 'Walk a Mile in Her Shoes' Marches." *Gender & Society* 24, no. 1 (February 1, 2010): 5–30.

———. "A Very 'Gay' Straight? Hybrid Masculinities, Sexual Aesthetics, and the Changing Relationship between Masculinity and Homophobia." *Gender & Society* 28, no. 1 (2014): 58–82.

Bridges, Tristan, and C. J. Pascoe. "Hybrid Masculinities: New Directions in the Sociology of Men and Masculinities." *Sociology Compass* 8, no. 3 (March 1, 2014): 246–58.

Brockes, Emma. "Chanel Miller on Why She Refuses to Be Reduced to the 'Brock Turner Sexual Assault Victim.'" *Guardian*, September 25, 2019. www.theguardian.com.

Brownmiller, Susan. *Against Our Will: Men, Women and Rape*. New York: Open Road Media, 2013.

Brumback, Kate. "Watch: Atlanta Police Hold Briefing on Spa Shooting." *PBS News Hour*, March 18, 2021. www.pbs.org.

Burke, Peter J. "Identity Control Theory." In *The Blackwell Encyclopedia of Sociology*, edited by George Ritzer, 2202–7. Malden, MA: Blackwell, 2007.

Burstein, Paul. "Attacking Sex Discrimination in the Labor Market: A Study in Law and Politics." *Social Forces* 67, no. 3 (March 1, 1989): 641–65.

Carian, Emily K. "The Inversive Sexism Scale: Endorsement of the Belief That Women Are Privileged." In *Male Supremacism in the United States: From Patriarchal Traditionalism to Misogynist Incels and the Alt-Right*, edited by Emily K. Carian, Alex DiBranco, and Chelsea Ebin, 21–47. New York: Routledge, 2022.

———. "Men's Rights Activism." In *The Wiley-Blackwell Encyclopedia of Social and Political Movements*, edited by David A. Snow, Donatella della Porta, Doug J. McAdam, and Bert Klandermans, 1290–93. Hoboken, NJ: Wiley-Blackwell, 2022.

———. "'No Seat at the Party': Mobilizing White Masculinity in the Men's Rights Movement." *Sociological Focus* 55, no. 1 (January 2, 2022): 27–47.

———. "'We're All in This Together': Leveraging a Personal Action Frame in Two Men's Rights Forums." *Mobilization* 27, no. 1 (March 30, 2022): 47–68.

Carian, Emily K., and Amy L. Johnson. "The Agency Myth: Persistence in Individual Explanations for Gender Inequality." *Social Problems* 69, no. 1 (2022): 123–42.

Carian, Emily K., and Tagart Cain Sobotka. "Playing the Trump Card: Masculinity Threat and the U.S. 2016 Presidential Election." *Socius* 4 (2018): 1–6.

Charles, Maria, and David B. Grusky. *Occupational Ghettos: The Worldwide Segregation of Women and Men*. Stanford, CA: Stanford University Press, 2004.

Cherlin, Andrew J. *Marriage, Divorce, Remarriage*. Rev. ed. Cambridge, MA: Harvard University Press, 1992.

Chowdhury, Romit. "Conditions of Emergence: The Formation of Men's Rights Groups in Contemporary India." *Indian Journal of Gender Studies* 21, no. 1 (February 1, 2014): 27–53.

Clatterbaugh, Kenneth. "Literature of the U.S. Men's Movements." *Signs* 25, no. 3 (April 1, 2000): 883–94.

Cohn, D'vera, Gretchen Livingston, and Wendy Wang. "Stay-at-Home Mothers on the Rise." Pew Research Center, April 8, 2014. www.pewsocialtrends.org.

Collins, Caitlyn, Leah Ruppanner, Liana Christin Landivar, and William J. Scarborough. "The Gendered Consequences of a Weak Infrastructure of Care: School Reopening Plans and Parents' Employment during the COVID-19 Pandemic." *Gender & Society* 35, no. 2 (April 1, 2021): 180–93.

Collins, Patricia Hill. "Learning from the Outsider Within: The Sociological Significance of Black Feminist Thought." *Social Problems* 33, no. 6 (1986): S14–42.

Coltrane, Scott R. "Household Labor and the Routine Production of Gender." *Social Problems* 36, no. 5 (December 1, 1989): 473–90.

Connell, Raewyn. *Masculinities*. 2nd ed. Berkeley: University of California Press, 2005.

Connell, Raewyn, and James W. Messerschmidt. "Hegemonic Masculinity: Rethinking the Concept." *Gender & Society* 19, no. 6 (2005): 829–59.

Coston, B. Ethan, and Michael Kimmel. "White Men as the New Victims: Reverse Discrimination Cases and the Men's Rights Movement." *Nevada Law Journal* 13, no. 2 (2013): 368–85.

Cotter, David A., Joan M. Hermsen, Seth Ovadia, and Reeve Vanneman. "The Glass Ceiling Effect." *Social Forces* 80, no. 2 (December 1, 2001): 655–81.

Cotter, David, Joan M. Hermsen, and Reeve Vanneman. "The End of the Gender Revolution? Gender Role Attitudes from 1977 to 2008." *American Journal of Sociology* 117, no. 1 (2011): 259–89.

———. *Gender Inequality at Work*. New York: Russell Sage Foundation, 2004.

Crenshaw, Kimberlé. "Demarginalizing the Intersection of Race and Sex: A Black Feminist Critique of Antidiscrimination Doctrine, Feminist Theory and Antiracist Politics." *University of Chicago Legal Forum* 1989, no. 1 (1989): 139–67.

———. "Mapping the Margins: Intersectionality, Identity Politics, and Violence against Women of Color." *Stanford Law Review* 43, no. 6 (1991): 1241–99.

Crosnoe, Robert. "Friendships in Childhood and Adolescence: The Life Course and New Directions." *Social Psychology Quarterly* 63, no. 4 (2000): 377–91.

Crossley, Alison Dahl. "Facebook Feminism: Social Media, Blogs, and New Technologies of Contemporary U.S. Feminism." *Mobilization* 20, no. 2 (July 22, 2015): 253–68.

———. *Finding Feminism: Millennial Activists and the Unfinished Gender Revolution*. New York: New York University Press, 2017.

Davis, Nancy J., and Robert V. Robinson. "Men's and Women's Consciousness of Gender Inequality: Austria, West Germany, Great Britain, and the United States." *American Sociological Review* 56, no. 1 (1991): 72–84.

de Boise, Sam. "'I'm Not Homophobic, 'I've Got Gay Friends': Evaluating the Validity of Inclusive Masculinity." *Men and Masculinities* 18, no. 3 (August 1, 2015): 318–39.

de Coning, Alexis, and Chelsea Ebin. "Men's Rights Activists, Personal Responsibility, and the End of Welfare." In *Male Supremacism in the United States: From Patriarchal Traditionalism to Misogynist Incels and the Alt-Right*, edited by Emily K. Carian, Alex DiBranco, and Chelsea Ebin, 142–63. New York: Routledge, 2022.

Dobbs v. Jackson Women's Health Organization. No. 19-1392. 597 U.S. ____ (2022).

Dragiewicz, Molly. *Equality with a Vengeance: Men's Rights Groups, Battered Women, and Antifeminist Backlash*. Boston: Northeastern University Press, 2011.

Edelman, Lauren B., and Jessica Cabrera. "Sex-Based Harassment and Symbolic Compliance." *Annual Review of Law and Social Science* 16, no. 1 (October 13, 2020): 361–83.

Eisen, Daniel B., and Liann Yamashita. "Borrowing from Femininity: The Caring Man, Hybrid Masculinities, and Maintaining Male Dominance." *Men and Masculinities* 22, no. 5 (December 1, 2019): 801–20.

England, Paula. "The Gender Revolution: Uneven and Stalled." *Gender & Society* 24, no. 2 (April 1, 2010): 149–66.

England, Paula, and Su Li. "Desegregation Stalled: The Changing Gender Composition of College Majors, 1971–2002." *Gender & Society* 20, no. 5 (October 1, 2006): 657–77.

Fahrenthold, David A. "Trump Recorded Having Extremely Lewd Conversation about Women in 2005." *Washington Post*, October 7, 2016. www.washingtonpost.com.

Faludi, Susan. *Backlash: The Undeclared War Against American Women*. New York: Three Rivers Press, 1991.

———. *Stiffed: The Betrayal of the American Man*. New York: Harper Perennial, 1999.

Farrell, Warren. *The Myth of Male Power: Why Men Are the Disposable Sex*. New York: Simon & Schuster, 1993.

Ferguson, Niall. "White Men Are Bad?" *Boston Globe*, April 2, 2018. www.bostonglobe.com.

Fisher, Bonnie S., Francis T. Cullen, and Michael G. Turner. "The Sexual Victimization of College Women." U.S. Department of Justice, 2000.

Flyvbjerg, Bent. "Five Misunderstandings about Case-Study Research." *Qualitative Inquiry* 12, no. 2 (April 1, 2006): 219–45.

François, Gloria. "Pass the Mic: Identifying and Eradicating Performative Allyship." *McGill Daily*, February 19, 2018. www.mcgilldaily.com.

Freedman, Estelle. *No Turning Back: The History of Feminism and the Future of Women*. New York: Random House, 2007.

Frenkel, Sheera, and Annie Karni. "Proud Boys Celebrate Trump's 'Stand By' Remark about Them at the Debate." *New York Times*, September 30, 2020. www.nytimes.com.

Friedan, Betty. *The Feminine Mystique*. Repr. ed. New York: Norton, 2001.

Fry, Richard, and Renee Stepler. "Women May Never Make Up Half of U.S. Workforce." Pew Research Center, January 31, 2017. www.pewresearch.org.

Gatwiri, Kathomi. "Racial Microaggressions at Work: Reflections from Black African Professionals in Australia." *British Journal of Social Work* 51, no. 2 (April 3, 2021): 655–72.

Gerstein, Josh, and Alexander Ward. "Exclusive: Supreme Court Has Voted to Overturn Abortion Rights, Draft Opinion Shows." *Politico*, May 2, 2022. www.politico.com.

Gilbert, Daniel T., and Patrick S. Malone. "The Correspondence Bias." *Psychological Bulletin* 117, no. 1 (January 1995): 21–38.

Ging, Debbie. "Bros v. Hos: Postfeminism, Anti-feminism and the Toxic Turn in Digital Gender Politics." In *Gender Hate Online: Understanding the New Anti-feminism*, edited by Debbie Ging and Eugenia Siapera, 45–67. London: Palgrave Macmillan, 2019.

Gökarıksel, Banu, Christopher Neubert, and Sara Smith. "Demographic Fever Dreams: Fragile Masculinity and Population Politics in the Rise of the Global Right." *Signs* 44, no. 3 (March 1, 2019): 561–87.

Goldin, Claudia. "A Grand Gender Convergence: Its Last Chapter." *American Economic Review* 104, no. 4 (April 2014): 1091–1119.

Goldin, Claudia, and Lawrence F. Katz. "The Power of the Pill: Oral Contraceptives and Women's Career and Marriage Decisions." *Journal of Political Economy* 110, no. 4 (2002): 730–70.

Gonzales, Richard, and Camila Domonoske. "Voters Recall Aaron Persky, Judge Who Sentenced Brock Turner." NPR, June 5, 2018. www.npr.org.
Goodwin, Jeff, James M. Jasper, and Francesca Polletta. "Emotional Dimensions of Social Movements." In *The Blackwell Companion to Social Movements*, edited by David A. Snow, Sarah A. Soule, and Hanspeter Kriesi, 413–32. Malden, MA: Blackwell, 2004.
Grauerholz, Elizabeth, and Gina M. Scuteri. "Learning to Role-Take: A Teaching Technique to Enhance Awareness of the 'Other.'" *Teaching Sociology* 17, no. 4 (1989): 480–83.
Gupta, Alisha Haridasani. "The Voices of Men Affected by Abortion." *New York Times*, June 25, 2022. www.nytimes.com.
Guzzo, Karen Benjamin, and Sarah R. Hayford. "Pathways to Parenthood in Social and Family Context: Decade in Review, 2020." *Journal of Marriage and the Family* 82, no. 1 (February 2020): 117–44.
Haas, Linda. "Parental Leave and Gender Equality: Lessons from the European Union." *Review of Policy Research* 20, no. 1 (January 2003): 89–114.
Hains, Rebecca. "Pride in Being a '#GirlDad' Is Good, but It Shows How Far We Still Have to Go." *Washington Post*, February 3, 2020. www.washingtonpost.com.
Handgraaf, Michel J. J., Eric Van Dijk, Riël C. Vermunt, Henk A. M. Wilke, and Carsten K. W. De Dreu. "Less Power or Powerless? Egocentric Empathy Gaps and the Irony of Having Little versus No Power in Social Decision Making." *Journal of Personality and Social Psychology* 95, no. 5 (November 2008): 1136–49.
Harding, Sandra. *Whose Science? Whose Knowledge? Thinking from Women's Lives.* Ithaca, NY: Cornell University Press, 1991.
Hartsock, Nancy C. M. "The Feminist Standpoint: Developing the Ground for a Specifically Feminist Historical Materialism." In *Discovering Reality: Feminist Perspectives on Epistemology, Metaphysics, Methodology, and Philosophy of Science*, edited by Sandra Harding and Merrill B. Hintikka, 283–310. New York: Kluwer, 1983.
———. *Money, Sex, and Power: Toward a Feminist Historical Materialism.* New York: Longman, 1983.
Hasday, Jill Elaine. "Contest and Consent: A Legal History of Marital Rape." *California Law Review* 88 (2000): 1373–1506.
Hastings, Zoe, David Jones, and Laura Stolte. "Involuntary Celibates: Background for Practitioners." *Organization for the Prevention of Violence*, May 2020. https://preventviolence.ca.
Hess, Cynthia, Jessica Milli, Hegewisch Ariane, Stephanie Román, Julie Anderson, and Justine Augeri. "Employment and Earnings." In *The Status of Women in the States: 2015*, 37–82. Institute for Women's Policy Research, 2015.
Hochschild, Arlie Russell. *Strangers in Their Own Land: Anger and Mourning on the American Right.* New York: New Press, 2016.
Hodapp, Christa. *Men's Rights, Gender, and Social Media.* Lanham, MD: Rowman & Littlefield, 2017.

Hollander, Jocelyn A., and Rachel L. Einwohner. "Conceptualizing Resistance." *Sociological Forum* 19, no. 4 (December 1, 2004): 533–54.

Hong, Nicole, Mihir Zaveri, and William K. Rashbaum. "Inside the Violent and Misogynistic World of Roy Den Hollander." *New York Times*, July 26, 2020. www.nytimes.com.

hooks, bell. *Feminism Is for Everybody: Passionate Politics*. Boston: South End, 2000.

———. *Feminist Theory: From Margin to Center*. Boston: South End, 1984.

Hsieh, Hsiu-Fang, and Sarah E. Shannon. "Three Approaches to Qualitative Content Analysis." *Qualitative Health Research* 15, no. 9 (November 2005): 1277–88.

Hunt, Scott A., and Robert D. Benford. "Collective Identity, Solidarity, and Commitment." In *The Blackwell Companion to Social Movements*, edited by David A. Snow, Sarah A. Soule, and Hanspeter Kriesi, 433–57. Malden, MA: Blackwell, 2004.

Ispa-Landa, Simone, and Barbara J. Risman. "The Gender Revolution on Greek Row." *Contexts* 20, no. 3 (August 1, 2021): 16–21.

Jackson, Robert Max. *Destined for Equality: The Inevitable Rise of Women's Status*. Cambridge, MA: Harvard University Press, 1998.

Jackson, Stevi, and Amanda Rees. "The Appalling Appeal of Nature: The Popular Influence of Evolutionary Psychology as a Problem for Sociology." *Sociology* 41, no. 5 (October 1, 2007): 917–30.

Jaye, Cassie. *The Red Pill*. DVD. Cleveland, OH: Gravitas Ventures, 2016.

Jerolmack, Colin, and Shamus Khan. "Talk Is Cheap: Ethnography and the Attitudinal Fallacy." *Sociological Methods & Research* 43, no. 2 (March 9, 2014): 178–209.

Johansson, Anna, and Stellan Vinthagen. *Conceptualizing "Everyday Resistance": A Transdisciplinary Approach*. New York: Routledge, 2020.

Jones, Angel M. "Conflicted: How Black Women Negotiate Their Responses to Racial Microaggressions at a Historically White Institution." *Race Ethnicity and Education* 25, no. 2 (May 4, 2021): 738–53.

Juhn, Chinhui, and Simon Potter. "Changes in Labor Force Participation in the United States." *Journal of Economic Perspectives* 20, no. 3 (2006): 27–46.

Kalmijn, Matthijs. "Sex Segregation of Friendship Networks: Individual and Structural Determinants of Having Cross-Sex Friends." *European Sociological Review* 18, no. 1 (March 1, 2002): 101–17.

Kerr, Emma. "For Scholars of Women's Studies, It's Been a Dangerous Year." *Chronicle of Higher Education*, February 11, 2018. www.chronicle.com.

Kimmel, Michael S. *Angry White Men: American Masculinity at the End of an Era*. Repr. ed. New York: Nation Books, 2017.

Kimmel, Michael, and Abby L. Ferber. "'White Men Are This Nation': Right-Wing Militias and the Restoration of Rural American Masculinity." *Rural Sociology* 65, no. 4 (December 2000): 582–604.

Kimmel, Michael S., and Thomas E. Mosmiller, eds. *Against the Tide: Pro-feminist Men in the United States: 1776–1990: A Documentary History*. Boston: Beacon, 1992.

Kitts, James. "Mobilizing in Black Boxes: Social Networks and Participation in Social Movement Organizations." *Mobilization* 5, no. 2 (2000): 241–57.

Kornfield, Meryl, and Hannah Knowles. "Captain Who Said Spa Shootings Suspect Had 'Bad Day' No Longer a Spokesman on Case, Official Says." *Washington Post*, March 18, 2021. www.washingtonpost.com.

Kovacs, Donna M., Jeffrey G. Parker, and Lois W. Hoffman. "Behavioral, Affective, and Social Correlates of Involvement in Cross-Sex Friendship in Elementary School." *Child Development* 67, no. 5 (October 1996): 2269–86.

Kurtzleben, Danielle. "More Than Twice as Many Women Are Running for Congress in 2018 Compared with 2016." NPR, February 20, 2018. www.npr.org.

Lamont, Michèle. *Money, Morals, and Manners: The Culture of the French and American Upper-Middle Class*. Chicago: University of Chicago Press, 1992.

Lamont, Michèle, and Ann Swidler. "Methodological Pluralism and the Possibilities and Limits of Interviewing." *Qualitative Sociology* 37, no. 2 (June 1, 2014): 153–71.

Leach, Colin Wayne, Naomi Ellemers, and Manuela Barreto. "Group Virtue: The Importance of Morality (vs. Competence and Sociability) in the Positive Evaluation of In-Groups." *Journal of Personality and Social Psychology* 93, no. 2 (August 2007): 234–49.

Levanon, Asaf, Paula England, and Paul Allison. "Occupational Feminization and Pay: Assessing Causal Dynamics Using 1950–2000 U.S. Census Data." *Social Forces* 88, no. 2 (2009): 865–91.

Levchak, Charisse C. *Microaggressions and Modern Racism: Endurance and Evolution*. London: Palgrave Macmillan, 2018.

Levin, Brian, and Kevin E. Grisham. "Final US Status Report: Hate Crime Analysis and Forecast 2016/2017." Center for the Study of Hate and Extremism, 2017.

Li, Victoria M., Katrina J. Heyrana, and Brian T. Nguyen. "Discrepant Abortion Reporting by Interview Methodology among Men from the United States National Survey of Family Growth (2015–2017)." *Contraception* 112 (August 2022): 111–15.

Linder, Chris, and Rachael C. Johnson. "Exploring the Complexities of Men as Allies in Feminist Movements." *Journal of Critical Thought and Praxis* 4, no. 1 (2015).

López, Francesca, Alex Molnar, Royel Johnson, Ashley Patterson, Lawanda Ward, and Kevin Kumashiro. "Understanding the Attacks on Critical Race Theory." National Education Policy Center, 2021.

Madden, Justin, Mark Oliver, and Maya Yang. "Pro-choice Demonstrators Rally across the US over Expected Reversal of Roe v Wade—as It Happened." *Guardian*, May 14, 2022. www.theguardian.com.

Major, Brenda, Alison Blodorn, and Gregory Major Blascovich. "The Threat of Increasing Diversity: Why Many White Americans Support Trump in the 2016 Presidential Election." *Group Processes and Intergroup Relations* 21, no. 6 (September 1, 2018): 931–40.

Mangan, Katherine. "'I Want to Hear Those Charges': Noted Sociologist Defers Award Until He Can 'Make Amends.'" *Chronicle of Higher Education*, August 1, 2018. www.chronicle.com.

Mantilla, Karla. "Gendertrolling: Misogyny Adapts to New Media." *Feminist Studies* 39, no. 2 (2013): 563–70.

Markiewicz, Dorothy, Irene Devine, and Dana Kausilas. "Friendships of Women and Men at Work: Job Satisfaction and Resource Implications." *Journal of Managerial Psychology* 15, no. 2 (2000): 161–84.

Martin, Patricia Yancey. "Gender as Social Institution." *Social Forces* 82, no. 4 (June 1, 2004): 1249–73.

Mason, Katherine. "Gendered Embodiment." In *Handbook of the Sociology of Gender*, edited by Barbara J. Risman, Carissa M. Froyum, and William J. Scarborough, 95–107. Cham: Springer, 2018.

Masquelier, Charles. *Critique and Resistance in a Neoliberal Age: Towards a Narrative of Emancipation*. London: Palgrave Macmillan, 2017.

McCall, Leslie. "The Complexity of Intersectionality." *Signs* 30, no. 3 (2005): 1771–1800.

McCormack, Mark. "Hierarchy without Hegemony: Locating Boys in an Inclusive School Setting." *Sociological Perspectives* 54, no. 1 (March 1, 2011): 83–101.

McIntosh, Peggy. "White Privilege and Male Privilege." In *Race, Ethnicity, and Gender: Selected Readings*, 2nd ed., edited by Joseph F. Healey and Eileen O'Brien, 377–85. Los Angeles: Pine Forge Press, 2007.

Mei, Gina. "21 Reminders That Women Are More Than Just Daughters, Mothers, and Wives." *Cosmopolitan*, October 8, 2016. www.cosmopolitan.com.

Menzies, Robert. "Virtual Backlash: Representations of Men's 'Rights' and Feminist 'Wrongs' in Cyberspace." In *Reaction and Resistance: Feminism, Law, and Social Change*, edited by Dorothy E. Chunn, Susan Boyd, and Hester Lessard, 65–97. Vancouver: UBC Press, 2011.

Messerschmidt, James W. *Hegemonic Masculinity: Formulation, Reformulation, and Amplification*. Lanham, MD: Rowman & Littlefield, 2018.

Messner, Michael A. "The Limits of 'the Male Sex Role': An Analysis of the Men's Liberation and Men's Rights Movements' Discourse." *Gender & Society* 12, no. 3 (June 1, 1998): 255–76.

———. *Politics of Masculinities: Men in Movements*. Lanham, MD: AltaMira Press, 1997.

Messner, Michael A., Max A. Greenberg, and Tal Peretz. *Some Men: Feminist Allies and the Movement to End Violence against Women*. New York: Oxford University Press, 2015.

Metinyurt, Tuğba, Michelle C. Haynes-Baratz, and Meg A. Bond. "A Systematic Review of Interventions to Address Workplace Bias: What We Know, What We Don't, and Lessons Learned." *New Ideas in Psychology* 63 (December 1, 2021): 1–9.

Meyer, John W., and Ronald L. Jepperson. "The 'Actors' of Modern Society: The Cultural Construction of Social Agency." *Sociological Theory* 18, no. 1 (March 2000): 100–120.

Meyer, John W., and Brian Rowan. "Institutionalized Organizations: Formal Structure as Myth and Ceremony." *American Journal of Sociology* 83, no. 2 (September 1, 1977): 340–63.

Moonshot. "Understanding and Preventing Incel Violence in Canada." September 1, 2021. https://moonshotteam.com.

———. "Violent Misogyny, Mass Murder and Suicide: It's Time to Save Incels from Themselves." September 10, 2019. https://moonshotteam.com.

Morris, Max, and Eric Anderson. "'Charlie Is So Cool Like': Authenticity, Popularity and Inclusive Masculinity on YouTube." *Sociology* 49, no. 6 (December 1, 2015): 1200–1217.

Morton, Jesse, Alexander Ash, Ken Reidy, Naama Kates, Molly Ellenberg, and Anne Speckhard. "Asking Incels (Part 1): Assessing the Impacts of COVID-19 Quarantine and Coverage of the Canadian Terrorism Designation on Incel Isolation and Resentment." International Center for the Study of Violent Extremism, January 21, 2021. www.icsve.org.

Moskalenko, Sophia, Juncal Fernández-Garayzábal González, Naama Kates, and Jesse Morton. "Incel Ideology, Radicalization and Mental Health: A Survey Study." *Journal of Intelligence, Conflict, and Warfare* 4, no. 3 (January 31, 2022): 1–29.

Mutz, Diana C. "Status Threat, Not Economic Hardship, Explains the 2016 Presidential Vote." *Proceedings of the National Academy of Sciences of the United States of America* 115, no. 19 (May 8, 2018): E4330–39.

Nadal, Kevin L., Marie-Anne Issa, Jayleen Leon, Vanessa Meterko, Michelle Wideman, and Yinglee Wong. "Sexual Orientation Microaggressions: 'Death by a Thousand Cuts' for Lesbian, Gay, and Bisexual Youth." *Journal of LGBT Youth* 8, no. 3 (July 1, 2011): 234–59.

Nelson, Libby. "The Strange History and Ugly Core of Donald Trump Jr.'s Skittles Tweet, Explained." *Vox*, September 20, 2016. www.vox.com.

Orbuch, Terri L. "People's Accounts Count: The Sociology of Accounts." *Annual Review of Sociology* 23, no. 1 (1997): 455–78.

Parker, Kim, Juliana Menasce Horowitz, and Renee Stepler. "On Gender Differences, No Consensus on Nature vs. Nurture." Pew Research Center, December 5, 2017. www.pewsocialtrends.org.

Pascoe, C. J. "'Dude, You're a Fag': Adolescent Masculinity and the Fag Discourse." *Sexualities* 8, no. 3 (2005): 329–46.

Passy, Florence. "Social Networks Matter: But How?" In *Social Movements and Networks*, edited by Mario Diani and Doug McAdam, 21–48. Oxford: Oxford University Press, 2003.

Pedulla, David S., and Sarah Thébaud. "Can We Finish the Revolution? Gender, Work-Family Ideals, and Institutional Constraint." *American Sociological Review* 80, no. 1 (February 2015): 116–39.

Peters, Lucia. "It Shouldn't Take Having a Daughter to Make Gender Equality Matter." *Bustle*, June 6, 2017. www.bustle.com.

Phillips, Amy. "'They're Rapists.' President Trump's Campaign Launch Speech Two Years Later, Annotated." *Washington Post*, June 16, 2017. www.washingtonpost.com.

Pinsof, David, and Martie G. Haselton. "The Effect of the Promiscuity Stereotype on Opposition to Gay Rights." *PLOS One* 12, no. 7 (July 13, 2017): 1–10.

Polletta, Francesca, and James M. Jasper. "Collective Identity and Social Movements." *Annual Review of Sociology* 27, no. 1 (2001): 283–305.

Prattes, Riikka. "Caring Masculinities and Race: On Racialized Workers and 'New Fathers.'" *Men and Masculinities* 25, no. 5 (January 17, 2022): 721–42.

Prentice, Deborah A., and Erica Carranza. "What Women and Men Should Be, Shouldn't Be, Are Allowed to Be, and Don't Have to Be: The Contents of Prescriptive Gender Stereotypes." *Psychology of Women Quarterly* 26, no. 4 (December 1, 2002): 269–81.

Pugh, Allison J. "What Good Are Interviews for Thinking about Culture? Demystifying Interpretive Analysis." *American Journal of Cultural Sociology* 1, no. 1 (February 1, 2013): 42–68.

Rachlinski, Jeffrey J., and Andrew J. Wistrich. "Benevolent Sexism in Judges." *San Diego Law Review* 58 (2021): 101–41.

Rafail, Patrick, and Isaac Freitas. "Grievance Articulation and Community Reactions in the Men's Rights Movement Online." *Social Media + Society* 5, no. 2 (April 1, 2019): 1–11.

RAINN. "Online Dating and Dating App Safety Tips." N.d. www.rainn.org.

Ralph-Morrow, Elizabeth. "The Right Men: How Masculinity Explains the Radical Right Gender Gap." *Political Studies* 70, no. 1 (February 1, 2022): 26–44.

Ratcliffe, Rebecca. "US Women's Rights Campaigner Accused of Sexual Harassment." *Guardian*, August 15, 2018. www.theguardian.com.

Ray, Victor. "A Theory of Racialized Organizations." *American Sociological Review* 84, no. 1 (February 1, 2019): 26–53.

Redden, Elizabeth. "Gender Studies Scholars Say the Field Is Coming under Attack in Many Countries around the Globe." *Inside Higher Ed*, December 5, 2018. www.insidehighered.com.

Reger, Jo. *Everywhere and Nowhere: Contemporary Feminism in the United States*. New York: Oxford University Press, 2012.

Rensin, Emmett. "The Internet Is Full of Men Who Hate Feminism. Here's What They're like in Person." *Vox*, August 18, 2015. www.vox.com.

Ridgeway, Cecilia L. "Framed Before We Know It: How Gender Shapes Social Relations." *Gender & Society* 23, no. 2 (2009): 145–60.

———. *Framed by Gender: How Gender Inequality Persists in the Modern World*. New York: Oxford University Press, 2011.

Ridgeway, Cecilia L., and Tamar Kricheli-Katz. "Intersecting Cultural Beliefs in Social Relations: Gender, Race, and Class Binds and Freedoms." *Gender & Society* 27, no. 3 (March 19, 2013): 294–318.

Risman, Barbara J. *Gender Vertigo: American Families in Transition*. New Haven, CT: Yale University Press, 1998.

Roberts, Steven. "Introduction: Masculinities in Crisis? Opening the Debate." In *Debating Modern Masculinities: Change, Continuity, Crisis?*, edited by Steven Roberts, 1–16. New York: Palgrave Macmillan, 2014.

Ross, Lee. "The Intuitive Psychologist and His Shortcomings: Distortions in the Attribution Process." *Advances in Experimental Social Psychology* 10 (1977): 173–220.

Rothermel, Ann-Kathrin, Megan Kelly, and Greta Jasser. "Of Victims, Mass Murder, and 'Real Men': The Masculinities of the 'Manosphere.'" In *Male Supremacism in the United States: From Patriarchal Traditionalism to Misogynist Incels and the Alt-Right*, edited by Emily K. Carian, Alex DiBranco, and Chelsea Ebin, 117–41. New York: Routledge, 2022.

Rottenberg, Catherine. "The Rise of Neoliberal Feminism." *Cultural Studies of Science Education* 28, no. 3 (May 4, 2014): 418–37.

Rudman, Laurie A. "Self-Promotion as a Risk Factor for Women: The Costs and Benefits of Counterstereotypical Impression Management." *Journal of Personality and Social Psychology* 74, no. 3 (March 1998): 629–45.

Rudman, Laurie A., Corinne A. Moss-Racusin, Julie E. Phelan, and Sanne Nauts. "Status Incongruity and Backlash Effects: Defending the Gender Hierarchy Motivates Prejudice against Female Leaders." *Journal of Experimental Social Psychology* 48, no. 1 (2012): 165–79.

Ruti, Mari. *The Age of Scientific Sexism: How Evolutionary Psychology Promotes Gender Profiling and Fans the Battle of the Sexes*. New York: Bloomsbury, 2015.

Samuels, Alex, Dhrumil Mehta, and Anna Wiederkehr. "Why Black Women Are Often Missing from Conversations about Police Violence." *FiveThirtyEight*, May 6, 2021. https://fivethirtyeight.com.

Sayer, Liana C. "Gender, Time and Inequality: Trends in Women's and Men's Paid Work, Unpaid Work and Free Time." *Social Forces* 84, no. 1 (September 1, 2005): 285–303.

Schmidt, Samantha. "'I'm Not a Sexist': Fired Google Engineer Stands behind Controversial Memo." *Washington Post*, August 10, 2017. www.washingtonpost.com.

Scott, James C. *Domination and the Arts of Resistance: Hidden Transcripts*. New Haven, CT: Yale University Press, 1990.

———. *Weapons of the Weak: Everyday Forms of Peasant Resistance*. New Haven, CT: Yale University Press, 1985.

Sheinin, Dave, Krissah Thompson, Soraya Nadia McDonald, and Scott Clement. "Betty Friedan to Beyoncé: Today's Generation Embraces Feminism on Its Own Terms." *Washington Post*, January 27, 2016. www.washingtonpost.com.

Sherman, Jennifer. *Those Who Work, Those Who Don't: Poverty, Morality, and Family in Rural America*. Minneapolis: University of Minnesota Press, 2009.

Smith, Carly Parnitzke, and Jennifer J. Freyd. "Institutional Betrayal." *American Psychologist* 69, no. 6 (September 2014): 575–87.

Snow, David A., E. Burke Rochford, Steven K. Worden, and Robert D. Benford. "Frame Alignment Processes, Micromobilization, and Movement Participation." *American Sociological Review* 51, no. 4 (1986): 464–81.

Somers, Margaret R. "The Narrative Constitution of Identity: A Relational and Network Approach." *Theory and Society* 23, no. 5 (October 1, 1994): 605–49.

Sommers, Christina Hoff. "Title IX: How a Good Law Went Terribly Wrong." *Time*, June 23, 2014. http://time.com.

———. *Who Stole Feminism? How Women Have Betrayed Women*. New York: Touchstone, 1994.

Sparkes, Andrew C., and Brett Smith. "Sport, Spinal Cord Injury, Embodied Masculinities, and the Dilemmas of Narrative Identity." *Men and Masculinities* 4, no. 3 (January 1, 2002): 258–85.

Speckhard, Anne, Molly Ellenberg, Jesse Morton, and Alexander Ash. "Involuntary Celibates' Experiences of and Grievance over Sexual Exclusion and the Potential Threat of Violence among Those Active in an Online Incel Forum." *Journal of Strategic Security* 14, no. 2 (2021): 89–121.

Sue, Derald Wing, Christina M. Capodilupo, Gina C. Torino, Jennifer M. Bucceri, Aisha M. B. Holder, Kevin L. Nadal, and Marta Esquilin. "Racial Microaggressions in Everyday Life: Implications for Clinical Practice." *American Psychologist* 62, no. 4 (May 2007): 271–86.

Sumerau, J. E., Tehquin D. Forbes, Eric Anthony Grollman, and Lain A. B. Mathers. "Constructing Allyship and the Persistence of Inequality." *Social Problems* 68, no. 2 (March 18, 2020): 358–73.

Tajfel, Henri, and John Turner. "The Social Identity Theory of Intergroup Conflict." In *Psychology of Intergroup Relations*, edited by S. Worchel and W. G. Austin, 7–24. Chicago: Nelson-Hall, 1986.

Taub, Amanda. "On Social Media's Fringes, Growing Extremism Targets Women." *New York Times*, May 9, 2018. www.nytimes.com.

Taylor, Verta, and Nancy E. Whittier. "Collective Identity in Social Movement Communities: Lesbian Feminist Mobilization." In *Frontiers in Social Movement Theory*, edited by Aldon D. Morris and Carol McClurg Mueller, 104–29. New Haven, CT: Yale University Press, 1992.

Totenberg, Nina, and Sarah McCammon. "Supreme Court Overturns Roe v. Wade, Ending Right to Abortion Upheld for Decades." NPR, June 24, 2022. www.npr.org.

Turner, Ralph H. "Sponsored and Contest Mobility and the School System." *American Sociological Review* 25, no. 6 (1960): 855–67.

Uwujaren, Jarune. "Why Our Feminism Must Be Intersectional (and 3 Ways to Practice It)." *Everyday Feminism*, January 11, 2015. https://everydayfeminism.com.

Vaisey, Stephen. "Motivation and Justification: A Dual-Process Model of Culture in Action." *American Journal of Sociology* 114, no. 6 (May 2009): 1675–1715.

Valentin, Iram. "Title IX: A Brief History." *Holy Cross Journal of Law and Public Policy* 2 (1997): 123–38.

Van Valkenburgh, Shawn P. "Digesting the Red Pill: Masculinity and Neoliberalism in the Manosphere." *Men and Masculinities* 24, no. 1 (April 1, 2021): 84–103.

Washington Post and the Kaiser Family Foundation. "Washington Post–Kaiser Family Foundation Poll—Feminism in the U.S." 2016. www.washingtonpost.com.

Weeden, Kim A., Mary Newhart, and Dafna Gelbgiser. "State of the Union 2018: Occupational Segregation." *Pathways*, 2018.

Weiss, Bari. "Meet the Renegades of the Intellectual Dark Web." *New York Times*, May 8, 2018. www.nytimes.com.

West, Candace, and Don H. Zimmerman. "Doing Gender." *Gender & Society* 1, no. 2 (June 1, 1987): 125–51.

Wetts, Rachel, and Robb Willer. "Privilege on the Precipice: Perceived Racial Status Threats Lead White Americans to Oppose Welfare Programs." *Social Forces* 97, no. 2 (December 1, 2018): 793–822.

Wiedeman, Reeves. "The Duke Lacrosse Scandal and the Birth of the Alt-Right." *New York Magazine*, April 14, 2017. https://nymag.com.

Williams, Christine L. "The Glass Escalator: Hidden Advantages for Men in the 'Female' Professions." *Social Problems* 39, no. 3 (1992): 253–67.

———. "The Happy Marriage of Capitalism and Feminism." *Contemporary Sociology* 43, no. 1 (January 1, 2014): 58–61.

Williams, Joan C. *Reshaping the Work-Family Debate: Why Men and Class Matter*. Cambridge, MA: Harvard University Press, 2012.

Woodly, Deva, Rachel H. Brown, Mara Marin, Shatema Threadcraft, Christopher Paul Harris, Jasmine Syedullah, and Miriam Ticktin. "The Politics of Care." *Contemporary Political Theory* 20, no. 4 (2021): 890–925.

Young-Jin Kim, Jennifer, Duoc Nguyen, and Caryn Block. "The 360-Degree Experience of Workplace Microaggressions: Who Commits Them? How Do Individuals Respond? What Are the Consequences?" In *Microaggression Theory*, edited by Gina C. Torino, David P. Rivera, Christina M. Capodilupo, Kevin L. Nadal, and Derald Wing Sue, 157–77. Hoboken, NJ: John Wiley, 2018.

Zamarro, Gema, and María J. Prados. "Gender Differences in Couples' Division of Childcare, Work and Mental Health during COVID-19." *Review of Economics of the Household* 19 (2021): 11–40.

Ziegler, Mary. *Dollars for Life: The Anti-abortion Movement and the Fall of the Republican Establishment*. New Haven, CT: Yale University Press, 2022.

INDEX

Aaron (interviewee), 133, 150, 155; on domestic violence, 145, 151; on gender wage gap, 152; on the golden rule, 148; men's rights movement for, 145–49, 154; on moral self-concept, 146, 147; rationality and, 145–54; on "red pill story," 149
Abe (interviewee), 123, 180
abortion, 1, 2, 13, 191–92
action: affirmative, 85–86, 122; collective, 92, 123, 126; direct, 128
active recruitment, for gender studies courses, 196
Adrian (interviewee), 158, 183, 188, 194–95, 198; on gender studies course, 156; mobilization and, 159–66; relationships with women, 174–75
advocacy, 158
affirmative action, 85–86, 122
Affordable Care Act, 145
African Americans. *See* Black Americans
"African storyteller" experience, 61
Against Our Will (Brownmiller), 170
agency, 132, 133–44; hyperagency, 125; morality and, 148; myth, 93; personal, 142, 200
aggrieved entitlement, 166
AIDS epidemic, 69
Alex (interviewee), 56, 62–70, 127, 152; men's rights movement for, 63, 67; moral identity for, 79–84; patriarchy on, 63; privilege renegotiation strategies for, 63, 68, 84
alimony, 99
allyship, of men, 6–7, 9, 17, 72, 203
altruism, 71
anger, 25, 33, 41, 49, 160; about birth control coverage, 145; as feedback, 29; Trump, D., and, 95; understanding, 31

anonymous online activism, 146
anti-abortion, 191–92
anti-Asian hate, 191, 205
antifeminism, 5–9, 185, 188, 193, 212; of Brian, 2; of Daniel, 173; misogyny of, 7; popularity of, 49
anti-trans legislation, 191
appropriate sexuality, 140
Ari (interviewee), 42, 177
Arnold (interviewee), 141
Asian women, 205
assault, sexual, 117, 163–65, 175–76
Atlanta shootings (2021), 205
awareness: gender, 131; racial, 57

backlash, 10, 203; organized backlash movements, 191
"bad guy," being seen as the, 26–28
beliefs: cultural, 91; feminism as, 131; gender, 91; in patriarchy, 1
benevolent sexism, 64
bias, 202
biological essentialism, 95, 99, 100, 101–2, 116, 117–18, 121–22
biology, 96–97, 101, 115, 119, 121
birth control, 145; insurance coverage for, 148; pill, 101
Black Americans, 53, 87; men, 55, 65, 84; women, 55, 82–83, 171
Black Lives Matter, 69, 83, 191
Blackness, 10
boundaries, moral, 138, 140, 152, 154
boundary making, 132
Bradley (interviewee), 155–56
Brian (interviewee), 1–4, 115
Brownmiller, Susan, 170
Butler, Judith, 194
bystanders, of sexual assault, 164

255

campfire tales, 97
Canada, 6
capital, social, 109–10
capitalism, 82, 123, 200
care: childcare, 39–42; politics of, 200–201
catcallers, 132
celebrities, 212
celebrity feminism, 46
change: identity, 186; identity control theory and, 29; social, 92, 98; structural, 123; technological, 98
Charlie (interviewee), 1–4, 6–7, 13–14
childcare, 39–42
childhood experiences, 25–26, 28
circumcision, 1
cisheteropatriarchy, 79, 200
cismasculinity, 56, 71
civil rights, 147; work, 30–31, 33
Clinton, Hillary, 212
collective action, 92, 123, 126
collective bargaining, 92
collective identity, 9–10, 48; formation, 141
collective organization, 131
college campuses, 72, 77, 180–82; feminist organizations on, 136; Greek organizations on, 71, 74–75, 109, 165, 195; Miller rape on, 163–64, 195–96
college-going women, 12, 14
colonialism, 200
colorblind racism, 197
computer science, 108, 149
Connell, Raewyn, 16, 17
consciousness: false, 9; gender, 168, 170; -raising groups, 137, 198
conservative organizations, 218
contraception. *See* birth control
corporate feminism, 46
COVID-19 pandemic, 12, 13
Craig (interviewee), 23–24, 33, 46, 50, 61, 188; discomfort for, 34–39; gender privilege to, 26–28; men's rights organizations for, 26–27, 34–39; privilege renegotiation strategy of, 35, 38–39
Crenshaw, Kimberlé, 55
criminal sentencing, 64
crisis of masculinity, 15–17
cross-sex friendships, 187–88

cues: verbal, 223; visual, 222
cultural beliefs, 91
cultural narratives, 25, 28, 34, 48–49, 80; contesting and creating, 203–7; of masculinity, 207
cultural norms, around masculinity, 72
culture: dual-process model of, 4; gender norms and, 118; homophobia of, 16; 1950s, 100; 1960s, 137; 1970s, 8, 137; rape, 81–82

Dakota Access Pipeline, 69
Daniel (interviewee), 158, 174, 188, 237n11; men's rights movement for, 171, 178; mobilization and, 167–73
data: analysis, 223–24; collection, 19, 222–23
declining fertility, 98–99
DeCrow, Karen, 34
Dedoose (qualitative analysis software), 224
defensiveness, 160
Democratic Party, 23
denial, 160
Diego (interviewee), 184
difference, systems of, 54–55
direct action, 128
discomfort, 25, 27, 52, 54, 62; for Craig, 34–39; dealing with, 34–43; for Gil, 39–43
discrimination, gender-based, 7–8
divorce, 180, 185; no-fault, 99
Dobbs v. Jackson Women's Health Organization, 191–92
"doing gender," 25
domestic violence, 8, 146; Aaron on, 145, 151; services for, 236n11
Doug (interviewee), 182
draft, military, 27
dual-process model of culture, 4
Duke University, 171

education, 189; higher, 56, 60, 172; social justice, 78
egalitarian relationships, 201–3
Elevatorgate, 3
embarrassment, 49
emotional intelligence, 124
emotion management, 114
emotions, 35, 83; moral, 48–49

empathy, 134, 178
Enlightenment, 5
entitlement, aggrieved, 166
equal protection clause, 8
essentialism: biological, 95; gender, 91
Evan (interviewee), 184
Eve (biblical figure), 90
everyday resistance, 11, 41–42, 50, 113, 131–32, 197
evolutionary psychology, 97–98, 116

Facebook, 217
false consciousness, 9
family, 172; gender performance and, 159; work-family balance, 132
family court system, 8
Farrell, Warren, 37, 168, 171, 182
fathers' rights movements, 217
fear mongering, 24
"feminazi," 185–86
The Feminine Mystique (Friedan), 28, 194
femininity, 10, 90; homophobia and, 16; as low-status, 14; traits, 154
feminism, 1; antifeminism, 2, 5–9, 49, 185, 188, 193, 212; as belief, 131; celebrity, 46; as confrontation, 30; as conscious choice, 127; corporate, 46; intersectional, 70–71, 78; as kindness, 23; mainstream popularity of, 6; mobilization interactions with, 180–86; as morality, 23–24; neoliberal, 6, 131–32, 141–42, 154; postfeminism, 49; profeminism, 8, 137, 193; radical, 31, 46; second-wave, 98; stakes in, 182. *See also specific topics*
feminist language, 74
feminist organizations, 136, 143–44, 157, 197–201
feminist spaces, 134–35, 143
fertility, declining, 98–99
First World, 101
folk norms, 91
4chan, 2
frames, 181, 183
Frank (interviewee), 50, 181
fraternities, 74–75, 107, 162, 183
freedom, 28, 35

Friedan, Betty, 28, 34, 194
friendships: cross-sex, 187–88; gender-segregated groups, 174; networks, 174–75, 183, 187–88

gay men, 166; stereotypes of, 140
gay rights, 69, 147
Gay Straight Alliance (GSA), 59, 77
gender, 167; beliefs, 91; as biological, 90; sex conflated with, 130; as social construct, 90, 96, 105, 108; structural understanding of, 181; understandings of, 21
gender awareness, 131
gender-based discrimination, 7–8
genderblindness, 25
gender consciousness, 168, 170
gender differences, 64
gendered violence, 175
gender equality, 3–4, 14
gender essentialism, 91
gender hierarchy, 74
gender inequality, 8–9, 14–15, 49–50, 91–93, 106, 113, 162; conceptualization of, 155; direct action for, 128; privilege renegotiation strategies and, 5, 11; reinforcement of, 22
gender norms, 109, 118
gender performance, 33, 109; benefits of, 111; family and, 159
gender privilege, learning about, 25–34
gender relations, 161
gender revolution, as stalled, 12–17
gender roles, 35
gender-segregated friend groups, 174
gender studies courses, 162–64, 183, 194–97
gender wage gap, 13, 84, 152–54
George (interviewee), 50, 116–17, 121–22, 183
Gil (interviewee), 23–24, 44, 46, 50, 61, 122; discomfort for, 39–43; gender privilege to, 30–34; men's rights movement for, 39–43
Global North, 15
golden rule, 147, 148
Greek organizations, 71, 74–75, 109, 165, 195
Green Party, 2
GSA. *See* Gay Straight Alliance

harassment campaigns, 7
Harrison (interviewee), 94, 124–25, 175, 178–79, 194; on gender norms, 108–9; on homophily, 106; on romantic relationships, 106–7; sense of self and, 104; structural lens for, 103–14; on "tough guy" hypermasculinity, 110
hate crimes, 64, 67
hegemonic masculinity, 16, 17
heteronormativity, 59
higher education, 56, 60, 172
high-status group: identities, 10, 20, 53–55, 58, 60, 69, 76, 78, 88, 174, 193; interest, 10; members, 10, 56, 198
Hodapp, Christa, 7
homophily, 106
homophobia, 16, 21, 59, 61
hooks, bell, 5, 7
household work, 39–40, 42
humility, 134
hybrid masculinities, 16, 17, 41, 75, 132
hyperagency, 125
hypergamy, 102
hypermasculinity, "tough guy," 110–11

Ian (interviewee), 124
identity: change, 186; collective, 9–10, 48, 141; high-status, 10, 20, 53–55, 58, 60, 69, 76, 78, 88, 174, 193; labels, 68, 82; moral, 70–88; personal, 48; politics, 169; racial formation, 57; self-concept and, 43–44, 46, 48, 130, 138, 146–47, 225; visibility of, 56–62; work, 20
identity control theory, 29, 45–46
identity-driven activism, limitations of, 127–32, 155–57; agency, 133–44; rationality and, 145–54
immorality, 45; privilege associated with, 25, 29
incels (involuntary celibates), 8, 205
inclusive masculinity, 15–17
individualism, 93
individual lens, 94–103, 115, 120
ingroup, 9, 29, 44; identifying, 186; masculine-typed, 156; positive conception of, 37, 44

Institute for Research on Male Supremacism, 228
Institutional Review Board (IRB), 215
insurance coverage, for birth control, 148
intelligence, emotional, 124
intensive mothering, 92
internalized status hierarchies, 139
intersectional feminism, 70–71, 78
intersectionality, 55
invisibility: of privilege, 10, 25, 56; of whiteness, 58
involuntary celibates (incels), 8, 205
IRB. *See* Institutional Review Board
Isla Vista shootings (2013), 212

Jackson, Stevi, 97
Jacob (interviewee), 176–77
James (interviewee), 89–90, 93
Japan, 227
jargon, 74, 199; avoiding, 183
Jeremy (interviewee), 119–21, 181
Jews, 87
Joe (interviewee), 125, 177
Johnson, Amy, 91, 93, 122
journalism, 205–6
justice: racial, 76; social, 56, 63, 69, 75–79, 87, 192

Ken (interviewee), 85–86, 227
Kimmel, Michael, 9, 232n30
kindness, feminism as act of, 23
King, Martin Luther, Jr., 148

labor: division, 39–40; force, 12–14, 91; market, 106; physical, 95; unpaid, 13
language: feminist, 74; jargon, 74, 183, 199; masculine, 155
Latino men, 172–73, 237n11
Lean In (cultural phenomenon), 212
Lenny (interviewee), 140
lived reality, of women, 52
"locker-room talk," 71–72, 122, 183
logic, 80
Lou (interviewee), 137
low-status group members, 80, 83, 88
Luke (interviewee), 69

mainstream popularity, of feminism, 6
"male feminist," 136, 137–38
male genital mutilation. *See* circumcision
male privilege, 74, 105
male sex drive, 181
male supremacism, 8, 21, 97, 102, 177, 179, 204–6
manhood, 167; achieving, 15; defining, 133, 155; rape and, 97; traditional, 155; Tyler on, 47–48
"the manosphere," 205, 212
"mansplaining," 66
"man's world," 26–27, 29
marginalization, 43
marital rape laws, 99
marriage, 174
masculine-typed ingroup, 156
masculinity, 9–10, 45, 51, 78, 82, 90, 134–35; cismasculinity, 56; crisis of, 15–17; cultural narratives of, 207; cultural norms around, 72; defining, 165–66; hegemonic, 16, 17; high status of, 8; hybrid, 16, 17, 41, 75, 132; inclusive, 15–17; language of, 155; moral, 132; as negative, 44; performing, 106, 108–9, 110; personal costs of, 201; power and, 108; primacy on, 156; rationality and, 151; as social construct, 108; "tough guy" hypermasculinity, 110–12; toxic, 63; traditional notions of, 75; traditional types of, 15; traits, 132, 154–55; value of, 14; white, 71, 75
Matthew (interviewee), 44, 51–52, 64, 84, 86, 234n1 (chap. 2); on patriarchy, 123; privilege renegotiation strategies for, 54
McIntosh, Peggy, 56
men: allyship of, 6–7, 9, 17, 72, 203; Black, 55, 65, 84; consciousness-raising groups for, 137, 198; friendship networks for, 174; gay, 140, 166; Latino, 172–73, 237n11; physical space and, 107; power imbalance between women and, 107; privilege taught to, 194–97; "real men," 108; stereotypes about, 51, 65, 140, 169–70; trans men, 96; wartime deaths of, 182
men-dominated space, 164
men going their own way (MGTOW), 8

Men's Rights, Gender, and Social Media (Hodapp), 7
men's rights movement, 211; for Aaron, 145–49, 154; for Alex, 63, 67; for Brian, 3; for Craig, 26–27, 34–39; cultural agenda for, 43; for Daniel, 171, 178; emergence of, 201; false consciousness and, 9; fundamental premise of, 7; for Gil, 39–43; golden rule and, 147; involvement in, 9; for Jeremy, 119; male supremacism and, 205–6; misogyny of, 8, 188; as organized backlash movement, 191; pathways to, 24, 62, 178; plausible deniability of, 204; as privilege renegotiation strategy, 20, 70, 204; rationality and, 148–49; "red pill story" and, 149; relationships with women and, 174; for Tyler, 152–53. *See also specific topics*
meritocracy, 93, 125
#MeToo, 46, 163, 180, 212
Mexicans, 24, 94–95
MGTOW (men going their own way), 8
microaggressions, 69, 78, 202
micromobilization, 187
Microsoft Word, 224
military draft, 27
Miller, Chanel, 163–64, 195–96
minimal involvement, in activism, 219
misogyny, 20, 193, 204, 224, 231n3; "feminazi" and, 186; individual lens and, 120; of men's rights movement, 8, 188; mobilization and, 188; popularity of, 7
mixed-gender spaces, 201
mobilization, 10, 158, 213; Adrian and, 159–66; Daniel and, 167–73; feminism interactions with, 180–86; micromobilization, 187; misogyny and, 188; relationships with women and, 174–80; social contexts for, 173–86; social movement, 141
Molyneux, Stefan, 205
moral boundaries, 138, 140, 152, 154
moral distinctions, 131
moral emotions, 48–49
moral framework, 147
moral identity: for Alex, 79–84; performing, 70–88; for Theo, 70–79

morality, 139, 147; agency and, 148; feminism as, 23–24. *See also* immorality
moral licensing theory, 234n25
moral masculinity, 132
moral self-concept, 130, 138, 146–47, 225
moral virtue, 150
Mother Jones, 212
mothers, 176–77
motivation, 38, 49; self-centered, 87; subconscious, 4, 20–21, 43, 79; unconscious, 143
Moynihan (Senator), 153
Muslims, 24, 64
The Myth of Male Power (Farrell), 37, 168, 171, 182

National Organization for Women (NOW), 1, 34–36, 46, 188
negative stereotypes, 51, 180
neoliberal feminism, 6, 131–32, 141–42, 154, 214
neoliberalism, 93, 125
neoliberal rationality, 6, 11, 199, 214
New York Times, 191–92, 212
Nick (interviewee), 127–31, 192, 225
1950s culture, 100
1960s culture, 137
1970s culture, 8, 137
Noah (interviewee), 124
no-fault divorce, 99
nonfamilial women, 176, 178
norms: cultural, 72; folk, 91; gender, 109, 118
NOW. *See* National Organization for Women

Obama, Barack, 154
Oliver (interviewee), 182, 183
online activism, anonymous, 146
organization, collective, 131
organizational/occupational involvement, in activism, 219
organizations: conservative, 218; feminist, 136, 143–44, 157, 197–201; Greek, 71, 74–75, 109, 165, 195; progressive, 218
organized backlash movements, 191

Pablo (interviewee), 121, 139–40
pair bonding, traditional, 96
parenthood, 174
paternalism, 237n17
patriarchy, 3, 46; Alex on, 63; belief in, 1; for Black women, 83; cisheteropatriarchy, 200; costs of, 49; Matthew on, 123; privilege as mechanism of, 200
Patrick (interviewee), 176, 178, 194, 225
peace movement, 9, 31
personal activism, 41
personal agency, 142, 200
personal identity, 48
Peter (interviewee), 84–85, 135–36, 194
Peterson, Jordan, 205
Phil (interviewee), 179–80, 185–86
physical abuse, 146
physical labor, 95
physical space, control over, 107
pickup artists, 8
police violence, 82–84
Politico, 191
politics: of care, 200–201; identity, 169; respectability, 114
postfeminism, 49
power: anti-men worldview for, 24; masculinity and, 108; physical space and, 107
power imbalance, between men and women, 107
power structures, resistance to, 11
presidential election, United States (2016), 64, 67, 72
privilege, 55, 85; fears of losing, 73; gender, 25–34; immorality associated with, 25, 29; invisibility of, 10, 25, 56; male, 74, 105; as patriarchy mechanism, 200; realization as social process, 160; relinquishing, 142; teaching men about, 194–97; unearned, 38; white, 59
privilege renegotiation strategies, 4–5, 11, 24, 43–50, 86, 126, 206; for Alex, 63, 68, 84; of Craig, 35, 38–39; gender identity and, 20; high-status group identities and, 174; for Matthew, 54; men's rights movement as, 20, 70, 204; responsibility and, 101; for Rick, 98, 103; social contexts and, 21; stalled gender revolution and, 12; white nationalism and, 87
profeminism, 8, 137, 193

progressive organizations, 218
progressive social movements, 148
Proud Boys, 239n13
pseudoscience, gender essentialism as, 91
psychology: evolutionary, 97–98, 116; social psychological theory, 29
public activism, 131, 132

"queer" label, 67
queerness, visibility of, 67

race, 52; hyperrational approach to, 82
racial ambiguity, 227–28
racial awareness, 57
racial identity formation, 57
racial justice, 76
racism, 20, 24, 30, 61; colorblind, 197
radical feminism, 31, 46
Ralph (interviewee), 86
rape, 98, 121, 170–71, 225–26; manhood and, 97; marital, 99; of Miller, 163–64, 195–96; by "real men," 108; reproduction and, 97
rape culture, 81–82
"rape gangs," 103
rationality, 132, 145–54; masculinity and, 151; men's rights movement and, 148–49; neoliberal, 6, 11, 199, 214
"real men," 108
reason, 80, 81
reasoning, feminist, 149
recreational involvement, in activism, 219
Reddit, 2
The Red Pill (documentary), 217, 223
the Red Pill (misogynist group), 212
"red pill story," 149
Rees, Amanda, 97
regret, 32
religion, 89, 123, 152–53, 182
reproduction: rape and, 97; sexual, 96, 98
research: access to participants, 214–20, *216, 220, 221*; challenges in, 224–29; data analysis, 223–24; data collection, 222–23; methods and sample, 213–14
resistance, 41–42; everyday, 131; to power structures, 11
respectability politics, 114

responsibility, 165; privilege renegotiation strategies and, 101; social, 237n17
Revolutionary War, 8
Richard (interviewee), 119, 124, 194, 203
Rick (interviewee), 96–102, 118, 121, 225–26, 229; privilege renegotiation strategies for, 98, 103; on Trump, D., 94–95
rights: civil, 30–31, 33, 147; fathers' rights movements, 217; gay, 69, 147. *See also* men's rights movement
rituals, for performing masculinity, 110
Roberts, Steven, 15
role-taking activities, 196
romantic relationships, 106–7
Rottenberg, Catherine, 6
Russell (interviewee), 117, 118, 225
Ruti, Mari, 98

Sam (interviewee), 68, 85, 175, 186
science: computer, 108, 149; pseudoscience, 91; social, 91; women in, 150
science, technology, engineering, and mathematics (STEM), 196, 211
second-wave feminism, 98
self, sense of, 160, 170, 175, 184
self-centered motivation, 87
self-concept, 43–44, 46, 48, 130; moral, 138, 146–47, 225
self-identification, 129–30, 214, 225
self-presentation, 226
self-reflection, 138
sense of self, 160, 170, 175, 184
sex: cross-sex friendships, 187–88; gender conflated with, 130; obsession with, 140
sexism, 3, 31, 33, 61, 140, 202; benevolent, 64; in criminal sentencing, 64; hooks on, 7
sexual assault, 117, 163–65, 175–76, 201–2. *See also* rape
sexual harassment, 116–17
sexuality, 55; appropriate, 140
sexual reproduction, 96, 98
Shapiro, Ben, 236n13
shootings: in Atlanta (2021), 205; in Isla Vista (2013), 212
Sid (interviewee), 136, 178–79
Silicon Valley, 212

Skittles metaphor, 52, 234n1 (chap. 2)
Skype, 215, 222
social capital, 109–10
social change, 92, 98
social construct: gender as, 90, 96, 105, 108; masculinity as, 108
social contexts: for cross-sex friendships, 187; of identity change, 186; for mobilization, 173–86; privilege renegotiation strategies and, 21
social difference, 68
social inequality, 24
socialization, 89–90, 109, 124
social justice, 56, 63, 69, 75–79, 87, 192
social media, 6, 127, 217, 219
social movements, 5, 10, 48, 92, 187; mobilization, 141
social networks, 179, 183, 187, 198
social processes, 119; privilege realization as, 160
social psychological theory, 29
social responsibility, 237n17
social science, 91
social structures, 112; oppressive, 81
"The Sociology of Gender" (course), 195
Sommers, Christina, 171
sororities, 107
spaces: feminist, 134–35, 143; men-dominated, 164; mixed-gender, 201; physical, 107
sports, 106, 117–18
standard narrative, 98
Stanford University, 163, 212–13, 215, 217
state agencies and actors, 205
state violence, 83
STEM (science, technology, engineering, and mathematics), 196, 211
stereotypes, 2, 53, 177–78; about men, 51, 65, 140, 169–70; of Asian women, 205; in color coding, 130; of gay men, 140; negative, 51, 180; of white men, 65
straightness, visibility of, 67
street cred, 109
structural change, 123
structural lens, 103–14, 181
structural solutions, 122, 125
structural support, 92
subconscious motivation, 4, 20–21, 43, 79
subjectivity, 10
supremacism, 5; male, 8, 21, 97, 102, 177, 179, 204–6; white, 21, 83, 87, 98, 200
Supreme Court, 12; on abortion, 13; *Dobbs v. Jackson Women's Health Organization*, 191–92
symbolic interactionism, 46
sympathy, 83

technological change, 98
Theo (interviewee), 87, 125, 194, 201, 203; on "locker-room talk," 183; moral identity for, 70–79; visible identity for, 56–62
Title IX, 204
"tough guy" hypermasculinity, 110–11
toxic masculinity, 63
toxic work environments, 73
traditional manhood, 155
traditional pair bonding, 96
traits: feminine, 154; masculine, 132, 154–55
transgender people: anti-trans legislation, 191; men, 96; women, 82
Travis (interviewee), 47–48, 141
Trump, Donald, 15, 66, 191, 212, 239n13; "locker-room talk" of, 71–72; Rick on, 94–95; supporters of, 64–65; Tyler on, 140
Trump, Donald, Jr., 234n1 (chap. 2)
Turner, Brock, 163, 164, 195
Tyler (interviewee), 155; agency and, 133–44; on manhood, 47–48; men's rights movement for, 152–53; as "the sole male voice," 134; on Trump, D., 140

unconscious motivation, 143
unearned privilege, 38
unfairness, 63
United States, 6, 54, 87, 192, 214; gender revolution in, 12; labor force in, 13; neoliberalism in, 93; presidential election (2016), 64, 67, 72; second-wave feminism in, 98
universities: Duke, 171; egalitarian relationships in, 201–3; Stanford, 163, 212–13, 215, 217
unpaid labor, 13

verbal cues, 223
victimhood, 68; claims to, 8
victimization, 43
Victim Olympics, 68, 152
Vietnam War, 23, 27
violence: Atlanta shootings (2021), 205; domestic, 8, 145–46, 151, 236n11; gendered, 175; Isla Vista shootings (2013), 212; police, 82–84; sexual assault, 117, 163–65, 175–76, 201–2; state, 83
virtue, moral, 150
visibility: of identity, 56–62; of queerness, 67; of straightness, 67. *See also* invisibility
visual cues, 222
Vox, 212

wage gap, gender, 13, 84, 152–54
"war on women," 148
wars: Revolutionary War, 8; Vietnam War, 23, 27; World War II, 86
wartime deaths, of men, 182
Watson, Rebecca, 3
white masculinity, 71, 75
white nationalism, 10, 86–87
whiteness, 10, 59, 61, 65; invisibility of, 58
white privilege, 59
white supremacism, 21, 83, 87, 98, 200

Who Stole Feminism? (Sommers), 171
Wikipedia, 149
womanhood, 161
women: Asian, 205; biological nature of, 90; Black, 55, 82–83, 171; college-going, 12; in everyday life, 161; lived reality of, 52; nonfamilial, 176, 178; oppression of, 35–36; power imbalance between men and, 107; relationships with, 174–80; in science, 150; trans, 82; "war on women," 148. *See also specific topics*
Women's March, 129, 132, 198
women's work, 13
work: activism as, 158; civil rights, 30–31, 33; egalitarian relationships in, 201–3; household, 39–40, 42; identity, 20; toxic environments, 73; women's work, 13
work-family balance, 132
working class, 102
World Atheist Convention, 3
World War II, 86

xenophobia, 24

#YesAllWomen, 46

Zoom, 222

ABOUT THE AUTHOR

EMILY K. CARIAN is Assistant Professor of Teaching in the Department of Sociology at the University of California, Irvine, and co-editor of *Male Supremacism in the United States: From Patriarchal Traditionalism to Misogynist Incels and the Alt-Right*. She earned her PhD in sociology from Stanford University. She is co-founder of the Institute for Research on Male Supremacism.

www.ingramcontent.com/pod-product-compliance
Lightning Source LLC
Chambersburg PA
CBHW031145020426
42333CB00013B/512